Richard Meier Architect

*Essays by Kenneth Frampton
and Joseph Rykwert*

1985/1991

Contents

Preface

Sitting on La Playa del Tejon at La Costa Careyes on the eve of
the last day of the year 1990, looking out at the steel blue sea,
the only white I find is the foaming surf gently touching sand
streaked with volcanic black. The great, dark rocks rise like
monuments from the waves, earth's fortress against the perpetual
seas. Cactus and palm, sturdy survivors of aridity, thrive among
rock and sand and gritty yellow-green.

The nearly cloudless sky looks transparent against the dense
horizon of the Pacific, perfectly horizontal, stretching from rock
to rock. The surf, its other definition, is like boiling lace, the
horizontal plane of constant motion whose surface ripples to the
edge of erosion. White becomes the signal of sea touching land,
of horizontal disappearing into vertical. White is the ephemeral
emblem of perpetual movement.

The white is always present but never the same, bright and
rolling in the day, silver and effervescent under the full moon of
New Year's Eve. Between the sea of consciousness and earth's
vast materiality lies this ever-changing line of white. White is the
light, the medium of understanding and transformative power.

Two little bodies bob up and down close to shore, delighting in
endless waterplay, making more white markings on their blue
playground. All three bodies, supremely unaware of each other's
nature, interacting, nonetheless, in fleeting moments of joy,
merge at the wave's crest. Laughter, indistinguishable from the
sound of the surf, from small bodies that feel themselves
creatures of the endless one. Reluctantly they emerge, at their
father's bidding, to be confronted by a question far from their
realm of present thought. "Look around you Joseph, what is
white?" "The waves sometimes when they are rough, their edges
are white. The clouds in the sky are white." Ana, being most

pragmatic, responds, "the paper on which you are writing is white, the towel is white, your hair is white, the stuff which you brought here is white."

Six years have passed since this question of "what is white" was first discussed. Despite age and circumstance, Joseph's and Ana's responses are similar to what they were before but in some ways, of course, they are different. Thus the ineluctable presence of white is ever-changing and yet the same, like the vision of childhood.

The importance of a book such as this is that it records an aspect of what it takes to make a significant body of architecture. This is distinct from, and one would hope more insightful than, a theoretical and distant stance a historian or critic might attempt to reconstruct. Therefore, it is important to thank the many people who were not only contributors but paramount in their involvement with the work and with the making of this book. My partners, Donald Barker, Robert Gatje, Michael Palladino, and Thomas Phifer are as maniacal as I am in attempting to insure the highest level of quality in everything that we do. My gratitude to them is immeasurable. The list of collaborators shows how many people have dedicated themselves to the art of architecture, and the result of their perpetual efforts is integral in both the realized buildings and in those unbuilt projects in which ideas are important to the world of architecture. This book, as a collection of ideas, would not have been realized without the dedication and conscientious efforts of Lisa Green, who was responsible for its compilation. My friend Massimo Vignelli was not only responsible for the precise and articulate design, but was my "kitchen cabinet" all through its creation. Abigail Sturges, who was also responsible for the final layouts of the first volume, continues to be an integral part of our team along with

Rizzoli editor David Morton, who conscientiously oversaw the writing of this volume.

Many, many others have mattered greatly to me, and I thank you all; especially Kate Gormley-Meier, who has been and continues to be a critical voice in all matters of importance, and lastly and most significantly Kenneth Frampton, my Boswell, my friend; the architect's teacher and the teacher's architect.

Richard Meier

Playa del Tejon, La Costa Careyes
Mexico

31 December 1990

Works in Transition

Kenneth Frampton

City Hall and Central Library, The Hague, The Netherlands. Richard Meier, 1986–1994. Axonometric study

Van Nelle Factory, Rotterdam, The Netherlands. Brinkman and Van der Vlugt, 1930. Perspective

Whether by accident or natural affinity, Richard Meier has become an American architect practicing in Europe or perhaps, one should say, a transcontinental architect who happens to live in America. The realization of the Museum for the Decorative Arts in Frankfurt (1979–85) seems to have been decisive in this regard, affording the final proof that Meier is a public architect of exceptional calibre and one who can be trusted with major commissions in the European scene. This reputation came into being through a series of competitions entailing, as always, as many failures as successes. Among the former one may count Meier's inexplicable exclusion from the limited Anglo–American competition for the British National Gallery (interviewed but not invited to compete) and his ironic "misplacement" in the 1983 open competition for the new Paris Opera. Thus, although some of Meier's current European work occurred through direct commission, from the headquarters project for Renault of 1981 to the facilities now under construction in Schwendi, Germany, for the industrialist Siegfried Weishaupt, the bulk of Meier's present continental practice was won in open contest.

Of the recent buildings and projects included in this volume, one of the most seminal is surely the Ulm Exhibition and Assembly Building won in competition in 1986—a project that brilliantly combines Meier's modernist syntax with an extremely sensitive approach to the site from the standpoint of the surrounding scale and rhythm. Aside from the Helmick House of 1984, this project also represents the first occasion in which a cylinder was employed as the principal unifying element. It is also the first building in which Meier was called upon to respond to the presence of a major architectural monument.

The self-contained authority of this work derives from the way in which it provides a modulated entry into the Munsterplatz, in part through the rhythmic syncopation of its cubic mass running down one side of the cathedral square, and in part through its tri-gabled glazed roof that caps the mass with a profile that is vaguely reminiscent of Gothic form. Thus, aside from providing top light to the nine-square exhibition volume beneath, this monitor roof incorporates two contextual gestures in a single form. On the one hand, it comprises three successive triangular gables that echo the traditional gable fronts flanking the *parvis*, on the other, it presents a series of peaks which spontaneously recall the pinnacles and spires of the cathedral. At the same time the latent propylea aspect of this structure is emphasized by two features: the piloti under the drum that serve to bound and articulate the outer limit of the Munsterplatz and the nine-square inner cube faced in stone that stands in strong contrast to the plastered, concentric surface of the drum.

The Hague City Hall and Central Library, won in the same year, could hardly be more removed in terms of size and extent from the diminutive scale of Ulm. It amounts, in effect, to the redesign of an entire urban quarter. Aside from its unusual size (approximately 820 feet long by 330 feet wide), one of the remarkable things about this project is the way in which it comes to fulfill an eighty-year-old ambition to erect a city hall on this site. Such a project was last seriously attempted in 1925 in a palatial proposal by Kalf and Wils. It says something for the colossal scale of Meier's present design that what was previously projected as an ornamental water garden symmetrically flanked by low-rise offices came to be recast some sixty years later as a twelve-story megastructure enclosing a vast atrium that is expected to serve as the new *res publica* for the city. Almost twice as big as the concourse of New York's Grand Central Terminal, this space will be the largest atrium in Europe— approximating the size of Piazza San Marco in Venice.

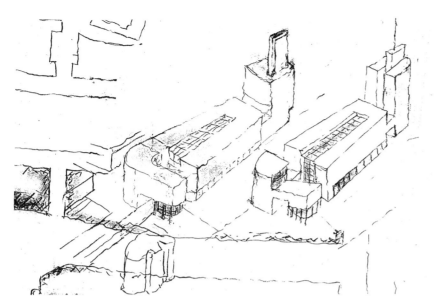

Appearing, at times, to be more of a "beached" transatlantic liner than a building in the traditional sense, one of the more heroic aspects of this design are the twelve-story, glazed curtain walls that enclose the atrium at its extremities. It is uncanny how certain features in this work appear to echo similar prominent forms in Brinkman and Van der Vlugt's canonical Van Nelle Factory, erected in Rotterdam in 1927—from the use of cylindrical or radial forms as terminals in a linear composition to the incessant repetition of the same fenestration and, last but not least, the use of wide-span, flying bridges. Assuming the form of conveyor belts in the case of the factory, these last become pedestrian passerelles in The Hague, spanning across the wings of the city hall. The idea of a ship or of a Corbusian *Unité* block is also implied by the four-story civic window let into the northern facade of the atrium.

Typical of the late-twentieth century city hall, this is more of a bureaucratic emporium than a public building, and Meier has had to fight in order to preserve those civic amenities that are essential to the public status of a municipal institution: the Council Chamber and the Wedding Room, both of which owe their present existence as much to the architect as to the client. Despite these features, the most dominant and rhetorical element is the public library which, combined with a large retail facility at grade, occupies the southwestern end of the complex.

The limitation of Meier's white-panelled, enameled metal syntax is perhaps most evident in this singular civic work, for while the three-by-six-foot curtain-wall module is surely appropriate to the cladding of rectilinear office space, it is relatively incapable of smoothly enclosing the more organic volumes that make up the library, that is to say the open loft space of the circular reading room and its public foyers.

Nonetheless, Meier's City Hall promises to be a success as a civic symbol mainly because it introduces a new horizontal scale into the fabric of the city in which the generous sweep of its horizontal form will more than make up for its excessive size. Through introducing a new scale into the neighborhood, it will also help to unify the somewhat piecemeal examples of urban renewal that have already risen on the adjacent sites.

Of late, the cylinder has come to play a particularly incisive role in focusing Meier's architecture, either as an all-embracing form, as in Ulm or the Arp Museum recently projected for Rolandswerth-on-the-Rhein, or as the container of a central honorific space, as in the Canal + Headquarters projected for Paris (won in competition in 1988) or the Museum of Contemporary Art projected for Barcelona from the same time. In Canal +, the cylinder, transposed into a cone, announces the presence of the screening room within, even if its battered form misleadingly suggests a volumetric penetration through the entire eight stories of the mass in which it is embedded. In Barcelona, on the other hand, a pure cylinder interrupts the three-story, rectiliner mass-form for its full height, even if this too is divided internally into galleries suspended above the entry foyer at grade. Here the volumetric continuity is assured by a double-height light slot running around the inner perimeter of the drum.

The other characteristic trope of Meier's recent work is the fully glazed ramp hall that effectively converts a given elevation into a dynamic display of the circulation, as though this singular public function spontaneously expressed the civic status of the institution. A ramp of this order occupies the front facade of the Barcelona Museum and a similar element plays an equally prominent role in the principal elevation of the new Museum of Ethnology projected for Frankfurt, in close proximity to Meier's

Canal+ Headquarters, Paris, France. Richard Meier, 1988-1991. Section

Museum of Contemporary Art, Barcelona, Spain. Richard Meier, 1987-1992. Section

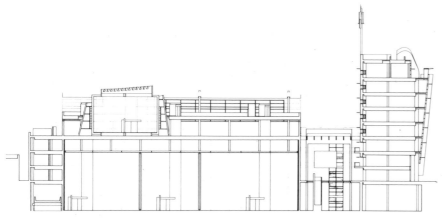

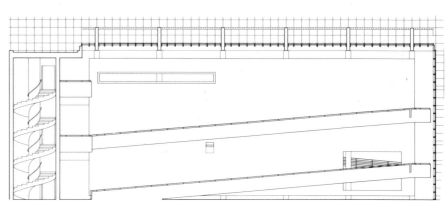

Museum for the Decorative Arts. One further motif also seems to determine the spatial character of Meier's recent work—namely, the presence of a pin-wheeling centroid, which, aside from establishing a central focus close to the point of entry, also radiates out as a set of complementary centrifugal spaces. These spiraling volumes serve to countermand, and even at times to undermine, the gridded spatial matrix of the work as a whole. Nowhere is this more evident than in the Barcelona Museum where the blade wall articulating the entry intercepts the central cylindrical volume in a dramatic but disruptive way. The resulting pin-wheel effect is offset in this instance by the spine wall of the main exhibition wing that, together with the ramp hall, counterbalances to the spiraling thrust of the entry volume.

Historically and topographically, Barcelona is the most intricate fabric in which Meier has been asked to intervene, and the museum's mass is appropriately inflected with regard to the surrounding pattern of streets and squares. The central drum and its attendant concave wall function jointly as a kind of valve between the garden court of the museum to the rear of the block and the entry front opening onto the Plaça dels Angels. This partially concealed *paseo* has been conceived as part of a pedestrian labyrinth that runs through the medieval fabric of the city, linking up various civic institutions in such a way as to constitute a kind of cultural promenade running throughout the central core. While Meier's perennial "villa syntax" reappears here in the unexpected superimposition of a domestic facade over the entrance and in the gratuitously organic feature that accentuates the northeastern corner of the block, this museum nonetheless remains one of Meier's most civic works.

The Barcelona Museum and Canal+ Headquarters testify to the fact that the expressive possibilities of metal-skin revetment are far from exhausted, just as Meier's painstaking perfection of enameled panel cladding—the shift, say, from neoprene caulked gaskets to open seams—has opened up new possibilities for the technical perfection of the technique. Evidence of this lies not only in the recent work of the office but also in parallel works achieved by others. I have in mind Fumihiko Maki's Tepia Pavilion completed in Tokyo in 1990 or Dominique Perrault's Technical School realized in Marne-la-Vallée in 1988. Although Perrault indulges in a somewhat superficial application of the Meier syntax, he has nonetheless advanced the expressive potential of the technique by cutting and piercing flat panels so as to suggest the illusion of a three-dimensional shape. In a similar way Maki's Tepia Pavilion departs from the round whiteness of the typical panel, engendering what Enrico Morteo has called a dematerialized "white light" aesthetic, in which glass and aluminum are interchangeably combined as though they are one and the same material—a kind of paper-thin, metallic ukiyo-e print.

With their subtle stereoscopic layering of clear, translucent, and white opaque glass and their superimposition of filigree *brise soleil*, made of lightweight cantilevered aluminum baffles, the facades of the Canal+ Headquarters enrich the familiar panel syntax, to come closer in spirit, if not in effect, to the tessellations of Maki's Tepia Pavilion. This feeling for an almost hallucinatory articulation of the surface finds itself reinforced in Canal+ by the perforated metal aerofoil canopy that crowns the roof, a trope that would reappear on a more monumental scale in Meier's highly rhetorical entry for the Bibliothèque de France competition.

Through membranaceous layerings of this order and through parallel slots of space cut into the prisms themselves, Meier's

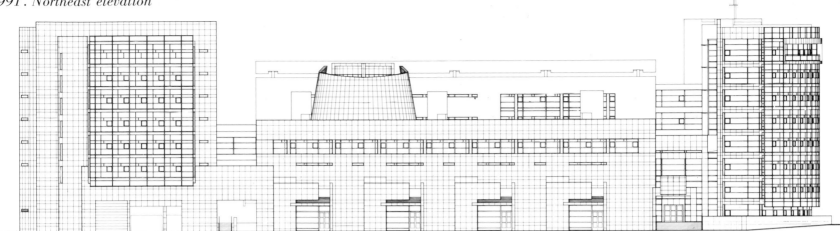

current work evokes a plaited quality that recalls Frank Lloyd Wright and, via Wright, albeit unconsciously, Gottfried Semper's theoretical elaborations on the theme of cladding: that is to say, Semper's idea of *Bekleidung* as a kind of petrified textile that at times glides over the outer surface of the structure, as in Otto Wagner's *Postparkassenamt* of 1906, or alternatively penetrates into its depth, as in Wright's canonical Larkin Building of 1904.

Among the most recent work, this oscillation between surface and depth shows up most clearly in the Barcelona Museum, for here, as in Canal+, a horizontal louvered screen initiates a series of shallow spatial layers that recede from the window-wall to become further articulated either in the recessive parallel planes of the ramps themselves (their spatial thrust being emphasized through horizontal balustrading), or through a sequence of carefully orchestrated light slots that penetrate the volume of the main gallery wing in section. These aforementioned slots are conceived like spatial "guillotines" that have to be traversed by visitors entering from the ramp hall to the major exhibition volumes, and then again towards the rear of the block, where the visitor has to cross a similar slot in order to gain access to the alcoves overlooking the double-height viewing space. In each instance, the slots are given definition by natural light filtering through glass-lensed bridges from monitors situated on the roof.

This lateral spatial interpenetration, occurring at regular intervals throughout the main wing, is offset around the central rotunda by a diagonal spatial axis passing across the *paseo*. Continual pedestrian movement through this passage is thus made visible not only from the central entrance lobby, but also from smaller gallery spaces located within the concourse wall. From this vantage point one will see both the *paseo* and the circular entry space within the cylinder—a rather unique kind of spatial

interchange as intense as any to be found within the general body of Meier's work.

It would seem that the Meier office has tried to develop its familiar white-on-white aesthetic in two distinct directions with decidedly varied results. In the first instance the practice has moved towards a kind of tessellated horizontal continuity compounded of light and surface, as is evident in Canal + or Barcelona; in the second, an attempt has been made to respond to the postmodern critique of the last decade by introducing the pierced window motif of traditional masonry construction. This revisionist ploy is evident in three recent works: in the somewhat cacophonous collage of Bridgeport Center (1984–1989), as autodestructive of the "house syntax" as Arata Isozaki's Tsukuba civic center; in the equally ill-proportioned, seventy-two-story high-rise complex proposed for Madison Square Garden, in Manhattan; and finally in the mixed fenestration, part pierced, part floor-to-ceiling, that appears in some of the more unresolved sections of the Getty Center.

While the occasional traditional window has long since served as a foil to the *fenêtre en longeur*, large areas filled with repetitive square openings are relatively ineffective for the modulation of oversized structures, as was long ago evident when Cass Gilbert ingeniously adapted the verticality of Gothic syntax to his canonical Woolworth Building of 1912—a skyscraper format that would be brilliantly developed in Rockefeller Center twenty years later. In these two canonical examples, prominent stone mullions and recessed spandrels jointly serve to unify the repetitive window into a rhythmically monolithic mass. Nothing could be further from this than the scalelessness of Meier's Madison Square Garden proposal or the equally scaleless repetition of disconnected square openings in the Getty Center and

Bridgeport, where the wallpaper pattern effect combined with other disjunctive modern tropes jointly have the effect of dissipating rather than unifying the overall *gestalt* of the form. Whether the Getty Center will eventually move closer to the surface elaboration evident in the Barcelona Museum and Canal + remains to be seen. In any event, such an illusory, volatile surface aesthetic compounded of light and tessellated form would seem to be more appropriately expressive of our late-modern times. It would also be a logical development of Meier's characteristic white-on-white manner, an aesthetic that in the last analysis has more to do with Laszlo Moholy-Nagy than with Balthasar Neumann.

Two works, in particular, reveal Meier's hitherto largely unforeseen capacity in the field of urban design: first, the Italian "hill-town" complex designed for the accommodation of the Getty Center on a prominent site overlooking the entire metropolitan region of Los Angeles and, second, a more recent competition design for the redevelopment of an area bounding the historic core of Aix-en-Provence in France. What is perhaps unique about both of these works is the way in which they successively adapt Meier's modernist syntax to traditional urban forms—to the avenue, the block, the street, the *rondpoint*, the *bâtiment d'angle*, and the arcade. While designed over very different time frames (the one, a long drawn out evolution, the other, a fast track *esquisse*), the two nonetheless demonstrate how modern idioms can be brought to respond to different contexts. To this end, many of modernism's organic tropes reappear in both the Getty Center design and the Aix-en-Provence proposal, from Aaltoesque auditoriums to Mendelsohnian corner buildings, from Russian constructivist cylinders to the more organic block layouts of Ernst May and Bruno Taut, and from the intersecting figure/ground formations pioneered by Colin Rowe to exotic plastic

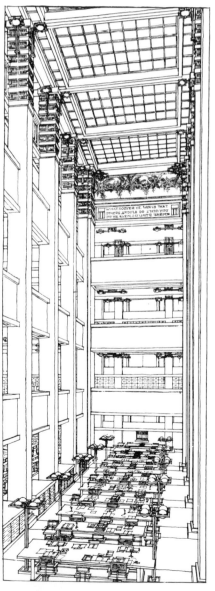

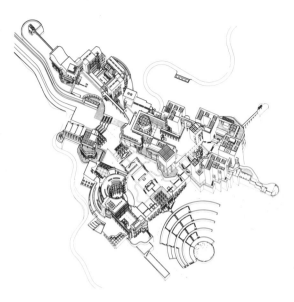

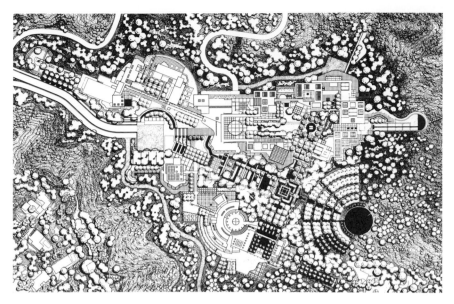

tropes derived from Oscar Niemeyer.

Where the proposal for Aix is essentially an introspective work in which the entire development is structured about a single tree-lined avenue, the famous Cours Mirabeau that extends as a continuous promenade from the *rondpoint* to the convention hall at the northern end of the site, the Getty is an extroverted assembly of semidetached buildings organized on an open, mountainous terrain about two intersecting axes, the one aligning with a dominant ridge and the other taking up the twenty-two-and-a-half degree shift of the San Diego Freeway as it travels north in a straight line from Los Angeles County Airport. The Getty Center is thus organized about two ridge formations as a set of three, loosely connected Italian "hill towns": the administration complex, the museum itself, and the research center. These aggregate clusters are accompanied by a limited number of freestanding institutions such as the food services building that juts forth on a promontory as a belvedere overlooking the Pacific. And yet for all the topographic informality and the evident play with the picturesque, this is a cultural acropolis in the Greek sense of the term. Its splendid isolation and its hierarchical otherness seem to be reflected in the main approach that, after arrival by car from the Sepulveda Boulevard, takes a different form for staff and visitors. While the staff, as guardians of the cult (curators, scholars and custodians, etc.), have the privilege of driving to the top of the acropolis, the visitors have no choice but to leave their cars in the propylea garage and ascend to the summit by an electrified tramway, taking some five minutes to ascend the 250 feet.

Of critical importance is the proposed cladding of all three clusters in a mixture of stainless steel and dressed stone, and the equally contextual terracing and planting of the site as though it

were a latterday Hadrian's Villa. We may speak here of two manifestations that formerly were suppressed in Meier's architecture—the tactility of the revetment as a crafted surface and the earthwork as an end in itself. These two, the fabric and the earth, display a more sophisticated attitude towards time and nature than that which was previously evident in Meier's practice, even if the museums in Frankfurt and Des Moines already hint at a more temporally responsive attitude in their use of stone. For where Meier's white-on-white aesthetic was conceived as eternally pristine, irrespective of the textual differences between stucco and metal panel, the two principal cladding elements in the Getty, steel and stone, are already envisaged as weathering in time. This acceptance of patina reflects a fundamental shift in the architect's attitude. In a recent report to the Getty, Meier was to be quite explicit about the contextual significance of the selected facing materials. "The metal panels will provide an elegant surface. The matte finish will emphasize the light, transparent qualities of the buildings without being highly reflective—without being shiny. At the same time, this material will offer both a contrast and a complement to the stone museum structures. And it will be a subtle reminder of the landscape I have grown so familiar with; I see these buildings as absorbing the blues and greens of the surrounding hills."

Surely nothing could be more picturesque than this account of the way in which the steel will go with the grey-veridian tone of the surrounding sky and mountains or the implication that the pale ochre stonework will match the sandy color of the arid, scrubby hilltop—the dialectic, as it were, between the substance of the building and the earth of its foundation, as the one fuses into the other over the passage of time. One is unexpectedly reminded at this juncture of Gianni Vattimo's late-modern disquisition on the nature of monumentality when he wrote:

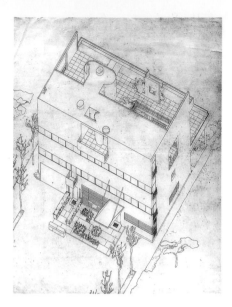

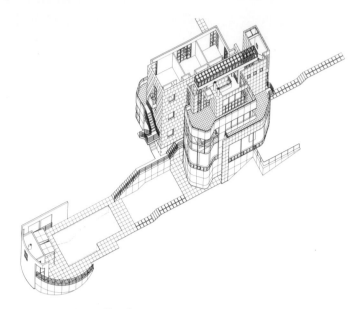

"...the monument is not, as Hegel would have it, a work in which form and content, inside and outside, idea and manifestation, are fully identified with each other, and which accordingly represents an eminent example of an accomplished actualization of freedom itself.... The monument is rather that which endures in the form of a funerary mask. The monument—and, historically speaking, neoclassical art is also this—is not the artistic casting of a full life, but rather a formula which is already constituted in such a way as to transmit itself, and is therefore already marked by its radical alienation: it is marked, definitively in so many words, by mortality. The monument formula is not constructed so as to "defeat" time, imposing itself on and regardless of time but so as to endure time instead...."

While Meier's debt to Le Corbusier is familiar, the exact way in which the original purist theme was transformed by Meier has perhaps been insufficiently studied. The generic character of the purist ramp, as this appears in the Villa Savoye of 1929 (a model of which graces Meier's New York office like an icon), demonstrates, as it were, the nature of Meier's creative misunderstanding, for neither its absolutely axial location nor its spiraling spatial form were to be strictly followed by Meier. So that while sculptural circulatory devices, be they stairs or ramps, certainly feature in Meier's early domestic work, they invariably gravitate away from the classical center towards the exterior—a passage, as it were, from introversion to extroversion. Despite the more or less central position of the ramp in the Atheneum in New Harmony, the general tendency of Meier's circulation is to gravitate towards the skin. The resultant agitation of the surface tends to leave the center strangely empty. Nothing could be further from the format of the purist villa, where the center is charged and the surface, while articulated with regulating lines, is hermetic and severe, save for decisive moments of projection

or recession. In this instance the energy released by the vortex at the center, be it a ramp or a stair, engenders a series of partially spiraling volumes, the animated *plan libre*, so to speak, as a metaphor for utopian socialist liberation.

We are witnesses here to the fundamental ideological differences separating Meier and Le Corbusier, above all their different attitudes towards the promise of the Enlightenment. For while purism is ideologically linked to the modern project as an architecture of Hegelian redemption, Meier's aestheticism is unconsciously related to the dissolution of this hope. Where Le Corbusier responded to this *dénouement* by going to ground, as it were, by retreating to the existentialist aesthetic of an intermediate technology that was neither progressive nor regressive, Meier has grounded his aesthetic in the belief that one may re-energize the language of a lost avant-garde without embracing its original utopian substance.

This comparison between purism and the evolution of Meier's architecture prompts one to see how *figure*, *field*, and *gestalt* have played entirely different roles in the work of these two architects, particularly where *figure* alludes to the spatial animation of the work (the plan as generator) and *field* refers to the modulated surface that assures the unity of the whole (regulating lines). The third term, the *gestalt*, arises out of the significant interaction of the figure with the field.

In Le Corbusier's purist period the figure is always contained, not to say concealed, by the field, by a hermetic skin that is occasionally eroded to reveal the spatial vortex of the figure within. In Meier, on the other hand, the figure invariably impinges on the surface, a manifestation that tends towards the disruption of the field. That this is always a latent risk in Meier's

Villa Stein, Garches, France. Le Corbusier, 1926. Axonometric

Westchester House, Westchester County, New York. Richard Meier, 1984-1986. Axonometric

Jean Arp Museum, Rolandswerth, Germany. Richard Meier, 1990. Etching

work is surely evident from the total dissolution of any field, as in the case of Bridgeport Center. We may construe this as proof of the way in which the gestalt of work, and hence its significance, depends, in a fundamental way, on the balance established between the figure and the field.

Meier's more recent work is particularly susceptible to being analyzed in terms of this hypothesis. In the Barcelona Museum, for example, the figure and the field interact at two different levels, each of which has a distinct impact on the overall gestalt. In the first of these, the figure of the central cylindrical core stands in clear contrast to the orthogonal field of the building. In the second, the spatial figure of the ramp as vortex, while impinging on the surface, is nonetheless contained by the surface screen of the fenestration and its *brise soleil*. The resultant gestalt, while inflected by other minor figures on the surface, depends ultimately on the balance established, between the eccentrically positioned cylinder and the orthogonal matrix of the principal mass. On the other hand, in the Ulm Exhibition and Assembly Building or in the Arp Museum, the figure of the cylindrical core expands to become the unifying form in itself. In this instance figure, field, and gestalt become a single unified whole.

Meier's recent emphasis on either the all-encompassing figure of the cylinder or on the hermetic scintillating field in the "high tech" aesthetic of Canal + and the Bibliothèque de France, seems to conform, in an unexpected way, to Vattimo's vision of the fate of the monument. Irrespective of whether it is announced in matte steel and stone or in shiny white enamel and aluminum, this fate is as much the destiny of occidental art in Los Angeles, as it is the more obvious high-tech efflorescence of televised media on the banks of the Seine.

The Second Installment

Joseph Rykwert

Richard Meier has often been praised for his consistency—but he has also been blamed for it. As the 1970s drew on, Meier's apparently obstinate development of his particular way of designing, with its proudly acknowledged debt to the architecture of the 1920s and 1930s, especially the "white" architecture (which many thought to have been quite discredited), seemed almost quixotic. Although the integrity of his vision was never impugned, Meier's position also became entrenched. Even a tyro could enumerate the elements that he might expect to find in any new building, the insistently recurring *stylemes* of which they were composed: structural elements and stairwells projecting out of a squared white enamel skin, the piano curves, the large panes of bent glass, the blunted corner, the nautical railings.

His compositional set of pieces is therefore deliberately frugal: it is not a repertory of standard details, but a formal vocabulary whose elements are all abstracted from the classics of early modernism and juxtaposed, much in the way a collage artist might use a piece of patterned wallpaper (or a printed advertisement or even a wooden molding): they are not edited or "treated," but left plainly recognizable. Moreover, their autonomy is emphasized by their being used both horizontally and vertically. Meier also had to exercise another *askesis*, and eschew proportional adventure in order to absorb the formal intrusions; he has relied instead on the square and its subdivisions, as well as on the use of the circle and its segments, in preference to more complex curves.

The whiteness and sparseness, generally seen as characteristic of his buildings, shroud them in a certain immateriality—a quality that was essential to his early achievement. Since the way forms were revealed to the spectator by the skillful modelling of light was the inherent virtue of his architecture, it was right that the

18

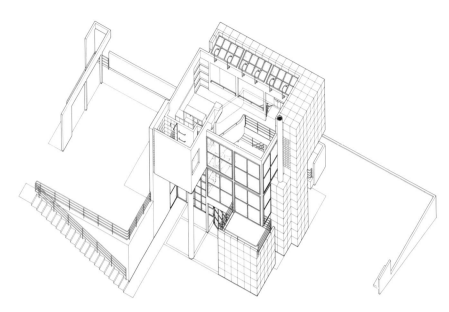

Giovannitti House, Pittsburgh,
Pennsylvania. Richard Meier,
1979-1983. Axonometric

buildings themselves should almost seem insubstantial, that they be the color of light, as it were.

Although Meier was considered *the* quintessentially "white" architect when the group of five New Yorkers took white as their banner or trademark in 1969, he never had to limit himself to that whiteness, in spite of the popular view of him. Indeed, it has become something of a cliché, imposed on him by his critics and by the prominent siting of certain buildings. White enamelled panels were singled out as branding his buildings with a personal mannerism; in fact they are a relatively cheap and enduring finish (though only one among several) which Meier uses to ennoble and sustain the surface of his buildings, even if those panels happen to have been used on his best-known and most visited ones. He has also used aluminum, stainless steel, and brick tile wherever they seemed appropriate (though not brick, which implies courses and is not an applied finish). The implicit immateriality is therefore deceptive since it is harnessed to an apparently contradictory and quite explicit concern with program and site.

That there should be such a thing as an art of architecture at all is a by-product of the inevitable contradiction between insubstantial form on the one hand and the demands of program and material on the other. The architect must recognize and attempt to resolve this very contradiction. It can be exorcised, as it was in the pierced vaults of Guarini or Vittone, or solemnized (ritualized almost), as in the flying buttresses of the high medieval cathedrals. In Meier's earliest work he adopted a number of tactics to enter this dialectic: by separating line and point supports very clearly, even pulling line support to the exterior of the building; or by isolating such functional elements as flues and stairwell out of the fabric of the building and turning them into almost emblematic devices.

Yet throughout his earliest work, it was the desire to impose form on material that dominated Meier's vision: timber siding, brick tile, stucco, and steel were homogenized into white and apparently immaterial shapes so that, perversely, glass became the only part of the fabric to retain its identity, the only coloristic substance. But as the balance of his commissions shifted from private work to public about 1970, so form became more conciliatory to material, finishes became more tactile. A dark brick tile had been chosen for two earlier projects: Twin Parks Northeast Housing and the Monroe Developmental Center. But later he used aluminum and enamelled panels in the minor scale of private houses as well, as on the Giovannitti House in Pittsburgh, and he has also begun to use a no-fines concrete block which can be tinted in a range of colors.

The formal complexity of his buildings has therefore been increasingly accomplished through the interweaving of different surfaces, and a thematic exploration of two or more textures has allowed him to play a formal counterpoint absent from his earlier work. This became apparent in the late 1970s, when, at the Clifty Creek Elementary School in Columbus, Ohio, Meier placed a *piano nobile* finished in grey concrete block over white enamel walls. The building stood on a sloping site, and the border between the two surfaces was drawn along the datum line of the higher level. This contrast achieves an elegance and a lightness which almost makes the building look as if it had been raised above ground.

The urge away from the abstraction of some of the earliest work has led Meier to explore another device, one that has been emulated by many of his contemporaries, by which the specific

19

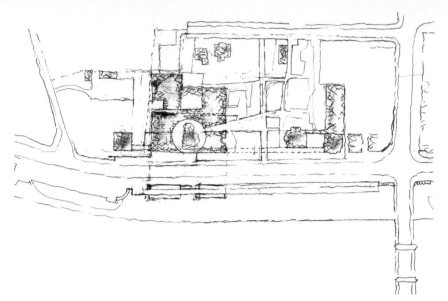
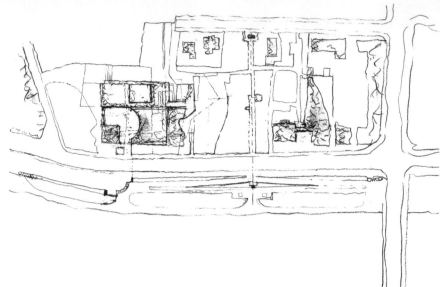

circumstances of a site generate the internal complexity of a building. In one of his first houses, the Hoffman House in East Hampton, he uses a diagonal access street to legitimize the exploiting of a 45-degree rotation of the volumes, and to work a wonder of complexity out of the challenge of a flat, square site in a suburban environment. It also became the generating device of the Atheneum in New Harmony, Indiana, the first of Meier's buildings to attract a great deal of public attention. Some years later, on an equally flat site in Frankfurt, he took the accidents of the surrounding street pattern to generate a plan of subtle complexity by eroding and articulating the square grid that extends from the compact cube of the Biedermeier Villa Metzler to the whole site.

Consistency is an easy prey for imitators; it is only worth having if you can develop from it (out of it, within it, or even on it—all these prepositions fit the case) the resilience to meet whatever challenge a new commission might offer—and Meier has been consistent above all in this ability to renew himself. Indeed, his famous consistency is in some ways like the old criterion of beauty—unity, which needs variety to temper it so as to seize and hold attention.

His variety is programmatic: in the first volume of Richard Meier's collected buildings, in which his consistency was established beyond any question, more than half the projects were either private houses or housing, and practically all of them were in the United States. In this second volume, in which his resilience will become more apparent, five houses are published, three of which are built, and there are no housing schemes. This last is partly a reflection of the changed political circumstances in which Meier has been working. Few countries are likely to commission a foreign architect to build public housing, and in

the USA the shortage of public money for such housing is notorious. He seems to be an architect who does not appeal to speculative housing builders; on the contrary, he is appreciated by the many public bodies and corporations that have commissioned him.

Of twenty public buildings, only a quarter have so far been completed, though four more, one in the United States, the others in Europe (another feature of Meier's recent work is the number of buildings outside the United States) are under scaffolding. Of the American buildings, the Bridgeport Center introduces an important new consideration: how to create urban conditions in a city dominated by the motorcar, but racked—effectively split apart—as Bridgeport is, by express throughways.

The Center lies at the entry of Main Street from the throughway: it is, in a sense, the town's gateway and sentinel. The small nineteenth-century Barnum Museum was on the site first, and had to be accommodated in the new development. The main planning decision was to align the buildings to the street grid on two sides, but then to fan out a quadrant radiating from the main entrance of the building towards the throughway to make a form strong enough to be legible to the passing driver. Of a different order was the decision to face some of the building in a granite similar to that of the Barnum Museum. This granite was used for the main office block, a square tower rising to a giant pergola. Connecting the Barnum Museum and the square tower is a white porcelain wing which dies in a piano-curve pavilion between the square columns at the foot of the tower. The main banking space—the hall and the office—focus on a small circle. This focal circle appears prominently on the facade as a negative half-cylinder cut into the grey enamel office building, nearly as tall as the granite tower. Unlike the granite-faced rectilinear parts, it is

supported on cylindrical pilotis. A white enamel block which contains elevators, stairways, and the general circulation spaces, which look out over the town and harbor, is determined by the section of the circle and radii drawn right through the building. The granite square tower and the gently curved circulation block are clearly perceived from the throughway. The outer building in the sequence, a long and lower block, is again on square pillars and faced in granite, while a white enamel link between the office buildings "rhymes" in alignment and in white enamel with the other link between the Barnum Museum and the tower.

The great fan shape of the parking garage in its grey enamel and concrete block is a buffer to the most spectacular space within the building, the three-story-high banking hall. The light troughs, which provide the filtered backlight in the banking hall, act as a moat between the parking areas and the office space. At the same time the grey enamelled part of the office building facing the throughway also follows the curve of the fan as it rises, so that even the most casual passer-by cannot fail to notice that play of the grey against the orthogonalities of the red granite and the white links between the elements. Such formal intricacy is an essential aspect of the building's urbanity, a quality, not often sought by contemporary architects, as has been pointed out by some of Richard Meier's critics as well as by his admirers.

Of the many European schemes, the City Hall and Central Library in The Hague seem to me the most important and the most urbane; it is close to completion. The Hague is a gentle and ancient settlement; the medieval castle of the counts of Holland is still at the center, and it later became the residence of *stadhouders* and kings, and, finally, the administrative center of the country. Yet as a city, it is relatively modern and already contains as many distinguished twentieth-century buildings as

older ones: the Gemeente Museum, H.P. Berlage's last masterpiece, and J.J.P. Oud's Congress Center Building are two well-known examples. A monumental building by a foreign architect, the Peace Palace, now the International Court, was designed in the first decade of the century by the Frenchman, L.M. Cordonnier.

The small seventeenth-century town hall had already been extended shortly after World War Two by M.J. Luthmann. Meier's much larger building has a narrow facade on the Spui, one of the arterial streets of The Hague, and a long one on the Kalvermarkt, which is two blocks south of the Binnenhof, the Palace and Parliament building on the site of the ancient castle. Meier's building is in fact something more than a town hall, since it contains the city library, housed in two pavilions at the west end of the block. One is curved, the other more or less rectangular, and the two are connected by a glazed bridge, itself trapezoidal, since it takes up the grid of the inner town towards the Spui; internally it is at a right angle to the line of the Kalvermarkt, which is the main entry into the block from the Spui. The library, like the rest of the building, has a recessed ground floor with a mezzanine above, while pilotis support the main block (four and five stories in the case of the library) through its double height. The curve is the exposed part of the circle on which the plan of the library is based. It has an added importance, in the urban texture of The Hague, since it echoes the facade of P.L. Kramer's Bijenkorf Store, another famous project of the pre-war period, which stands at the other end of the same block.

The northern facade of the main building houses the actual town hall and its offices, while the south wall contains more offices, as well as the mayor's parlor. The two "walls" rise nine stories over

a ground-floor and mezzanine enclosing a large atrium; pilotis tie the two recessed lower floors into a colonnade, making the atrium an explicitly public and enclosed space. On the top two stories of the outer faces of the building it is echoed by a glazed wall recessed behind the columns to create a running "penthouse" parallel to those ground-floor colonnades, which are animated shops opening to the streets, while bars and restaurants open to the atrium. Various "incidents"—the curved council chamber which projects into it at the west end over four stories, and the ceremonious stairway which rises to the wedding registry—articulate and play on this public character of the atrium; it is also partitioned by two ranges of bridges which connect the two office "walls."

The idea of the atrium space grew in the 1960s and 1970s out of the nineteenth-century concept of the arcade, and it has become a commonplace of shopping malls and hotels. An arcade keeps out rain and snow, while an atrium allows temperature control as well and offers the possibility of creating a public space for all weather. Strangely enough, it has been neglected by most of the major architects of our time; Meier is one of the very first to incorporate it into an architectural conception of great quality.

The atrium of the city hall will be used not only by its workers but also by those in the adjoining ministries, as well as by visitors to the library and the neighboring theaters, or by passers-by. The entries are therefore quite crucial. One, which has already been mentioned, is the rather solemn one under the bridging block of the two libraries; another one, largely pedestrian, is focused by a fountain on the axis of the Victorian Gothic church across the Spui. It leads the visitor between the library on the left and the wall of the atrium on the right, which continues the splayed angle of the adjoining theater building.

Beyond the building, the visitor looks through the pilotis into the Kalvermarkt. The space, which may seem a little constricted on the model, is, at ground level, open to both the main streets and into the atrium proper through a glazed porch on the entrant's right. At the east end of the building, a block of rentable space makes another forecourt towards the Kalvermarkt, where the visitor looks through the block and under the pilotis into the pedestrian street.

What is perhaps more difficult to appreciate from the published drawings is the remarkable community this project has with some of the best Dutch architecture of the inter-war years. It comes perhaps closest to the work of Brinkman and Van der Vlugt, whose Van Nelle factory in Rotterdam, built sixty years ago, although still producing its quota of chocolate and coffee, remains one of the few truly monumental ensembles of our time. This community of style, this sympathy, is all the more remarkable since Meier achieves it without the slightest compromise of his very specific idiom.

Already much better known, though at the time of this writing site work has barely begun, is an American project for the Getty Center in Los Angeles. It will certainly be seen as the summa of Meier's approach and of his method. Without suggesting that there is any linear "progress" in Meier's work, it is still possible to see much of what he has done as "leading up to" this large and prominent scheme. It is prominent for all sorts of reasons: because the Getty Trust is perhaps the richest "cultural" foundation in the world; and also because, perched as it is overlooking the junction of the San Diego Freeway and Sunset Boulevard, the Getty Center will inevitably become one of the "sights" of the West Coast.

The Hague City Hall and
Central Library, The Hague,
The Netherlands. Richard
Meier, 1985-1994. Rendering

De Volharding Office Building,
The Hague, The Netherlands.
Buys and Lürsen, 1928.

De Bijenkorf Department Store,
The Hague, The Netherlands.
P.L. Kramer, 1926.

Van Nelle Factory, Rotterdam,
The Netherlands. Brinkman and
Van der Vlugt, 1930.

But there is yet another reason: the Center will certainly become a focus for pilgrimage—and I use the word advisedly. Like many of his contemporaries, Meier has been seduced by Corbusier's vision of the Florentine Charterhouse at Galluzzo in the Val d'Ema; now disused, it still looks like a walled, miniature city perched over the countryside, so that its windows overlook the treetops, much as Corbusier's later *immeuble-villas* were to do. More important for Corbusier (and by analogy for Meier in the Getty Center) was the way in which the monastery achieved a balance between privacy (even solitude) for the individual and the generosity of public space; that balance is almost the keynote of the Getty project.

The Getty is in fact a collection of institutions, of which the Museum and the Getty Center for the History of Art and the Humanities (the research center) are only the best known. But there is also a school of conservation, which houses an important aspect of the foundation's activities. Moreover, various enterprises that would normally occupy a full-scale publishing house are added to the normal work of the administration.

All this is vastly bigger, of course, than anything which the original Malibu building and its grounds could possibly have housed. Yet even at Malibu access had become a problem and the Pompeian villa-museum had to be treated as a kind of hanging garden over a car park. At the new Center, the decision was taken to exclude the car as far as possible. Visitors will park at the entrance off the San Diego Freeway, a quarter of a mile to the north of the main buildings, and will make their way up to it by tram; this arrangement may well (paradoxically, in Los Angeles) be a token of urban conditions in the future, in which private automobiles will have given way to public and electronic transport. Inevitably, since 2000 people, almost all of them

Angelinos, will find employment (and another estimated 4000 enjoyment) in these buildings daily, road access and parking are provided for the business users and for suppliers. However, within the enclave all movement will be pedestrian.

Once the visitor has alighted from the tram, he or she will come into the forecourt of the museum, and this forecourt will be flanked on the left by auditoriums and administration buildings, while on the right will be the restaurants and coffee shops. The buildings on the left will be aligned on a due north-south line, which is also the center line of the ravine that begins on the site; but the museum proper, which visitors will face directly, will be at an angle of twenty-two-and-a-half degrees to them, the angle which picks up the grid lines of western Los Angeles.

This forecourt, in so far as it will be appreciated as a defined shape, will be trapezoidal. To the right will be an access ramp to the main level, but directly before the visitor will be the steps up to the glazed museum entrance, through which the transparent cylinder of the main hall and the gardens beyond will be visible at ground level, while its opaque clerestory will project above the entrance. The part of the building that overhangs at entrance level, on the visitor's left, picks up the twenty-two-and-a-half degree angle against the orthogonals of the building, and urges the visitor into the museum, but it also continues, in a gentle curve, to draw attention to another garden, or rather a promenade, which lies between the museum and the research center; it then descends to a pergola, beyond which a semi-circular theater-orchard, an arcadia, opens onto a panorama of the city. For an "orchestra" or "stage," this theater has a circular pool fed by a discontinuous conduit that springs near the entrance and descends through a number of rectangular basins and channels. It is the climax, or perhaps the resolution, of the

composition, and one of the three dominant circles within it: the plan of the museum hall, the central courtyard for the research center, and finally that "orchestra."

The circular cortile makes the research center the most explicitly centered part of the whole complex, and this is evidently deliberate and indicative of the nature of that institution. It opens inward, and the radii of the circle are the ordering devices. Most obviously, in the interior, they provide the plan of the reference library; on the exterior, they allow Meier to develop abrupt and varied groupings within a very tight scheme.

There are other circular figures essential to the organization of the plan. The tramway station stands within a segmental courtyard; the administrative buildings on a semi-circular platform. Indeed there is a kind of symmetry between the orthogonal administration on its semi-circular platform and the circularly organized research center, which is enclosed by the two axial orthogonalities. Though axial may not quite be the right word, these lines, which I mentioned earlier when describing the entrance to the building, are directives, rather; they organize the buildings very clearly. One line, which goes from the circle of the helipad to the museum entrance, is deflected (as all these lines are when they meet one of the crucial circles) through the cylindrical hall, and continues down the avenue-garden to the circular pool in the arcadia where it is crossed by the line of the pergola which is the cut-off point of the whole urban texture, through which the theater and the edge buildings of the museum and of the research center extend on either side of the theater. The museum crests the hill as if it were the castle to this town; the research center descends more gracefully into a miniature garden suburb.

The other line, at twenty-two-and-a-half degrees, is notionally drawn though the center of the museum: it provides a datum to which the museum buildings as well as the restaurant block refer. It begins at the entrance, passes right through the museum, and like the other line, ends in a series of much smaller, rectangular descending pools beyond the pergola wall. Throughout the building the contrasting angles are reiterated through pavilions which, by their placing, recall the variations, even harshly at times.

Increasingly, as I tried to show both in the case of the Bridgeport Center and The Hague City Hall, Meier has relied on circular geometry as an ordering device, though nowhere as thoroughly (or at any rate, pervasively) as he has at the Getty. In a sense, the directing lines, which are not axes, since they are never continuous but are taken through a number of breaks and twists, are subordinated to the circles which are the nodal points of the building.

Very explicit, precisely because it is so small in scale, is Meier's use of a circle to organize the plan of the Grotta House in New Jersey. The type is one that he had worked out fully in his earliest houses: the public portion, the duplex "front" (living, dining, etc.) is opened to the landscape through large windows, while the private and service part is contained between two parallel walls. The entrance is through that second section, while the two parts of the house are articulated by an interspace, which is quite often top-lit. However, in the Grotta House, the rectangular private service section backs onto the rising lawn behind the house, a kind of private garden, and not the access road, so that entry to the higher floor is along a ramp, and from there to a staircase which leads to the lower floor and the center of the cylindrical "public" part. Here it meets the entry from the

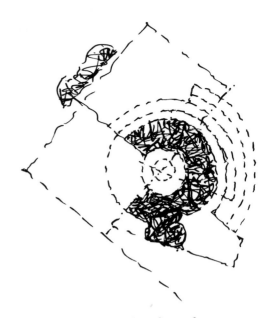

garages along a pergola from one side of the house, and a door into the garden and lawn which rise around the house. The geometry is almost brutally explicit: a public cylinder set almost tangentially to a private rectangle, the two solid bodies set to one side of a square podium. The two entries cut a quadrant out of the circle and meet at its geometrical center. Curiously, when you are in the house, the spaces required for its very individual working seem to be comfortably accommodated, the lines drawn in the most obvious, the most "natural" places. The geometry only obtrudes as you inspect the plan.

Of the abandoned projects, there is one which I particularly regret, that for the Eye Center for the Oregon Health Sciences University at Portland. Its attraction may well be partly accidental: the modest building, much smaller than many of Meier's schemes in Germany or France, straddles the main university entrance, and is therefore a gateway to the whole complex; consequently, it also includes a large parking garage for some 300 cars, which is built into the slope of the adjoining hill. A covered walkway connects the Eye Center with the other hospitals at roof level.

The particular requirements of this building have led Meier to invent formal devices he has not had to use elsewhere. The control of daylight is more crucial here than in his other buildings, and he has provided for it through panels "pulled out" of the outer walls, layered to allow top light to penetrate through interstices between them, while the windows proper are narrowed to horizontal slits and screened from direct sunlight by external screens. All this gives the building a rhythmic animation intensified by the contrast with the one big westward window overlooking the rest of the campus. It is another instance of Meier's accomplishment in extracting a vigorous stylistic turn

from what might have seemed constraining and awkward circumstances.

I have insisted on the continuity and the consistency in Meier's work, and this may seem a departure. That is not so. It is a clear demonstration of the other quality which I attribute to him: the capacity to innovate within the very tight and spare formal vocabulary that he has adopted. As I pointed out earlier, since antiquity writers on art have demanded that unity, that essential ingredient of beauty, be tempered with variety. To have achieved the intense concentration and the discipline of his consistency, and yet to have found a way to respond to locality, to specific constraints of program, even to the vagaries of his clients without departing from it in any way, singles Meier out among his contemporaries as having achieved the requirements set by the masters of his art—a classic.

Private Buildings and Projects

Westchester House

Westchester County, New York
1984–1986

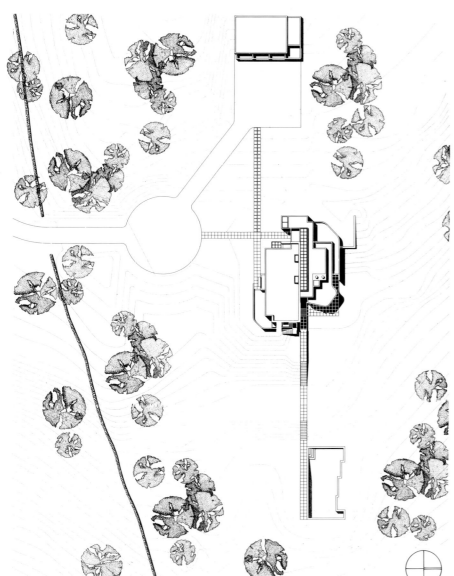

The rolling hillside site of this house has views to a landscape interlaced with fieldstone walls. The house, garage, and pool are located just below the highest point and are organized on an east-west axis that bisects the house and extends into the site as a bounding wall. A perpendicular approach leads to the house; inside, there are spectacular views to the northwest and northeast through undulating glass walls.

Unlike the Smith (1965) and Douglas (1975) houses to which it is related, this house does not face one direction. Instead, the *parti* consists of two more-or-less rectangular volumes that "slide" past each other in an east-west direction on either side of a top-lit stair hall that runs parallel to the same axis.

In contrast to the fully glazed living volume, the kitchen, study, and the private spaces on the upper levels are all enclosed in heavyweight masonry walls pierced by corner windows and relatively small openings. These walls relate in scale, color, and texture to the fieldstone works on the site.

In juxtaposition to the three-story private wing, the curvilinear metal and glass enclosure of the public space flows up past a suspended mezzanine floor to culminate in a series of overlapping roof terraces that run along the northern face of the house.

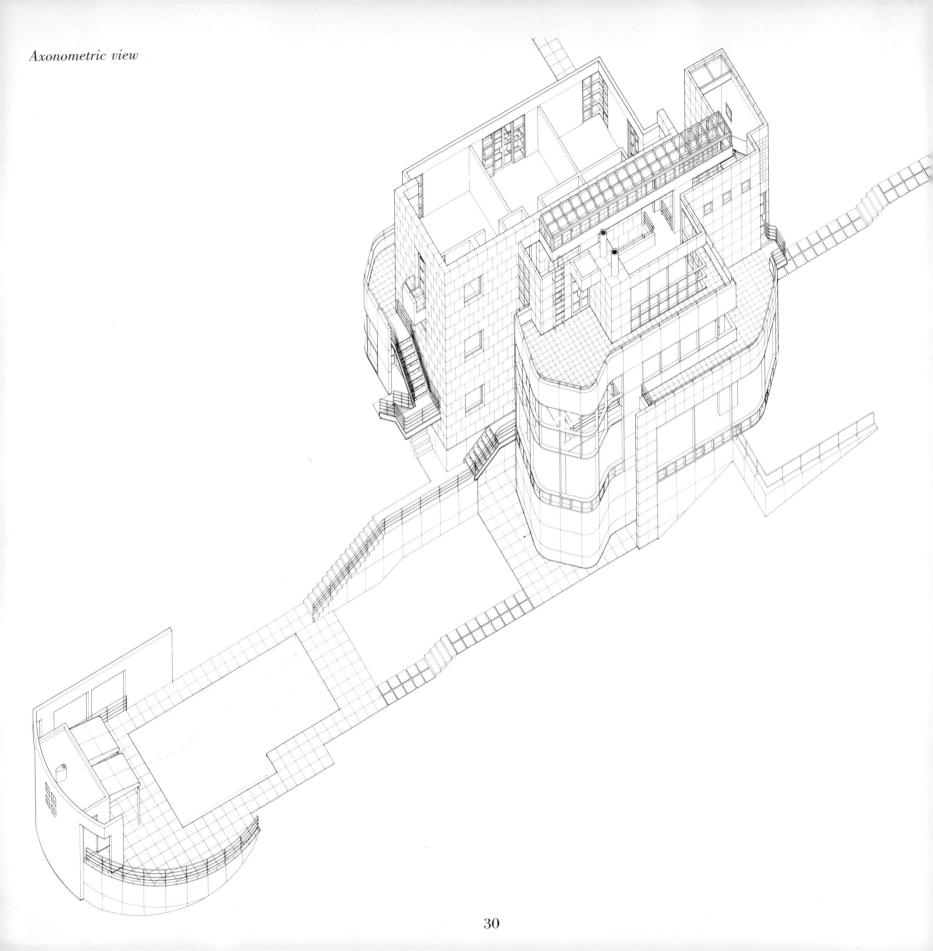

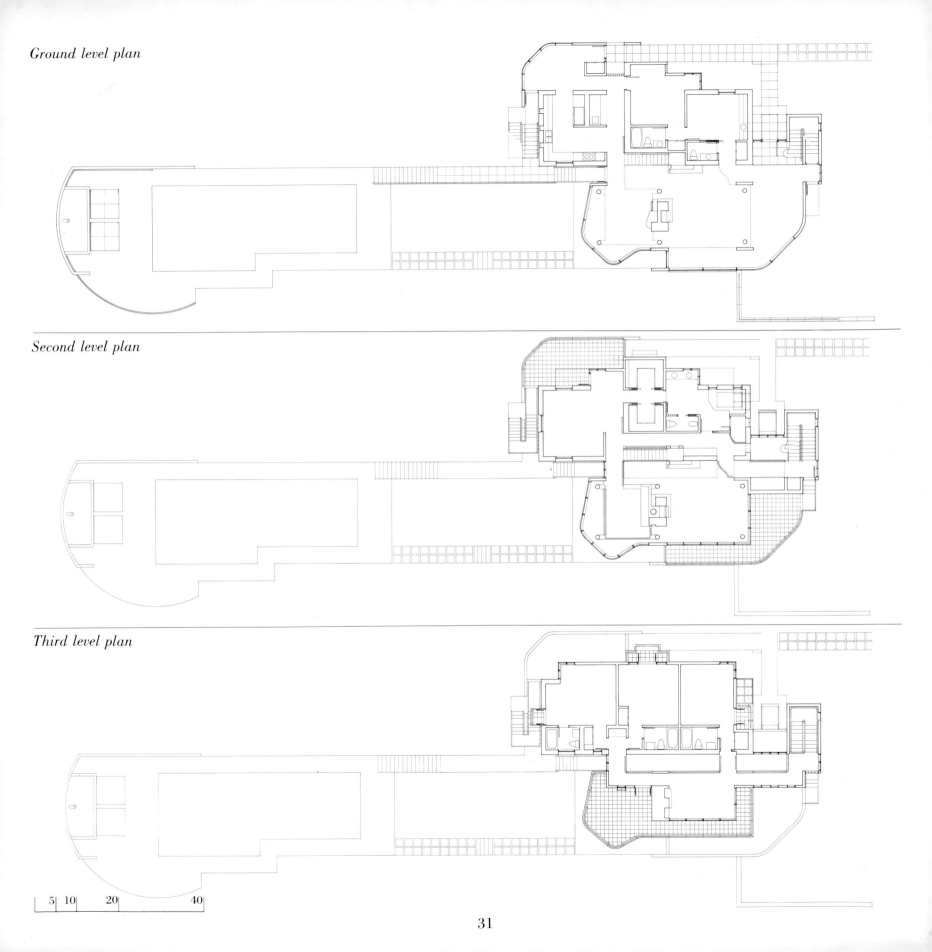

Ground level plan

Second level plan

Third level plan

5 10   20   40

31

While it is the client's responsibility to find a site, it is the architect's responsibility to make something of it, to make it better because of the architecture that is placed there. In this, our last private residence of the 1980s, the procession through this truly sensational one-hundred-acre site—from the public road through the woods and fields, along the old stone walls demarcating the pastures, and to the entry of the house—is a special experience to be remembered and contemplated from the house itself.

Cross section facing east

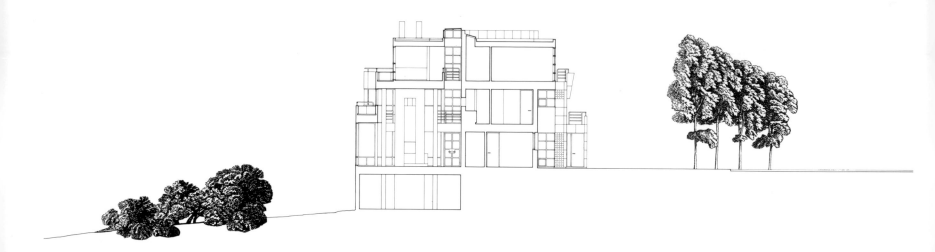

Longitudinal section facing south

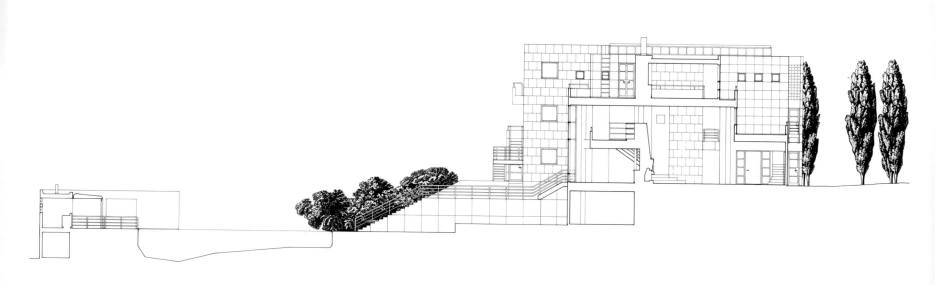

10| 20| 40|

The house faces north to the
verdant hills of Westchester,
where the views of the
countryside are ever-changing.
Within the large glazed walls of
the public spaces, one seems
perched on top of the world.

The path from the pool to the house bisects and denotes the top-lit circulation spine which separates the private, walled-masonry sector from the public, curvilinear portion of the house.

Stained glass becomes integral to the architecture when it is rectilinear, open in pattern, and simple in design. A small amount of color goes a long way. This double glazing at the clerestory level of the living room projects the red and blue into an otherwise monochromatic interior space.

Architecture comes into being in a variety of ways, through competitions, via the interview process, and by direct commission. For me, the latter is the most effective, for it allows both architect and client to know one another on a more personal level. When the patron is a childhood friend, as was the case for this house, the relationship of architect and client takes on an even richer quality of shared experience and appreciation of our past and future.

The sky-lit circulation spine opens through the home's three stories and bridges the living spaces and bedroom spaces on each of the upper floors. It expresses dramatically the individuality of the two parts of the house and their spatial connections. Along this light-filled path, the solid rectilinear house shears away from the more fluid and curvilinear glazed volume.

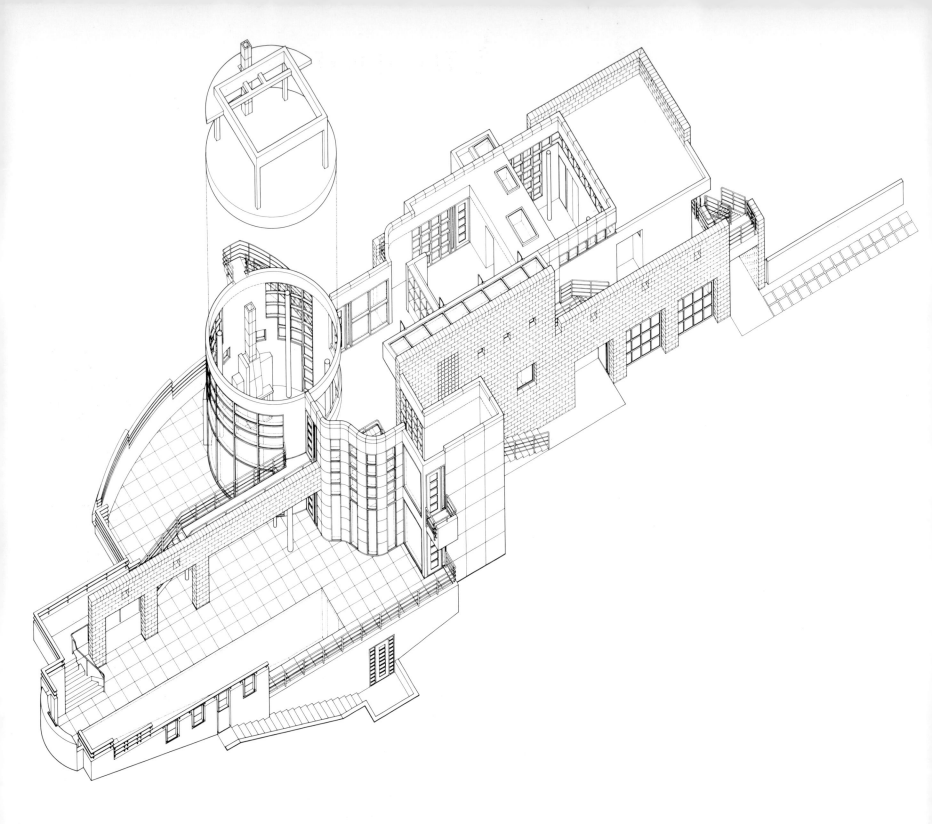

Helmick House

Des Moines, Iowa
1984

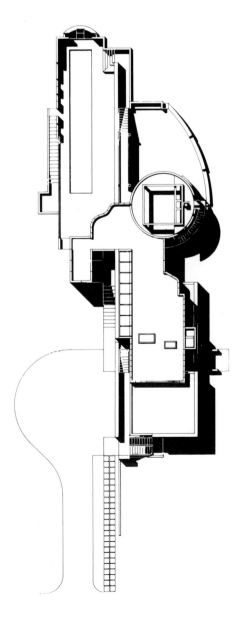

The narrow, suburban site of this project is bordered on the north by a bird sanctuary which, in addition to providing a natural screen, accounts for the orientation of the interior volumes. A new masonry wall running from east to west provides closure to the south and is the principal axial device around which this linear scheme is organized. Although designed for this specific place, this house has an organization and a quality that transcends the site.

After passing along the south face of the masonry wall, one enters the house through a metal-paneled vestibule. The entrance hall gives a view of the lap pool, and a glazed, serpentine surface links this space to the double-height, cylindrical living room, which is the central focus of the house.

The circulation, on both levels, is on the north side of the masonry spine, with a ramped entry stair linking the ground-floor, two-car garage to the kitchen, dining, and living room above. An enclosed main stair clad in metal paneling connects this principal floor to the exercise room, guest and master bedroom suites on the second floor. This floor has direct access to the pool by means of an open-air passerelle north of the masonry spine.

While this is the first Meier work to be orchestrated around a central cylinder, its overall surface treatment relies on a subtle interplay between concrete block, rendered walls, and precisely delineated areas of white enameled metal paneling. Although unbuilt, this project was important as a forerunner of later works.

First level plan

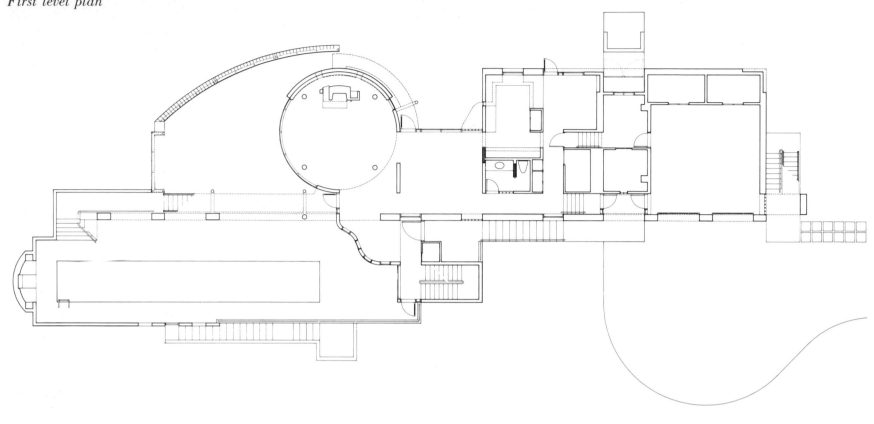

Second level plan

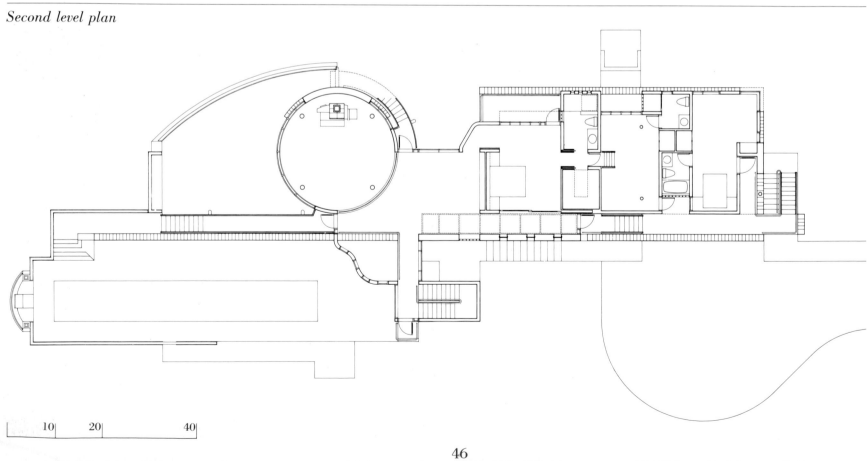

10 20   40

Ackerberg House

Malibu, California
1984–1986

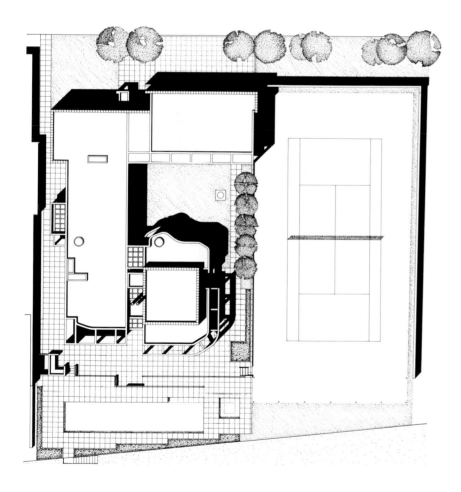

This house mediates between the mountains along the coastal highway to its north and the ocean beach front to the south. Related to the indigenous courtyard houses of Southern California, it is planned in relation to three adjacent courts. The L-shaped house is thus able to take full advantage of the marvelous, temperate climate with its living room opening directly onto an internal patio facing the water. This free-flowing spatial sequence is complemented by a pre-existing tennis court to the south and a new, narrow swimming pool west of the house.

The main approach is from the north, where, passing through a sheltered entry, one enters a double-height entrance hall faced in glass block. This space provides immediate access to the living room and patio. In general, there is a high level of interpenetration between exterior and interior space, especially in the public areas of the house.

In order to modulate and inflect the changing California light, the house has ample clerestories and skylights. A system of *brise soleil* integrated with the ground floor loggia is arrayed along the southern face of the house in order to frame the ocean panorama and to provide protection from high-angle sun.

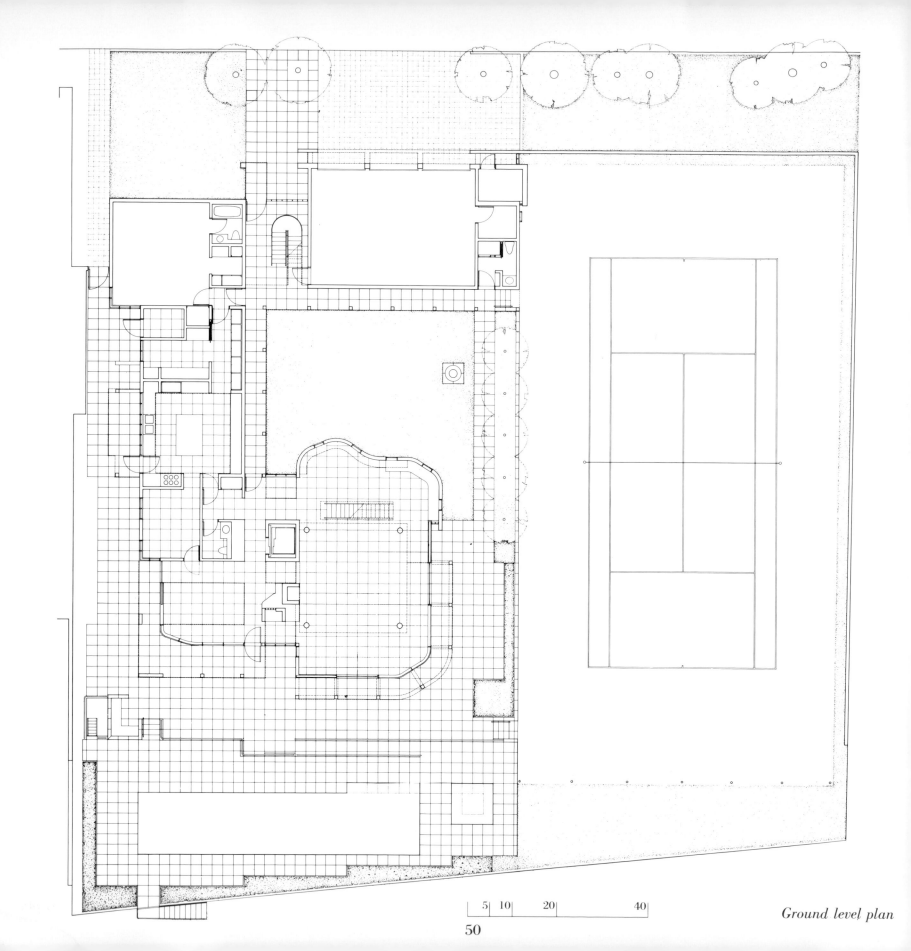

5 10   20   40

50

Ground level plan

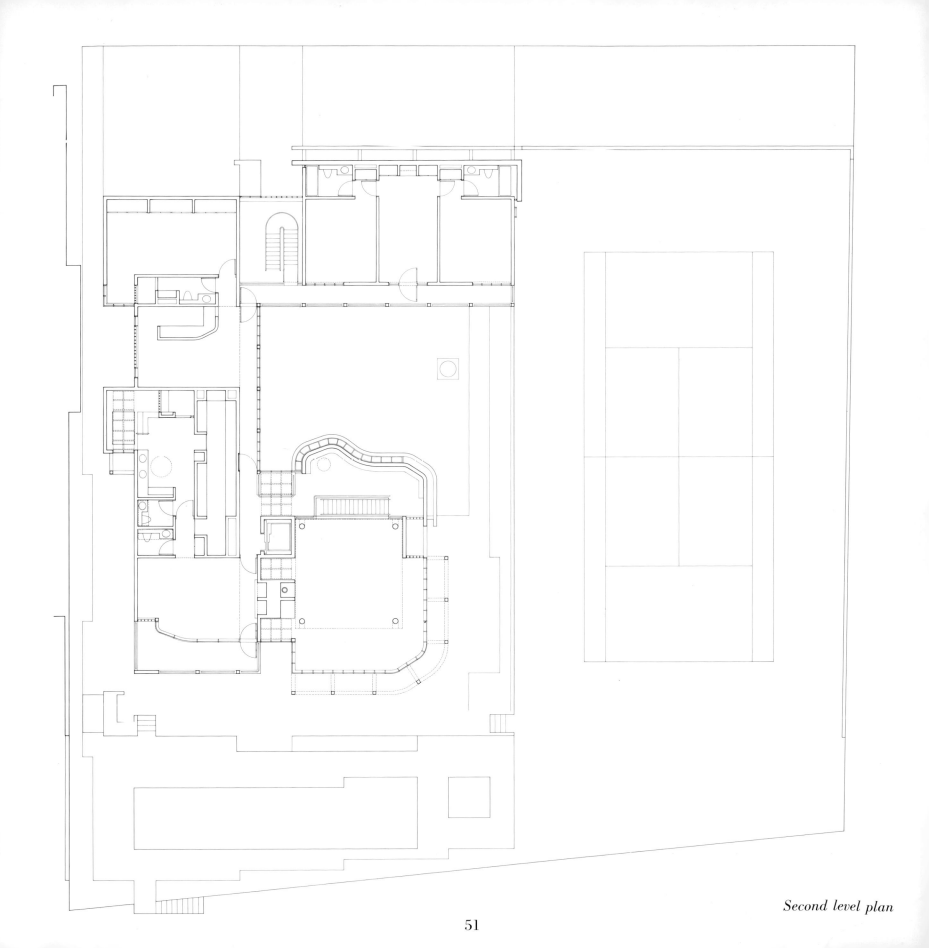

Second level plan

Malibu is an urban waterfront lined with row houses, with a visual order of absolute chaos. Each house—all ramshackle beach bungalows—differs from its neighbor. When looking for the Ackerberg House, all one has to seek is the white wall. Just inside this pristine wall, the sequence from the entry to the sea evokes a Mediterranean sensibility. One passes undercover from the roadside entry door through the inner courtyard to the front door. At this point, the sea and sand reveal themselves as the house becomes fluid and, at the same time, a powerful frame.

Longitudinal section facing west

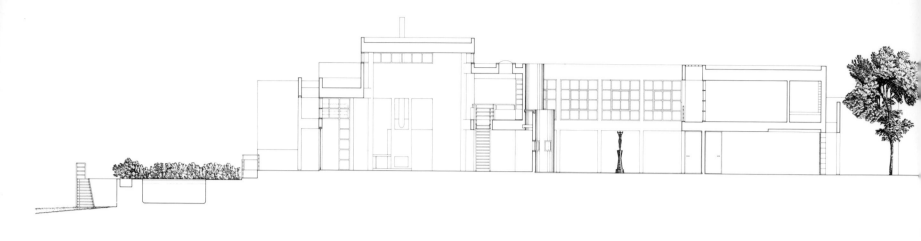

Cross section facing north

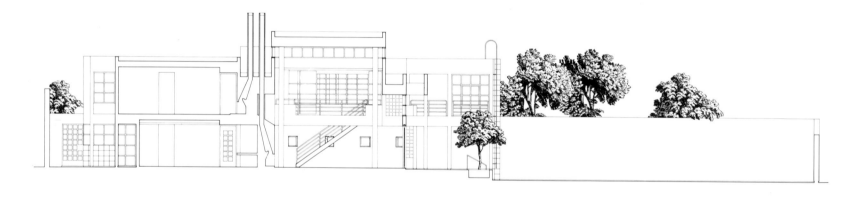

North elevation

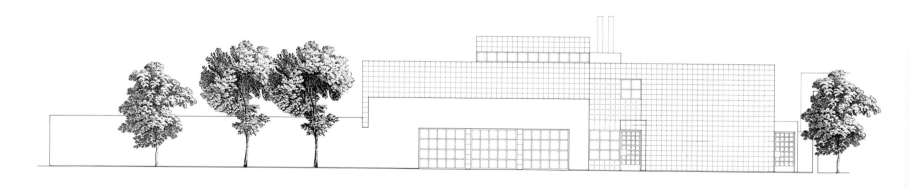

| 5 | 10 | 20 | 40 |

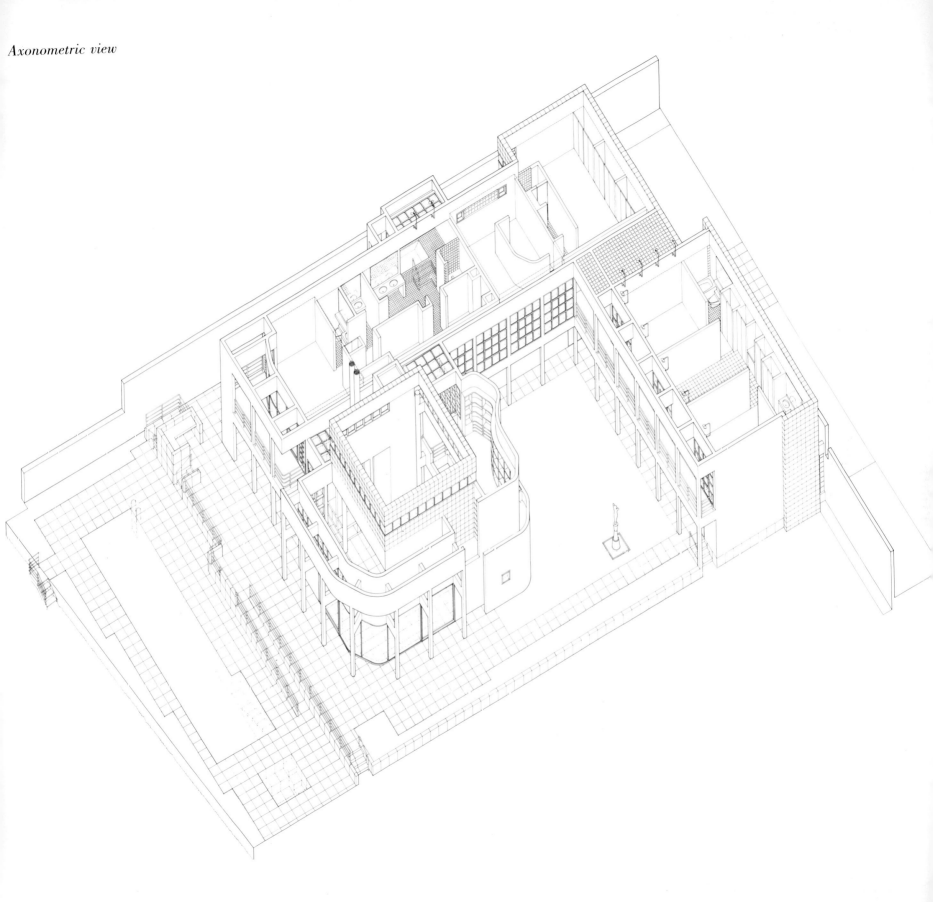

Each client brings something special to the making of a particular place—lifestyle, cultural necessities, material belongings, social aspirations, and family obligations. Rarely does architecture integrate all of these elements and also exist as a meaningful work of art on its own terms. With inspired clients, the making of a house is often a process full of joy.

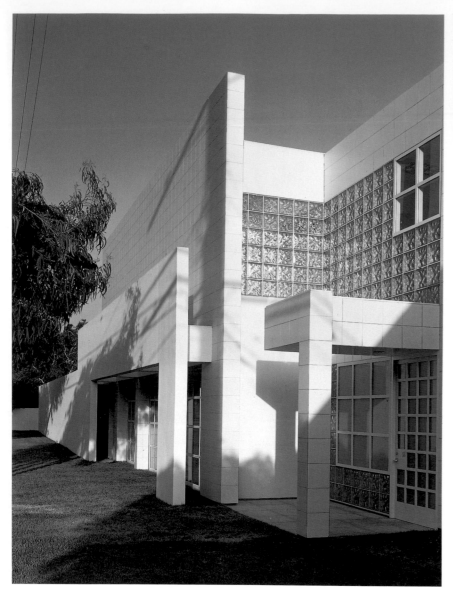

Grotta House

Harding Township, New Jersey
1984–1989

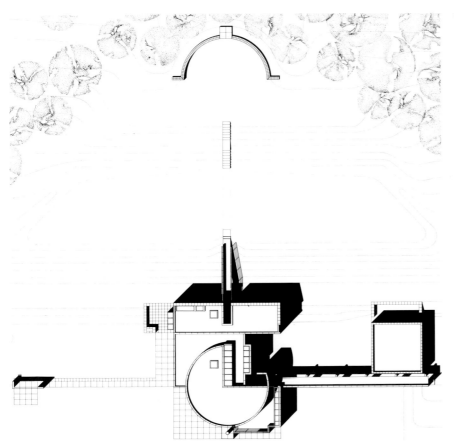

The site for this house is a seven-acre sloping meadowland with wooded areas to the northwest and scenic views towards the south and east. Two perpendicular axes extend from the center of the house to distant locations within the site, thereby extending the internal volumes into the landscape and establishing the house in a particular location within the site.

Like the Helmick House, this building is structured around a central cylindrical, double-height space, although this volume is partially absorbed by the orthogonal corpus to which it is attached. The living room, at the intersection of these two bodies, is divided into two different areas: a high, rectangular platform and a low, semicircular sitting area that surrounds a freestanding chimney.

A covered walkway connects the garage to the house, bisecting the house in plan and shearing it in section. Immediately upon entering, a perpendicular, sky-lit staircase establishes a countervailing axis that leads to an open-air passerelle which runs out to the upper garden level. These sequential changes in level are reflected in a number of sectional displacements throughout the ground floor.

Unlike previous houses, the range of materials employed here varies from the ubiquitous white enamel to grey enamel paneling and extensive wall areas of ground-faced concrete block at the back of the house.

First level plan

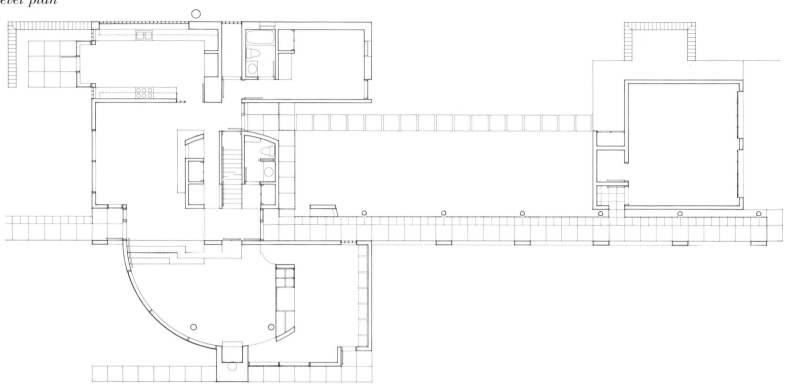

Second level plan

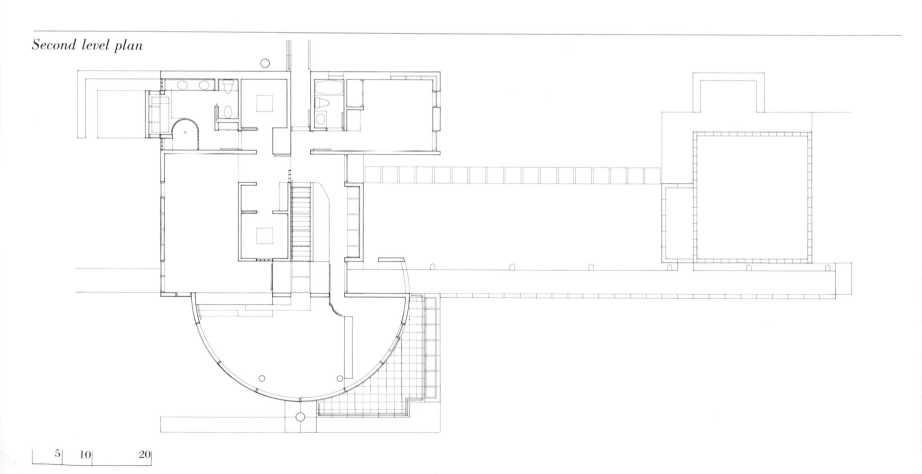

5 10   20

70

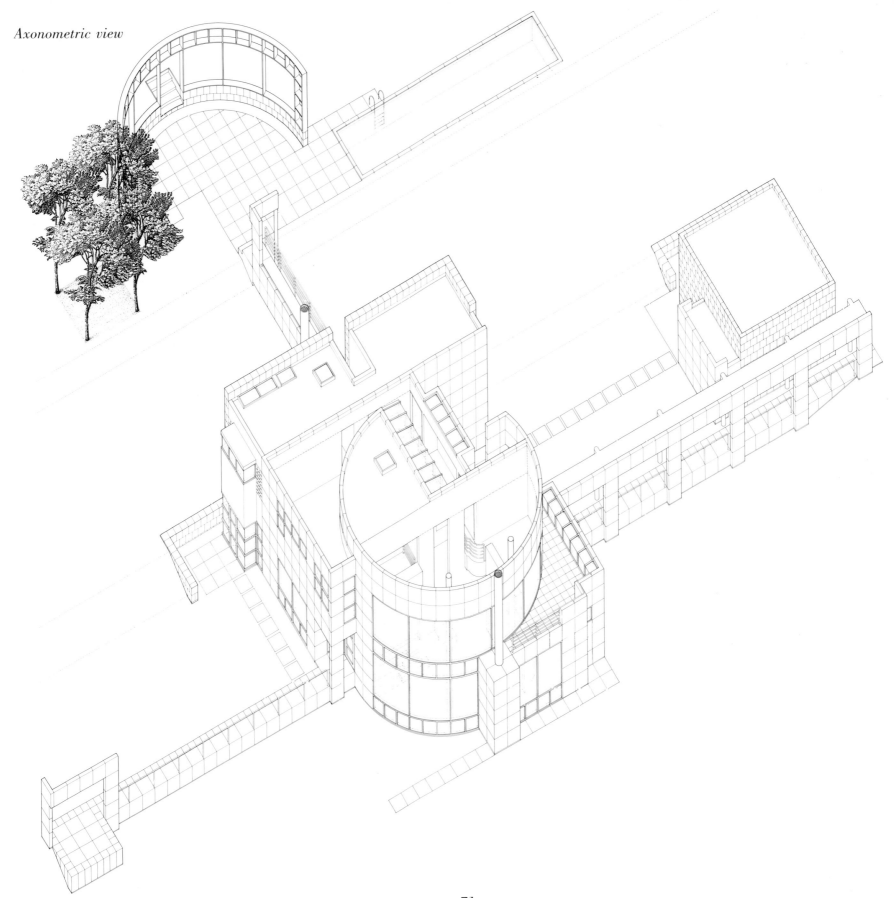

Axonometric view

71

74

Alighting a gentle ridge and surrounded by fields of gold, the Grotta House rests elegantly in the pastoral landscape of New Jersey's countryside.

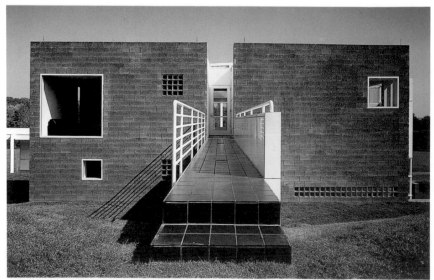

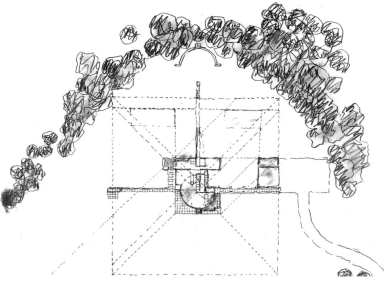

A simplified diagram of this house's plan would be a circle overlaid by a square. The intersection of these two forms creates the circulation space. Another path slices through the square, perpendicular to the initial field created by the overlap. This axis becomes the stairs.

The elegant precision of the
interior creates a sensual
juxtaposition with the more
earthbound forms of the owner's
outstanding contemporary craft
collection.

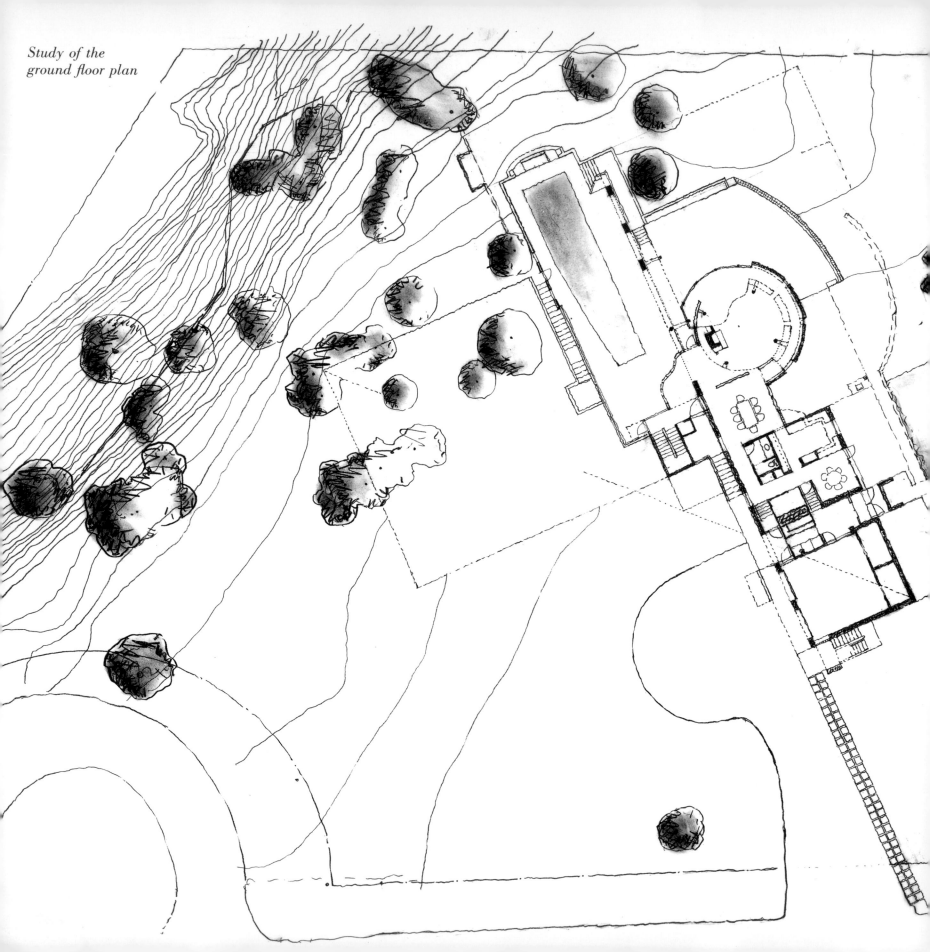

Study of the
ground floor plan

Rachofsky House

Dallas, Texas
1985

Unlike most of the previous houses that have a rectangular or cubic form, this house has more in common with the linear organization of the Helmick House (1984) and even the Old Westbury House (dating back to 1971). Clearly, much of this organization derives from the narrow suburban site and from its somewhat awkward orientation.

The house extends to the west while opening out towards the north over an irregular, picturesque lake. These conditions, in addition to the preservation of outstanding trees on the site, largely determined the linear organization. Thus, the house begins at one end with the carpark/portico and terminates at the other in a three-story, cylindrical living room. This familiar motif is crowned by a circular viewing terrace overlooking downtown Dallas. At the third story, it is modulated by a free-form platform that doubles as a study and is linked to the master bedroom suite directly above the children's rooms and the guest quarters on the second floor. The entire house stands on a granite podium, and its linear form is augmented by a lap pool that extends into the garden.

First level plan

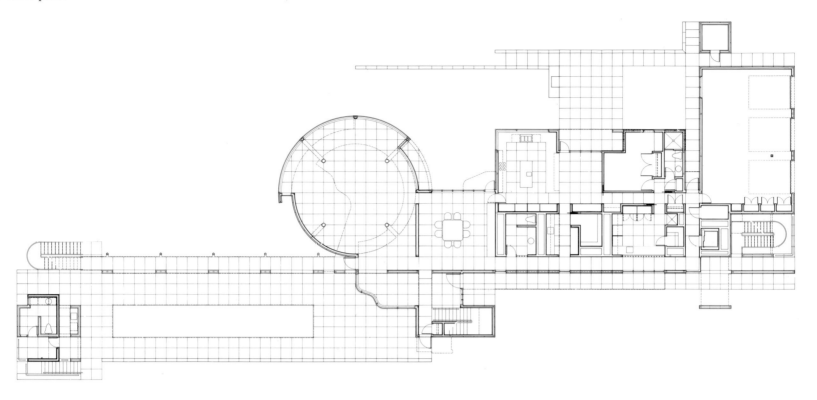

Second level plan

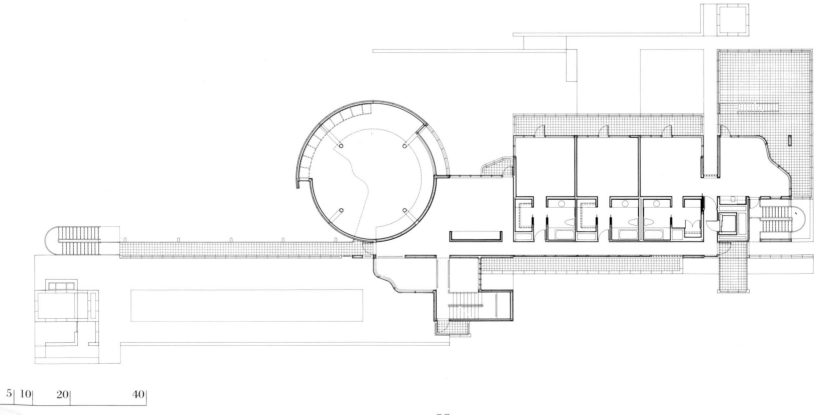

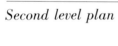

Third level plan

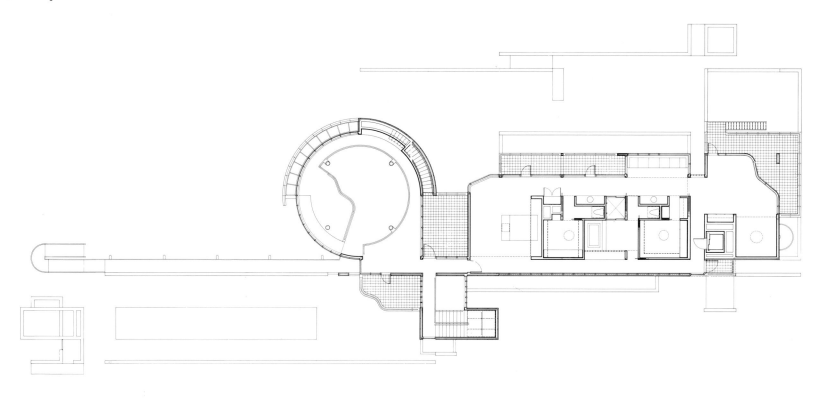

Roof level plan

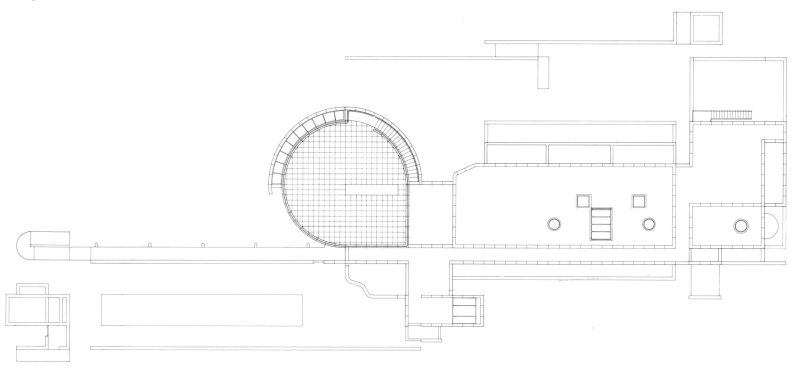

North elevation

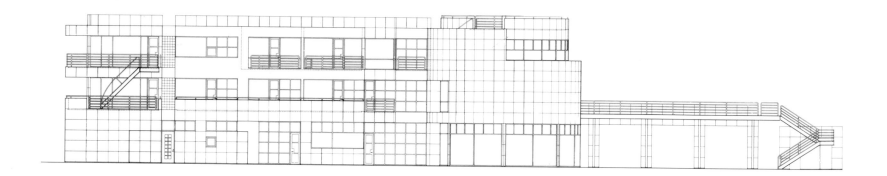

South elevation

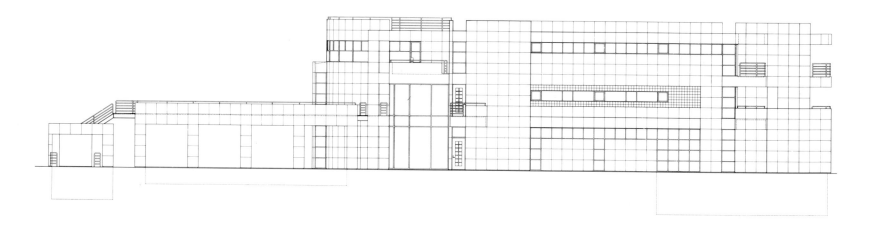

East elevation   *West elevation*

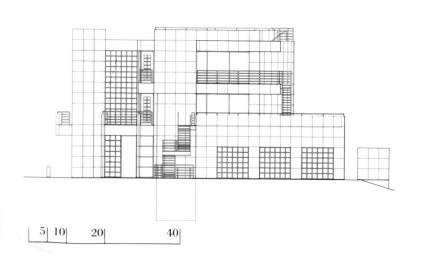   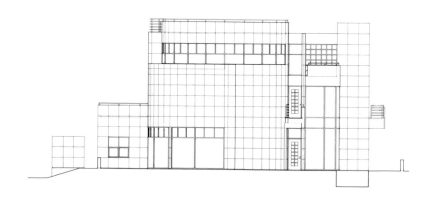

5| 10| 20| 40|

90

Cross section facing south

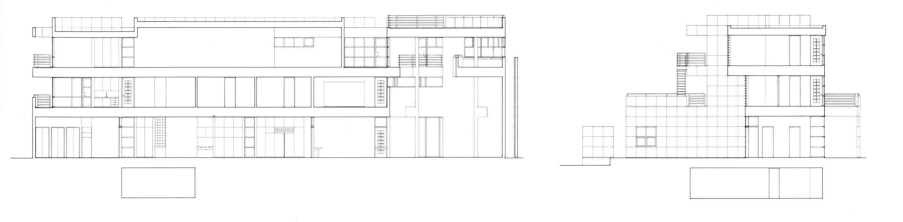

Cross section facing east

Cross section facing east

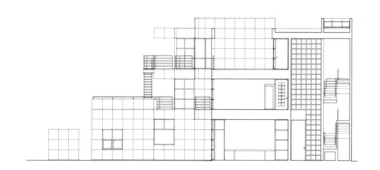

Cross section facing east

Cross section facing west

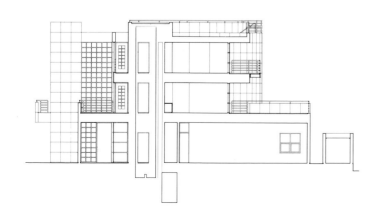

Cross section facing west

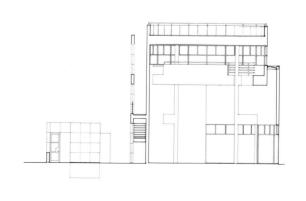

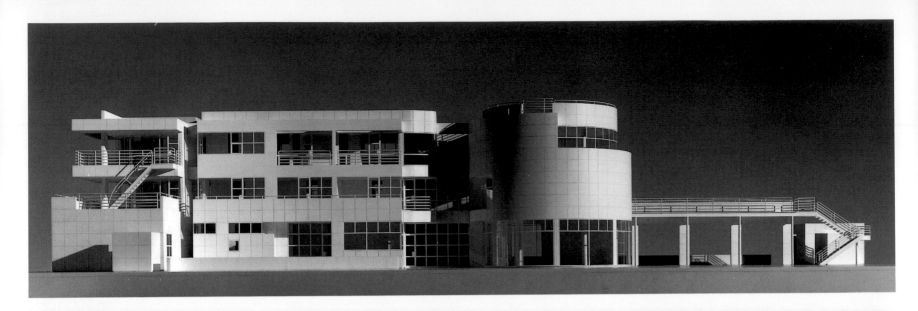

The program of this house,
grand in its conception and
scale, reflects the cultural
climate of the 1980s. Had the
Rachofsky House been designed
today, its forms would be
reduced in scale and would
more clearly express its formal
organization.

Dallas is a strange place. It would seem that those who live there do not always know where "there" is and often change their mind about their there. Nevertheless, it is a place we love to hate and would hate to be without. This house is Texas—vast, ambitious, larger than life, and yet unrealized. It still may come into being, perhaps in a different guise. Every time I say that I will never do another house, a client comes along, willing to take that leap of faith with me to grasp that moment when the house becomes the distillation of the most compelling ideas that are rattling around in my brain. What a wonderful way to make architecture. Thank heaven for crazy Texans.

Museum for the Decorative Arts

Frankfurt am Main, Germany
1979–1985

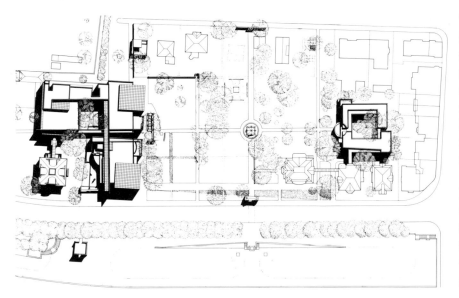

The character of the surrounding environment had a decisive impact on the form of this building, not only in terms of the topography but also with respect to the local *doppel villa* topology. Designed as a part of a new cultural district—the so-called *Museumsüfer*—on the banks of the river Main, this museum was a transitional work in more ways than one; first, because it represented a shift in the kind of commissions coming into the office, and second, because it was part of the wholesale conversion of a residential quarter to public use.

By accommodating the program within a limited area, much of the site could be treated as a park, open to the community, to Sachsenhausen in the south, and to the city across the river in the north. In addition, precisely articulated pathways and vistas were used to reorganize the site in order to overcome the barrier formed by the villas lining the Main River.

The skewed organization of the plan was based on two intersecting geometries: on an orthogonal grid deriving from the nineteenth-century Villa Metzler, and on a discrepant second grid taken from the alignment of the river. The villa is further incorporated into the new composition by being inscribed into one quadrant of a sixteen-square grid that includes the whole complex. This initial grid was then overlaid by a second grid of exactly the same size, but rotated 3½ degrees to align with the embankment.

The general organization of the museum has a specifically didactic character, with visitor circulation counterclockwise through a prescribed series of spaces that outline the history of European decorative art. Specific openings are framed in various ways to sustain a sense of discovery, but objects are always presented in the scale of their immediate environment.

97

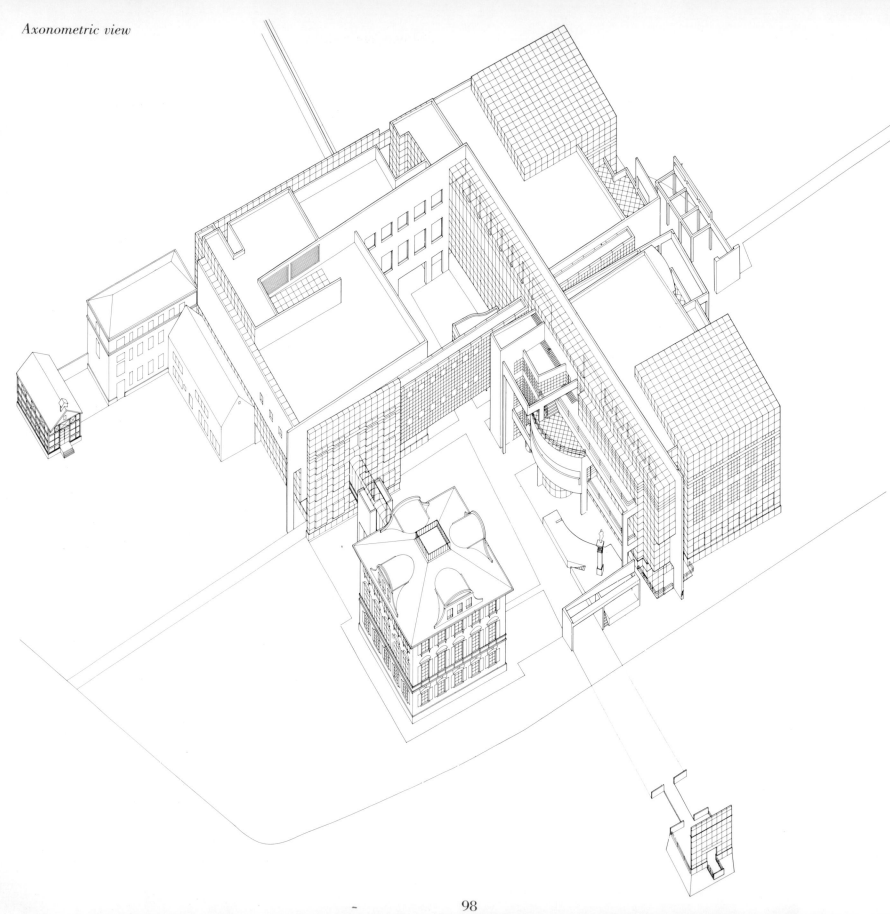

Ground level plan

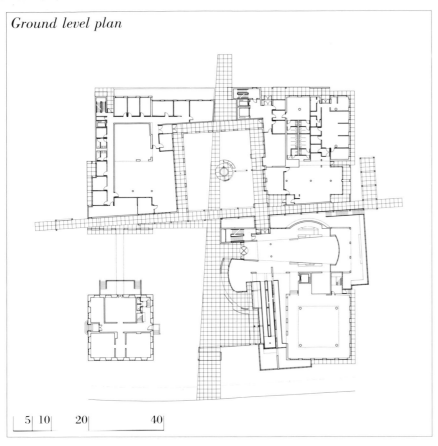

5| 10| 20| 40|

First level plan

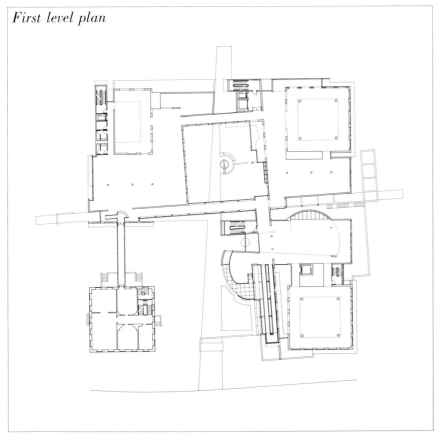

Second level plan

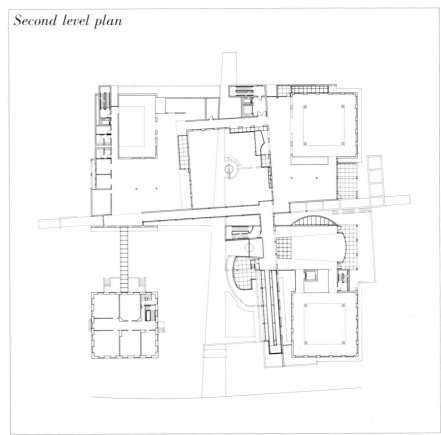

Roof plan

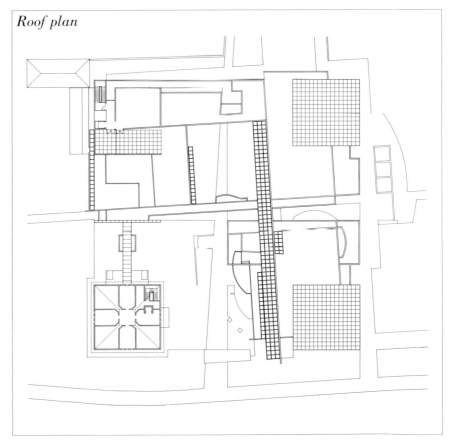

99

Facade study of Villa Metzler

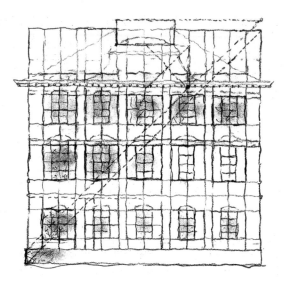

Facade study of new building

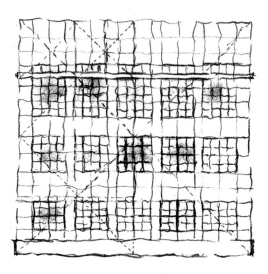

Facade of Villa Metzler with overlaid grid

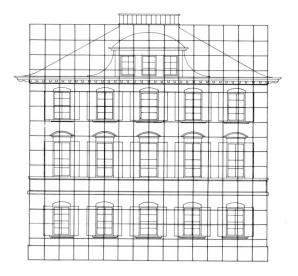

Panel and fenestration grid of new building

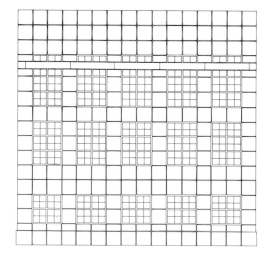

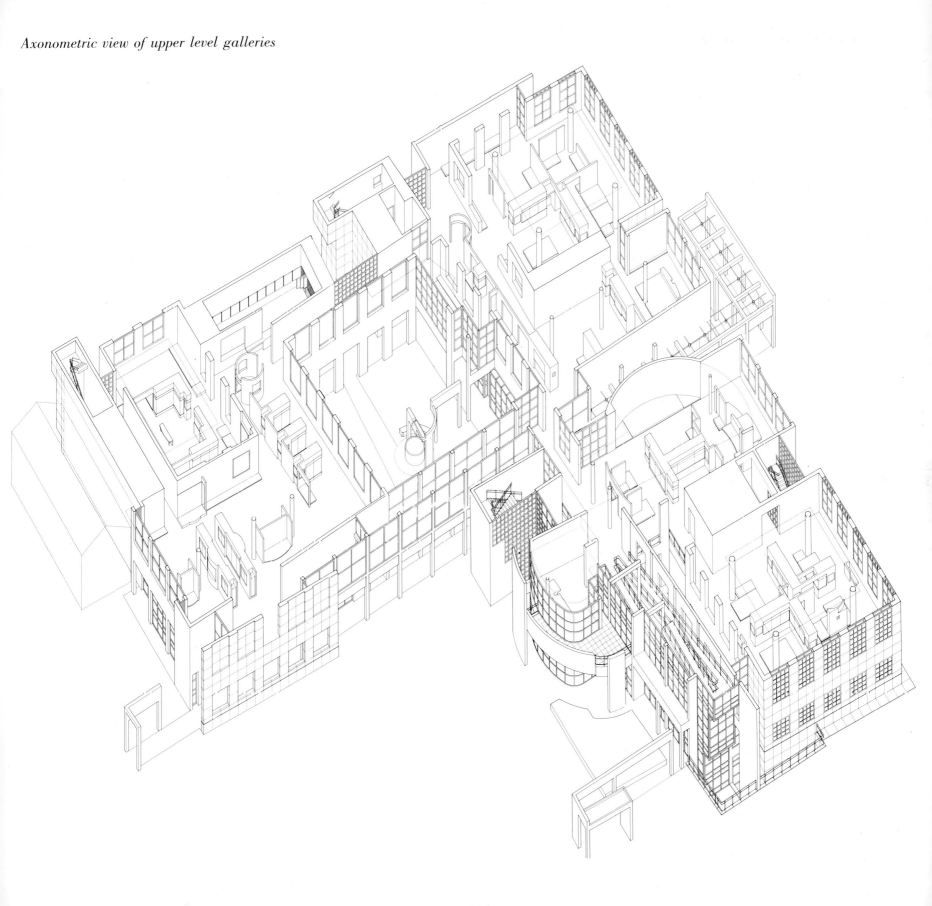

Axonometric view of upper level galleries

The urban fabric of Frankfurt and the program of the museum became an opportunity to work with a confluence of scales that have tremendous resonance. The European idea of a museum as a series of rooms, like a great palace, and the domestic scale of the objects in this museum, made it even more fitting that this building be like a house in a garden or a pavilion in a park.

103

Building in Germany at this particular moment was an opportunity to construct a very important bridge, a link between the old and the new, between history and the present, and between what was and what could be. For me it was a way of dealing with my own family's roots and the significance of their departure from Germany. The project allowed me to make a work of art that forms a meaningful continuity with a broken cultural heritage.

Des Moines Art Center Addition

Des Moines, Iowa
1982–1984

The Des Moines Art Center, designed in 1948 by Eliel Saarinen, consisted of a U-shaped single-story gallery and a double-height gallery to its west terminated by a two-story annex. In 1965, in order to create an internal sculpture court, I.M. Pei added a block, facing a public park to the south, that closed the original U-plan. Due to the slope of the site and its proximity to the earlier education wing, the Pei building could rise two full floors without overwhelming the low profile of the original building. Since the Saarinen building is visible from the downtown approach, the problem was to design a new addition that would respect the generally horizontal profile of the center; consequently, it was decided to articulate the new addition as a series of separate volumes that would not produce a large mass. Thus, three new additions were located, mostly north of the earlier complex, in such a way as to reinforce the formal order of the Saarinen scheme.

The program called for permanent and temporary exhibition spaces, maintenance/facilities rooms, additional storage, and a public restaurant that could also double as a meeting room. The east-west entry axis of the existing museum is strengthened by a new courtyard pavilion accommodating the restaurant/meeting room which now activates the previously underutilized court by opening it to the patio in warm weather.

A glass-enclosed link along the north-south axis leads to the main new addition, which houses most of the additional gallery space. It is larger and volumetrically separate from the Saarinen building, and is vertically condensed in such a way as to leave the preferred view of the existing museum unobstructed. The largest of its three levels, the temporary exhibition gallery, is below grade and provided with light slots to admit natural light.

The overall plan of this addition derives from a nine-square grid, in which the central square is pushed up to provide a four-column internal atrium, lit by clerestory windows and perimeter skylights. This cubic volume is sheathed in granite and covered by a flattened pyramid that is a foil to the butterfly-section roof employed by Pei. A third, smaller addition, accommodating services and additional gallery space above, is attached to the west wing of the Saarinen building, thus completing the discrete amplification of the complex by three separate additions of different sizes.

This project, clad in four foot square panels of metal and granite, is the first in which granite was used as a primary facing material. A pink-beige stone was selected to blend with the exterior masonry of the Saarinen building. Elsewhere, where curved forms are introduced, they are finished in white porcelain-enameled steel, in contrast to the gray finish and orthogonal profiling of the granite.

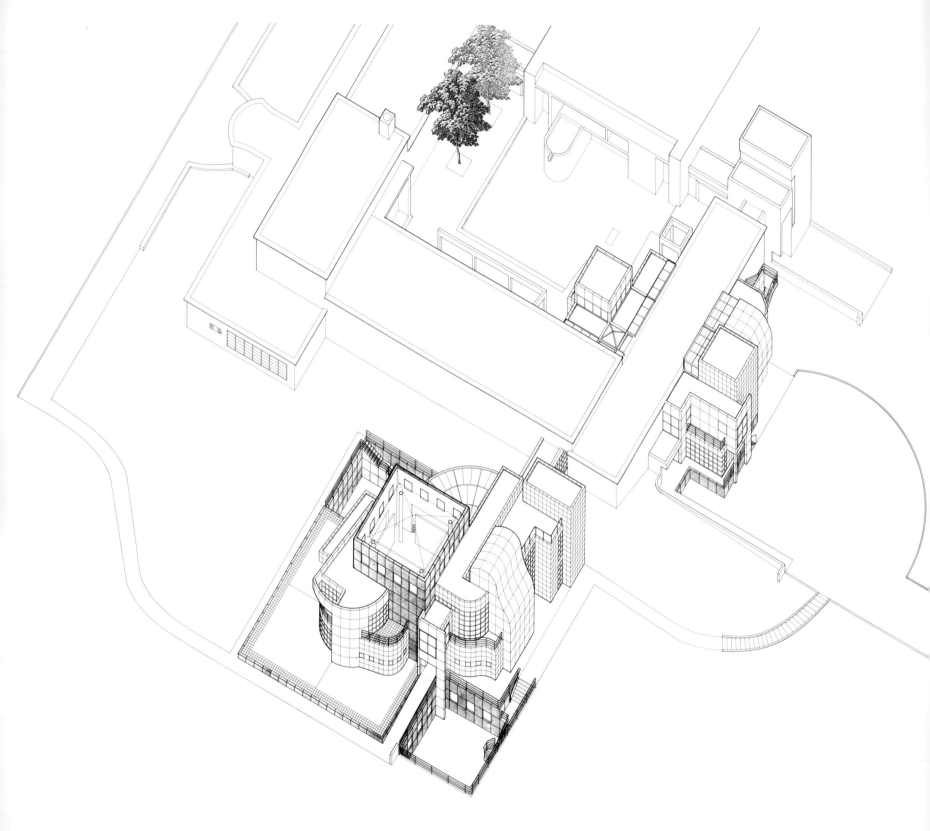

Axonometric view

Ground level plan

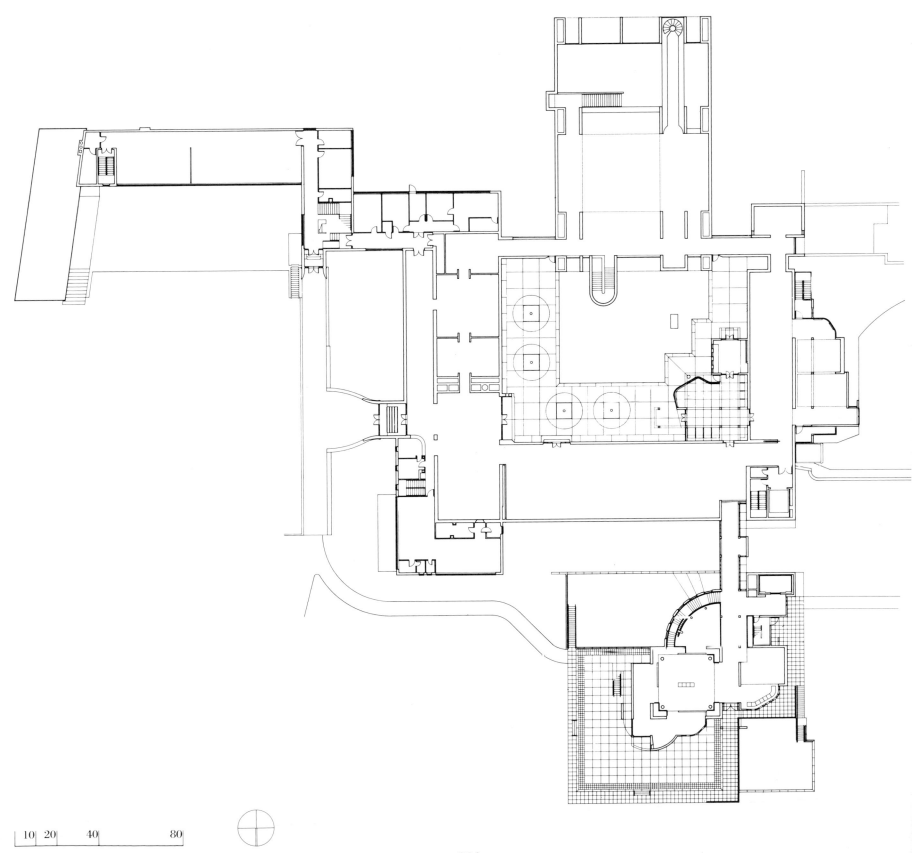

10 20   40   80

The challenge here was to build a museum space as an addition to the works of two greatly respected architects. There were two ways to deal with the context. One was to try to replicate that which existed. The other was to create a counterpoint which is respectful, but which has its own existence and projects a conscious presence. I chose the latter.

North elevation

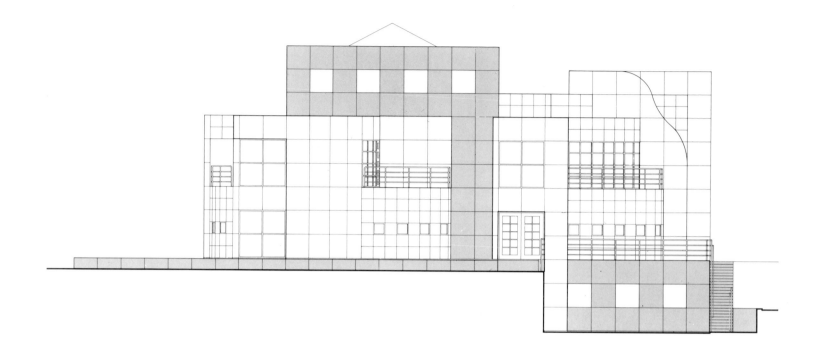

South elevation

5 10   20   40

Section facing north

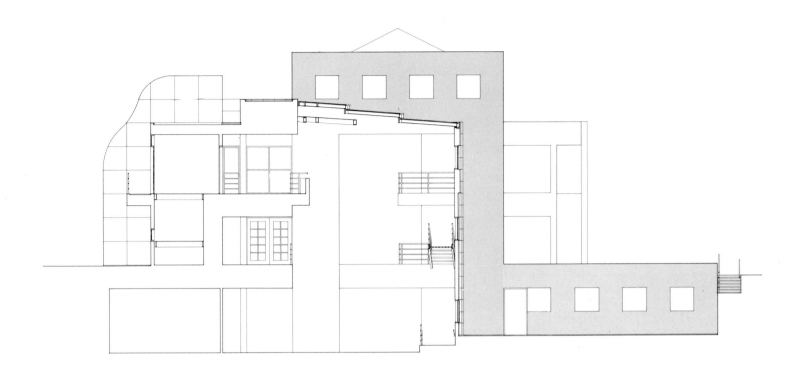

Section facing west

Section facing north

Section facing west

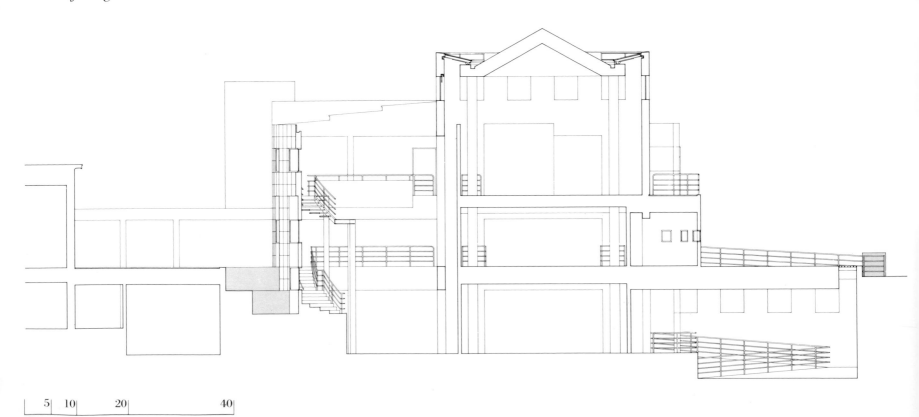

5 10   20   40

West elevation

East elevation

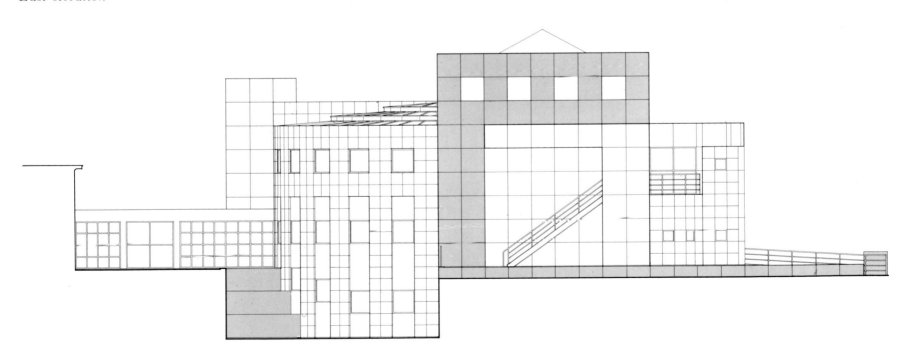

Architecture is the thoughtful making of space, space that we exist in, move through, and use. Spatial ideas are the oxygen of our universe. My concerns have been and continue to be about spatial constructs. However, when I speak of space it is not in the abstract, for my work is always related to light, human scale, and the culture of architecture.

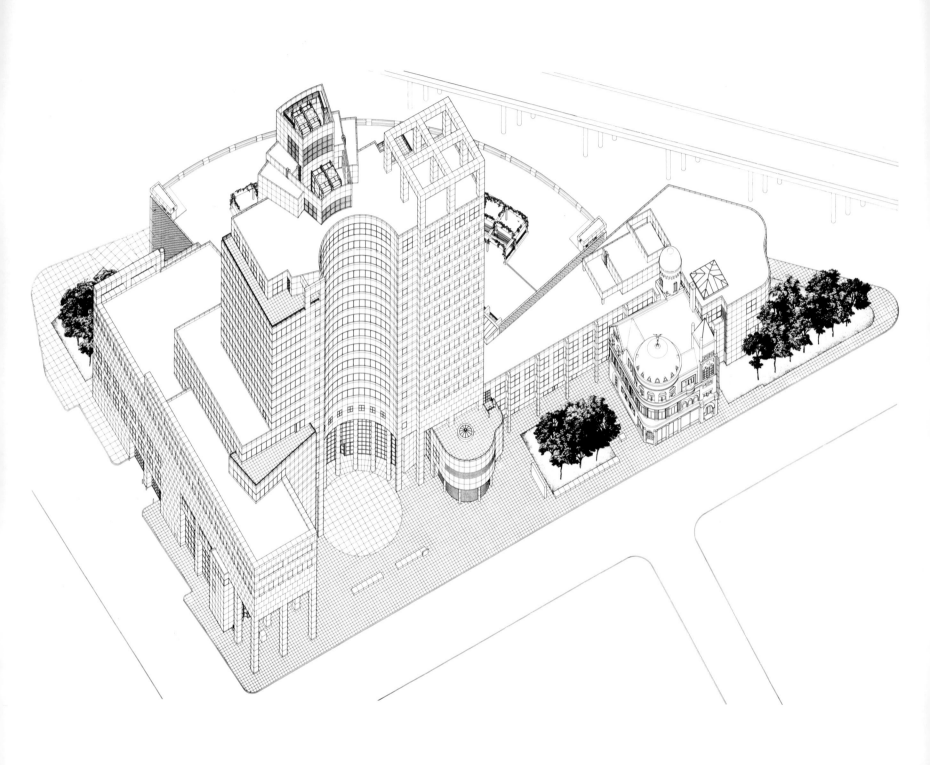

Bridgeport Center

Bridgeport, Connecticut
1984–1989

Bridgeport Center takes a new approach to the problem of redevelopment in a deteriorated urban context. Eschewing the single, monolithic edifice, this complex was conceived as an assembly of heterogeneous buildings designed to echo the form and scale of the city fabric. Bridgeport Center is designed as a continuous fabric of low to mid-rise structures, with different surfaces, to relate to its context. The assembly responds both to the overall view of the downtown area from the highway, and to the pedestrian experience of the building from the central spine of Main Street.

The internal focus of the building is a five-story atrium that links the lobby and elevators to the parking garage and serves as the distribution core for the sixteen-story office tower rising above.

The adjacent Barnum Museum has been restored as a historic landmark and linked to the Bridgeport Center by a wing with gallery space at grade, a training center on the second floor, and an employee cafeteria above.

Faced in white and gray porcelain steel panels, red granite and clear insulating glass, Bridgeport Center is a demonstration of the way in which "cities in miniature" can revitalize decaying urban areas while still harmonizing with their context.

Ground level plan

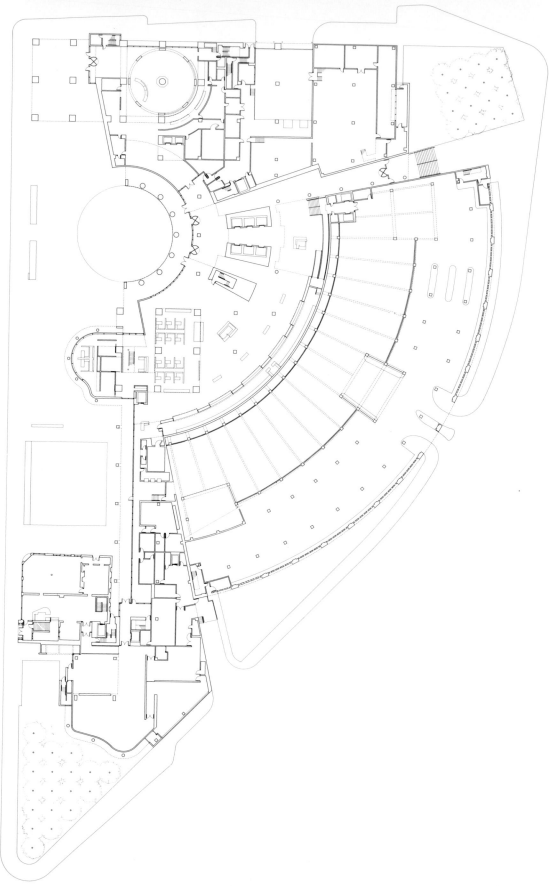

5|10| 25| 50|

Third level plan

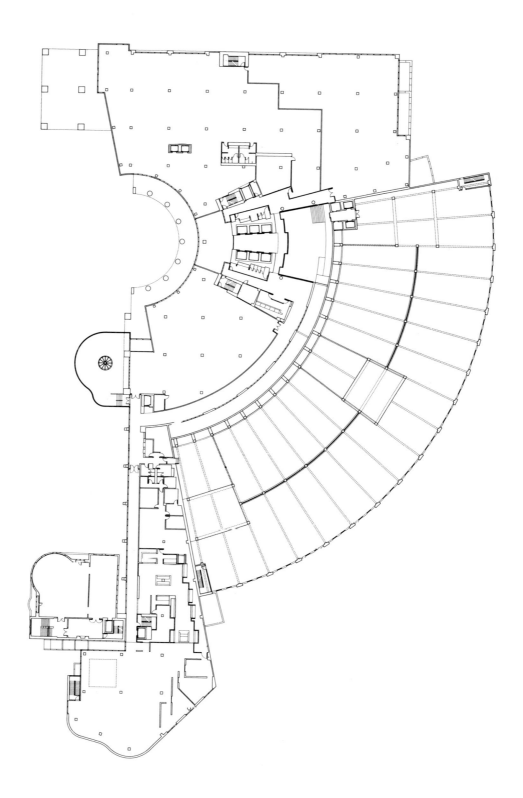

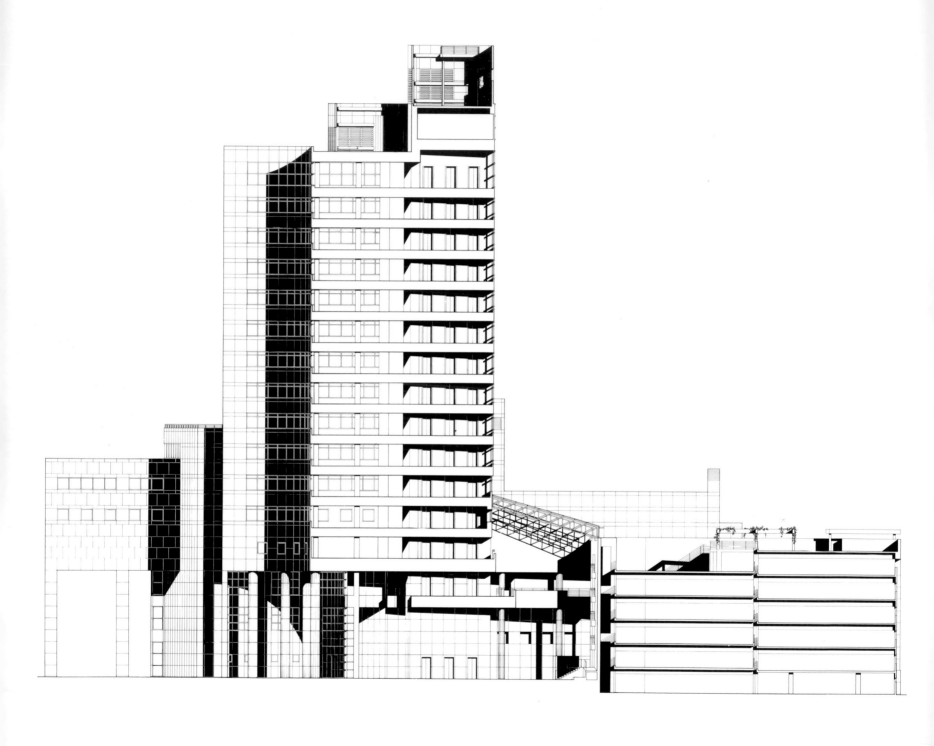

5 10   20   40

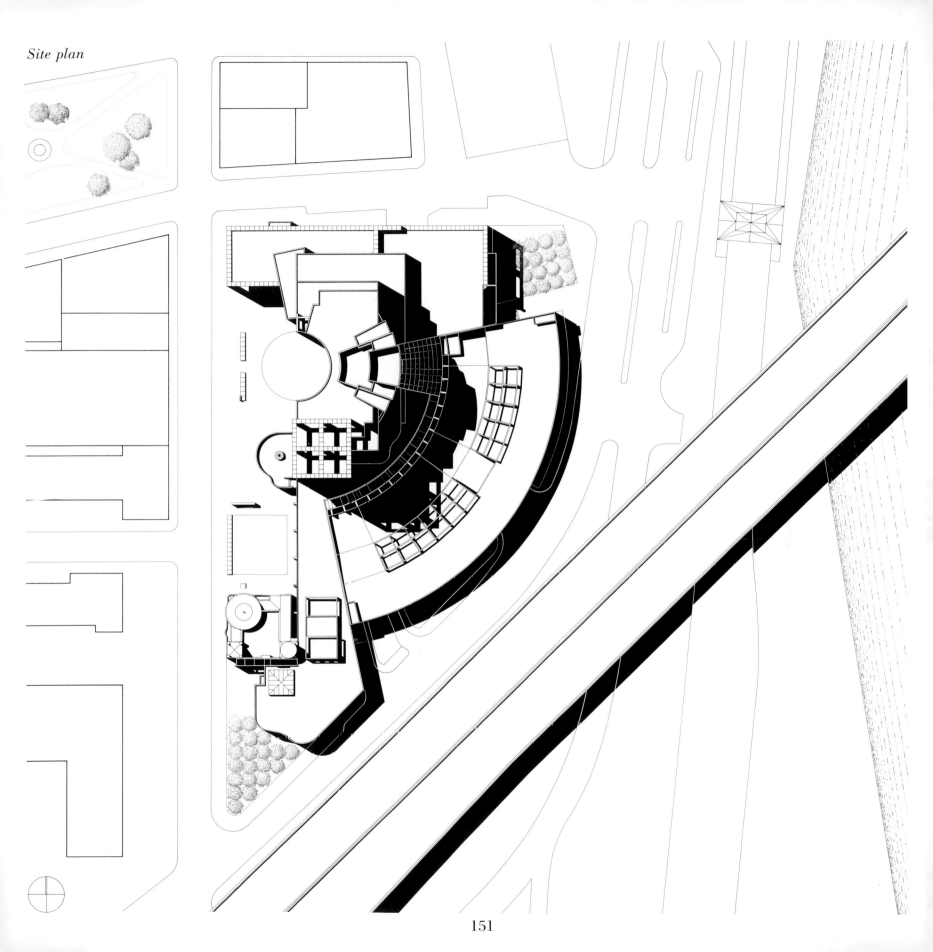

Site plan

The concave form of the building acts as a kind of focus, gathering pedestrians into its radiant interior. At the crossroads of the city, the building displays various faces reflecting its contextual richness.

The People's Bank building at Bridgeport Center functions as a beacon. It has an illuminated interior for those who work and bank there, but it also has a symbolic dimension in its location adjacent to Interstate 95, the main autoroute between New York and Boston. It is not only a symbol of hope to the depositors and customers of the bank, but it represents the spiritual and conceptual renewal of the downtown area.

The main hall is full of light.
It is the core of the building's
circulation space, connecting
parking, office, lobby, and
entry spaces with the heart of
the building—the banking hall.

*The building is intended to be
an assemblage of various
disparate elements connected to
one another and to the city.*

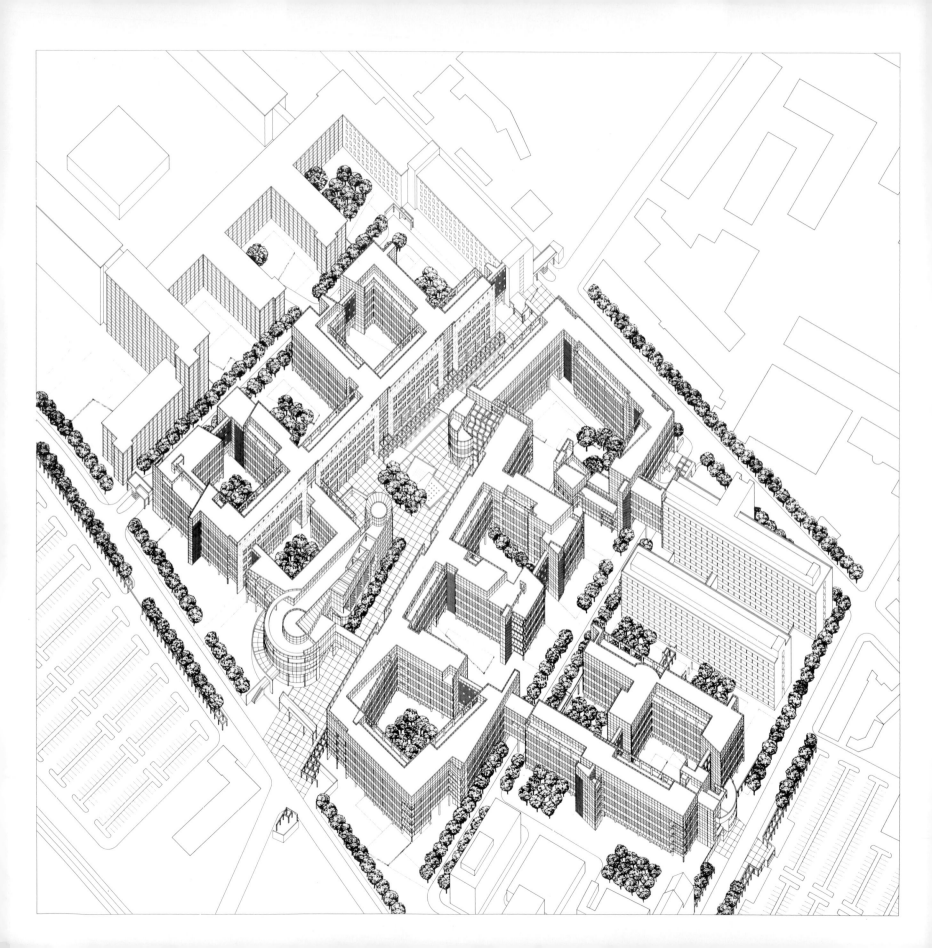

Office and Laboratory Facilities for Siemens AG

Munich, Germany
1985–1989

Built as the first stage of a master plan for the full expansion of an industrial headquarters dating from the 1960s, this seven-story office complex and research facility replaces a number of older buildings that no longer meet the requirements of the company. In addition to general offices, this phase also houses a cafeteria, a library, a medical center, conference rooms, and exhibition spaces.

The master plan for the ultimate development of the site is based on two orthogonal grids at an angle to each other. These grids, which derived from the dimensions, setting, and structural bays of the buildings on the site, have been used to determine the modular order and alignment of the present phase. Clad throughout in white aluminum panels, the overall envelope is relieved by stucco and granite facings.

The Siemens office complex employs a series of extrusions organized to form urban courtyards. These building blocks are made up of repetitive, rectilinear offices. Like a Navajo blanket weave, the pattern gives way at moments of symbolic importance. The windows, for instance, breathe life into the whole by breaking the grid and expressing the special nature of the place.

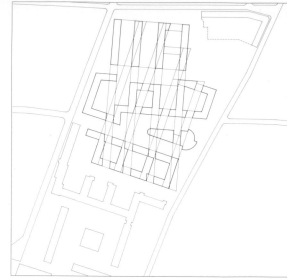

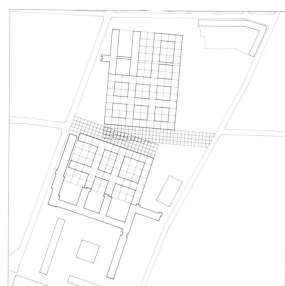

Existing situation

Existing buildings create two different axes that intersect along the east-west axis created by the connection of the two streets

Overlapping axes created by the existing structures aid in establishing the massing of the planned structures

Two grids are created in an analysis of the structures of the existing buildings

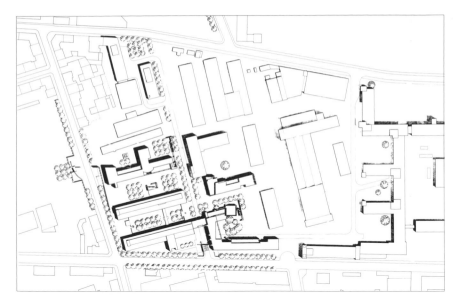

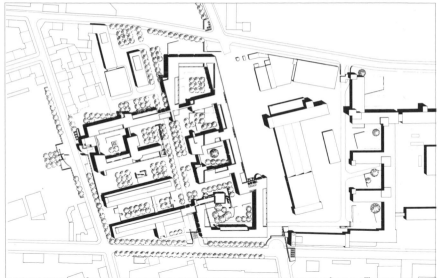

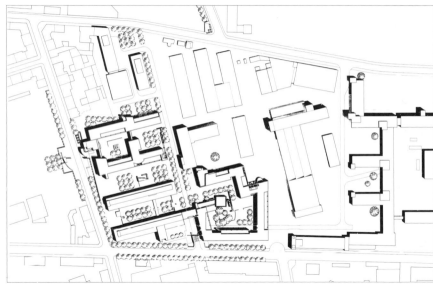

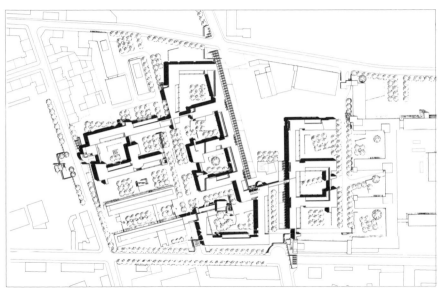

Site plan phase one

Site plan phase two

Site plan phase three

Site plan phase four

In 1984, I was invited by Siemens to participate with a Swiss and a German architect in a competition for their new world headquarters building in Munich. I won that competition, but nothing happened while the plans shuttled their way through the city's approval process. Two years later, I was asked to prepare a scheme for rebuilding an office and laboratory complex far from the center of the city, a project which was intended to be built more or less continuously over a number of years. The first phase was the only piece of the whole to be constructed. There it ended. Now, six years later, the first commission for which I won the competition is about to resume.

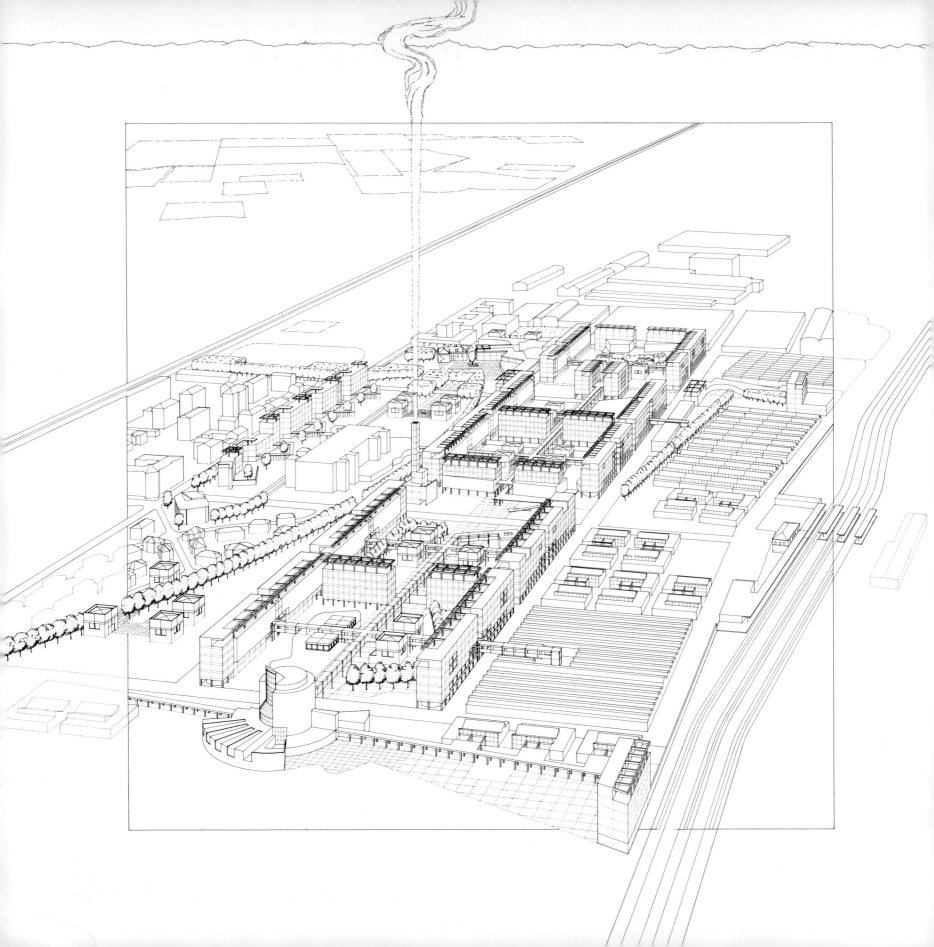

Progetto Bicocca

Milan, Italy
1986

The Pirelli Bicocca site, although removed from the center of
Milan, is well connected to it by major transportation routes. The
rail yards to its east and the Zara-Testi axis to the west establish
the boundaries and the linear nature of the site. However,
through the partial realization of various master plans in the past,
the satisfactory identity and integrity of this industrial area was
never achieved. The purpose of this competition was to clarify
the site's topographical and functional relationships and give
them architectural form.

As the competition organizers gave no specific program for the
site, this proposal organizes the area through the development of
a fairly wide range of industrial and techno-scientific building
types. The linear core is composed of a mixture of residential,
administration, and service buildings linked by an elevated
service spine and walkway. This mall, which contains all the
public functions of the project, is structured about a 7.5-meter
grid that maintains the existing street and block dimensions so
that phasing can proceed incrementally, and the basic
infrastructure can be preserved and augmented where necessary.
To the east there are industrial sheds and work spaces close to
the railway, while to the west a long park separates the new work
areas from the housing and commercial activities that will
naturally gravitate to Viale Sarca.

In this proposal the urban character of the present industrial
complex is combined with a low-density, parklike setting
appropriate to tertiary activities and to the integration of the site
with the northern outskirts of Milan. Only the most useful
structures would be kept, to permit a comprehensive, unified,
and flexible scheme. This high-tech center would also allow
public access along the Via Emanueli, thereby connecting the
train station to the Pirelli Exhibition Hall and other facilities.

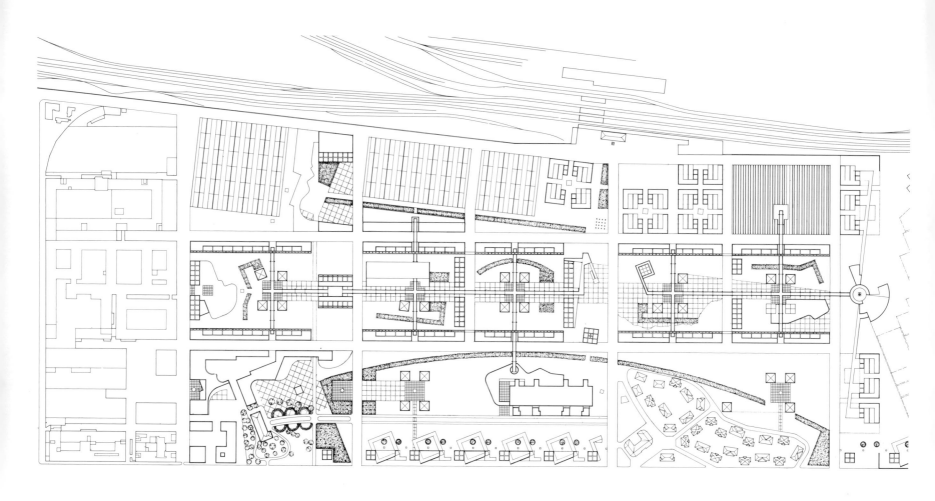

Axonometric view

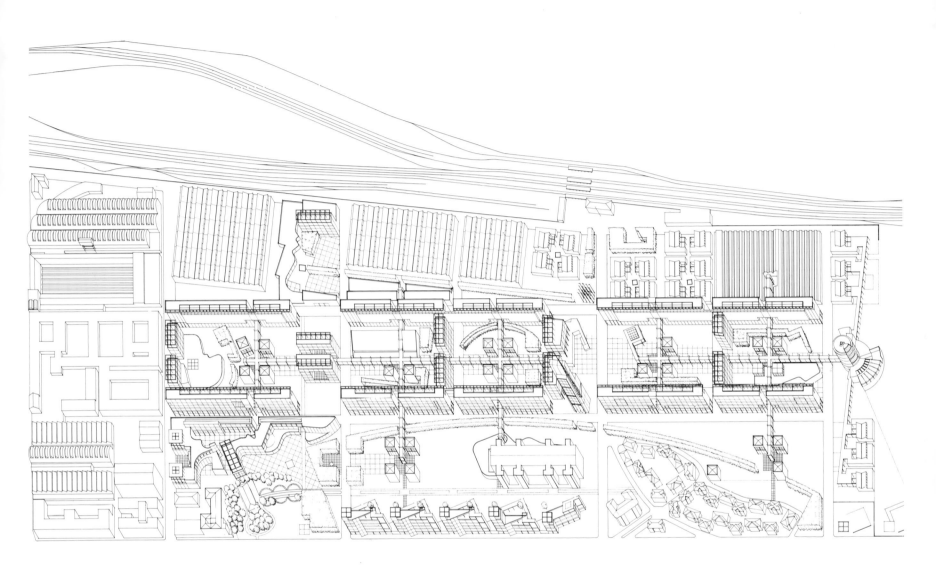

Ulm Exhibition and Assembly Building

Ulm, Germany
1986–1992

Existing situation

Geometry

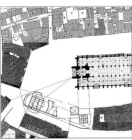

Volumetric relationships

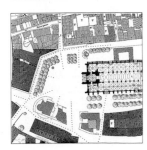

Pedestrian connections

This design is conceived as a foil and a complement to the Munsterplatz. It is based on a nine-square plan enclosed on three sides by a number of circular screens. These are modified and curtailed by a series of intersecting axes and frontage lines, derived in part from the cathedral, the general geometry of the square, and its immediate surroundings. Placing the open form of the building on the southwest corner of the square draws attention to the intersection of the main space and Hirchstrasse, inviting entry into the square. The interplay between the building and the square is enhanced by small, outdoor spaces and framed views into the square.

In the entry foyer are the city's tourist office and ticket agency, and a main stair and elevator leading to the lecture hall/assembly room on the first floor and to two levels of exhibition space above. A covered loggia/bridge at ground level connects the restaurant to the entry foyer. The main assembly space on the first floor has oblique views to the cathedral. The central, nine-square, reinforced concrete cube is faced in natural stone and the curved portions and the restaurant annex are clad in stucco.

The building is complemented by the refurbishing of the Munsterplatz, and above all by its new paving grid, which is derived from the cathedral. This *parvis* has been kept free of furniture, and its northwest periphery is planted with sycamore trees to give a more intimate scale to the commercial frontage. An asymmetrically placed fountain is the third point of a conceptual triangle connecting the cathedral tower to the center of the building.

181

Site plan

182

Axonometric view

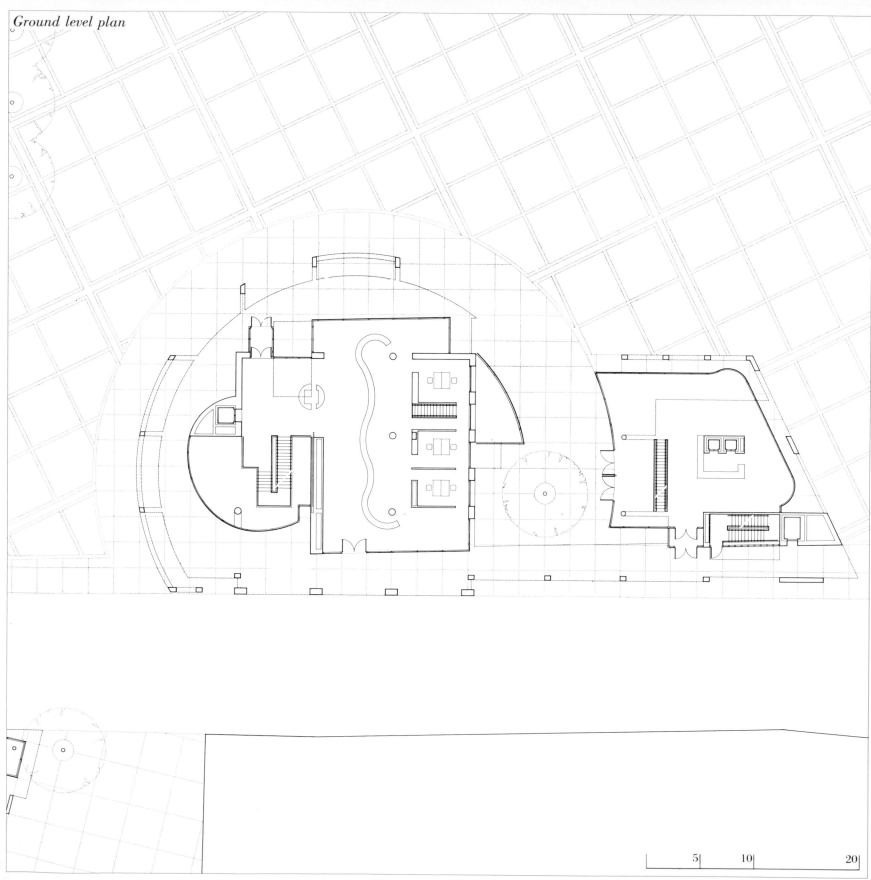

Ground level plan

5| 10| 20|

184

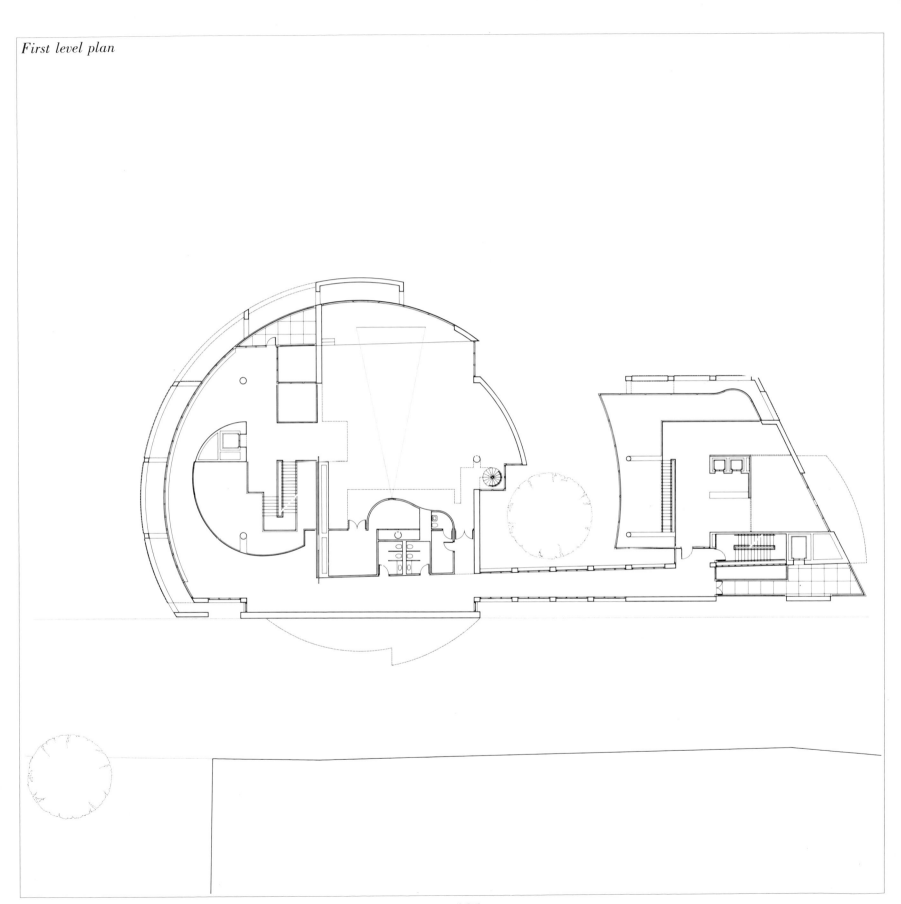

First level plan

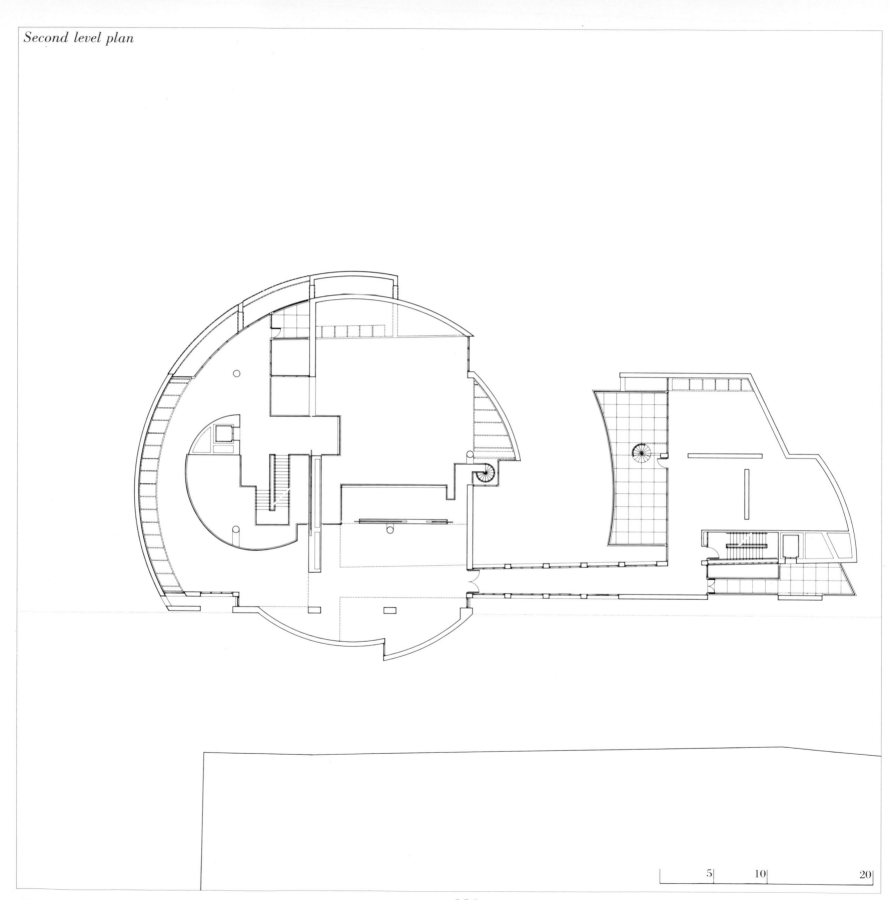

5 10 20

Third level plan

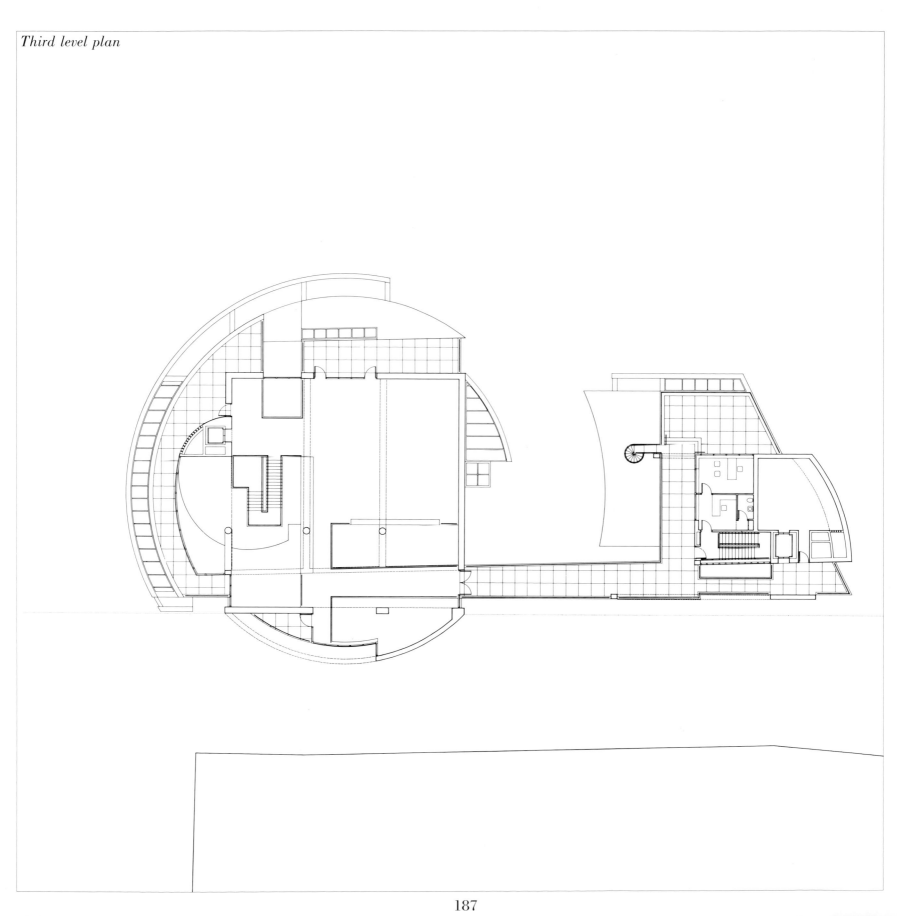

East elevation

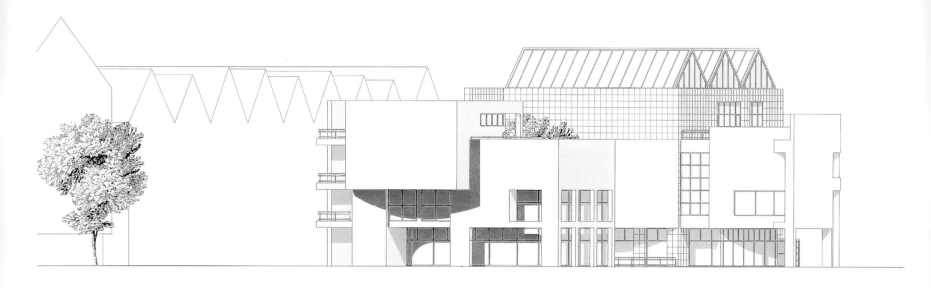

Southwest elevation

5　10　20

Northwest elevation

Northeast elevation

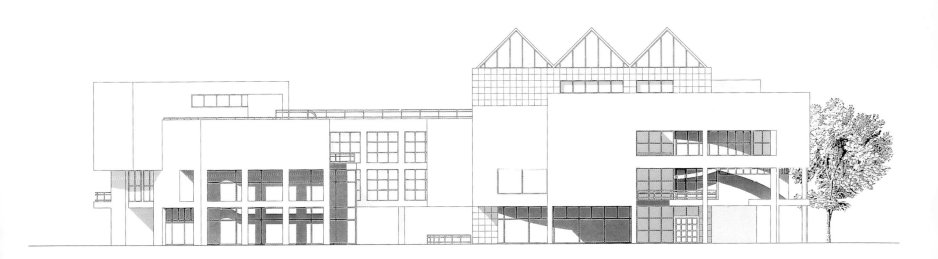

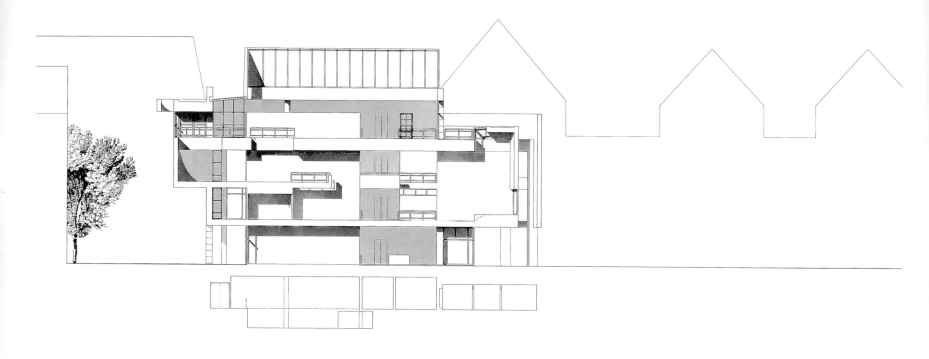

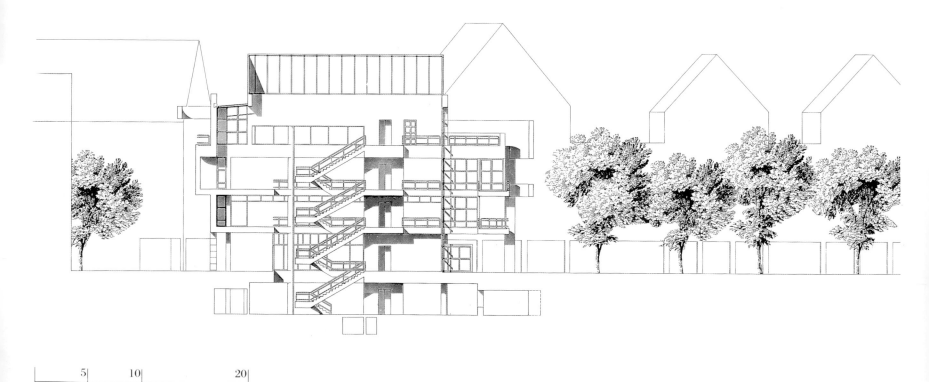

5   10   20

Cross section facing northwest

Cross section facing southwest

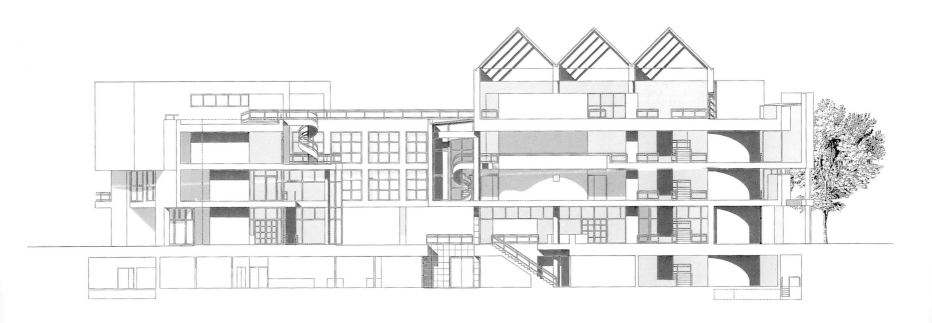

192

In the past one hundred years there have been seventeen competitions to complete the plaza in front of one of the greatest Gothic cathedrals in Germany. On being asked to participate in yet another competition for the site, my first reaction was to ask why the winning entry should be realized when the past has produced so many failures. Since winning the final competition, six years and dozens of political referendums have passed. The will of Mayor Ludwig and Mayor Schaber and the enthusiastic support of the young people in Ulm have prevailed. Democracy wins again. Construction has begun.

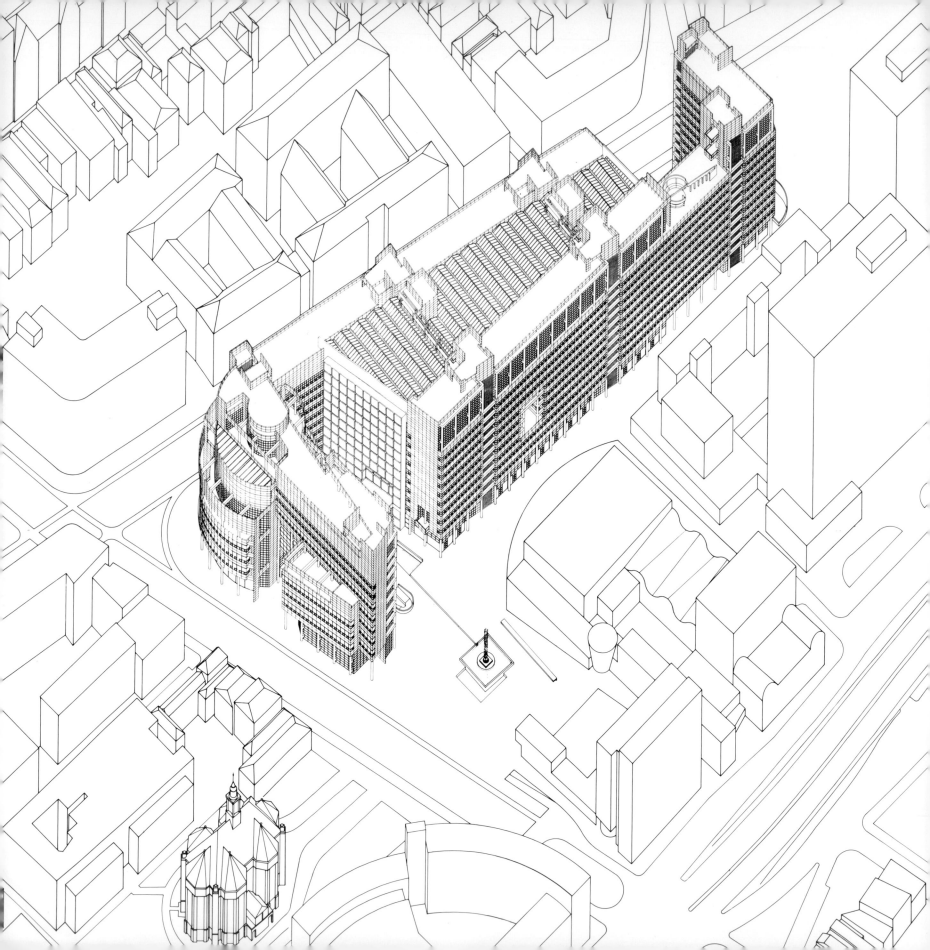

The Hague City Hall and Central Library

The Hague, The Netherlands
1986–1994

The two grids that organize this complex are derived from the outline of the wedge-shaped site, situated between Kalvermarkt and Turfmarkt. The surrounding urban fabric is structured according to the same divergent, but orthogonal geometry.

This continuous structure, measuring 800 feet by 250 feet, includes a council chamber, a city wedding room, a central public library, and a large number of local government offices. The elements of this mega-facility are combined with a semi-independent rental office building at its northeastern end and extensive shops throughout the ground floor. The main twelve- and ten-story horizontal office slabs, which diverge from each other at an angle of 10½ degrees, flank a large, internal atrium that forms the new *res publica* of the city known as the Citizens Hall. This large, wedge-shaped hall's entrance is either from the center of the city at the northeastern end of the site, or from the historic core, where one enters from a plaza at the western end of the site. The vast room is modulated by two tiers of aerial bridges linked to the elevator cores.

The main library, with its concentric semicircular plan, is the head building at the extreme northwestern corner of the site, where its dynamic form imparts a strong character to the principal plaza that it also encloses and defines. Another element on the plaza at this point is a furniture store that will be rebuilt and expanded beneath the library. The plaza extends into the library where there are a reception/orientation area and a cafe. From there, entrance to other floors is strictly organized. Free-standing escalators provide circulation between floors, and as in the City Hall, this sequence progresses from the more public at grade to more private, administrative services at the top.

Throughout the building, open office space is in a reinforced concrete, intercolumniated structure with loadbearing cores. Inside and out, the structure is clad in white, 90 x 90 centimeters porcelain-enameled metal panels.

The glass roof of the atrium is supported by free-spanning laminated timber trusses incorporating sun screens, maintenance walkways, and light fixtures. The aerial bridges spanning the atrium, together with the elevator and stair cores, are of white painted steel, the lightness and elegance of which is intended to give the impression of a light screen subtly subdividing the large volume.

The northeastern plaza, which is more intimate than its southwestern counterpart, serves as the quiet back yard extension of the atrium. From the larger, urban standpoint, the complex is linked, along the Turfmarkt, to the central station by a connection that is reinforced by a canal and a line of sycamore shade trees running parallel to the sidewalk.

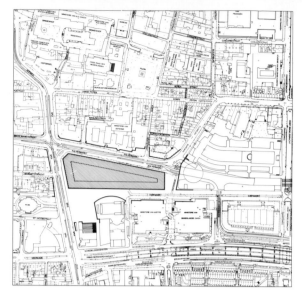

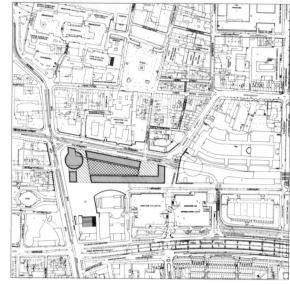

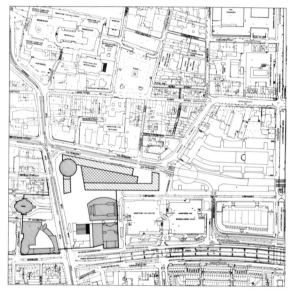

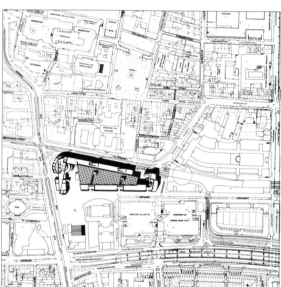

Building site

The building's organization grid follows the two grids of the city; the new building is the intersection between the two grids.

The creation of open spaces on the site and in the building was in response to the formal organization of the existing built environment.

The city hall and library building completes the "culture square" precinct of The Hague.

The positioning of open spaces on the site also relates to the building's main entrances.

Site plan within the urban fabric of the city.

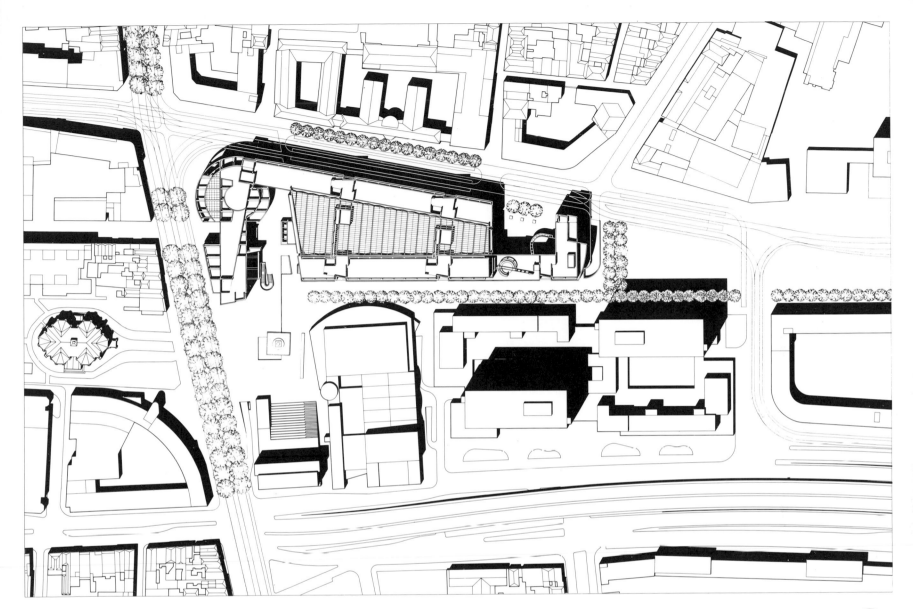

Site plan

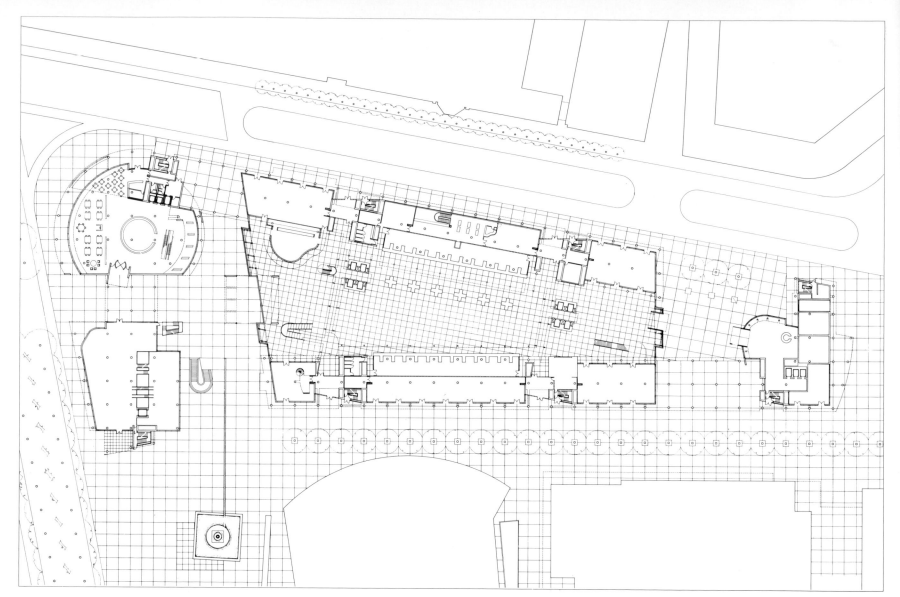

Ground level plan

5 10   20   40

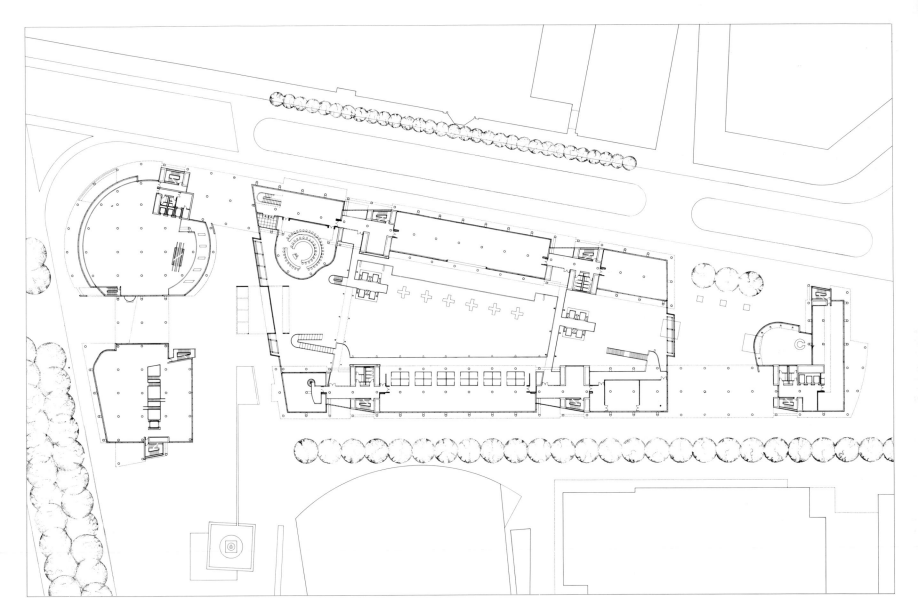

First level plan

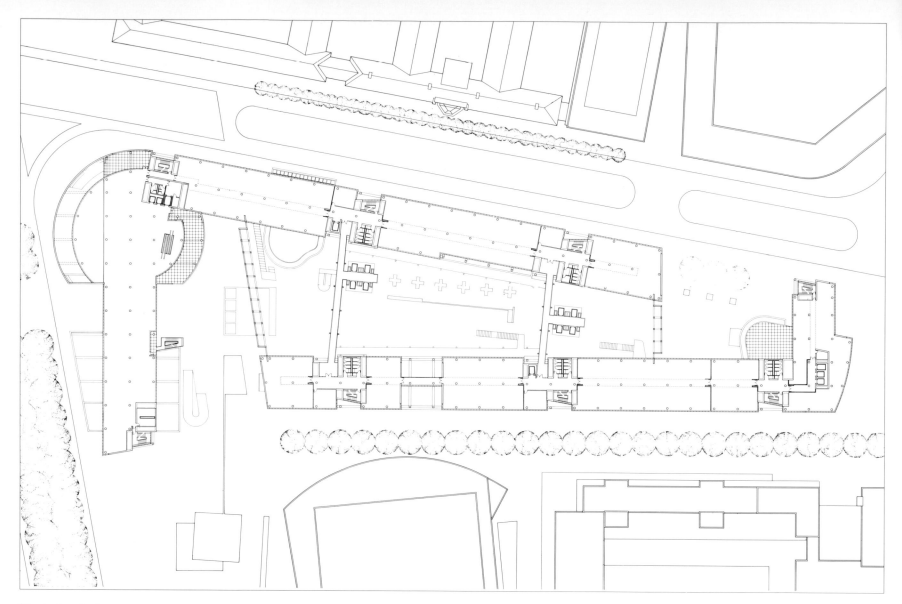

Sixth level plan

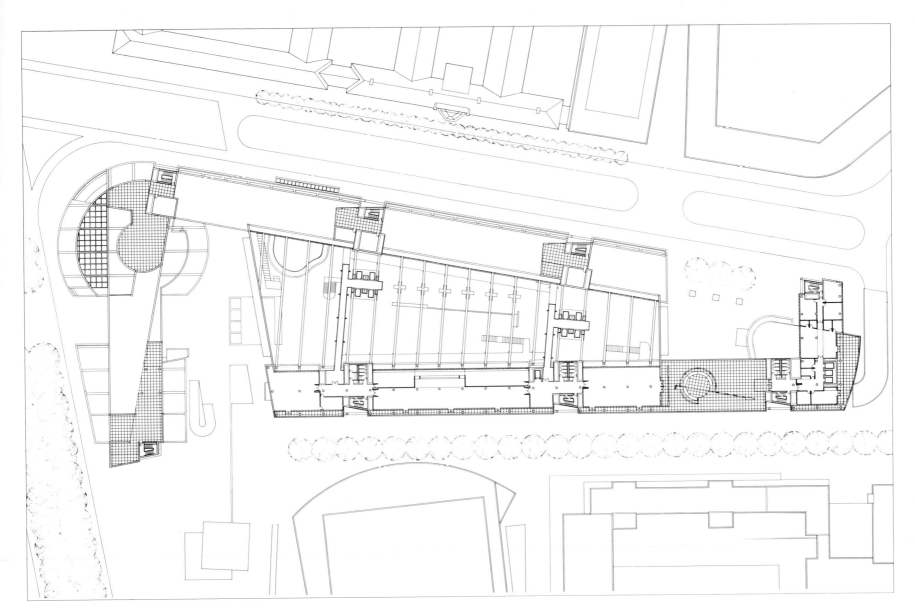

Eleventh level plan

Southwest elevation

Cross section through the entrance square facing the library

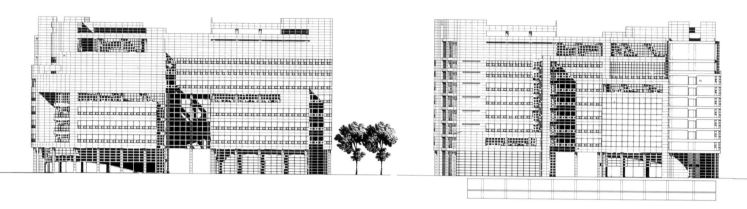

Southeast elevation

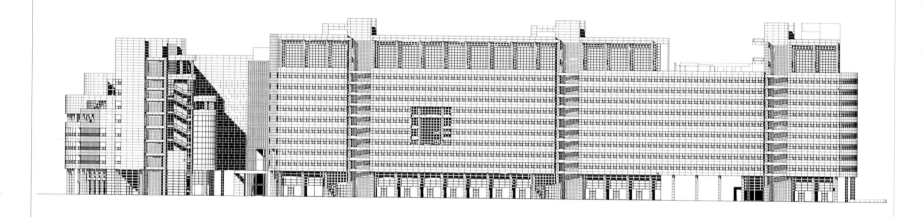

5| 10| 20| 40|

Northeast elevation

Cross section through the court near Kalvermarkt

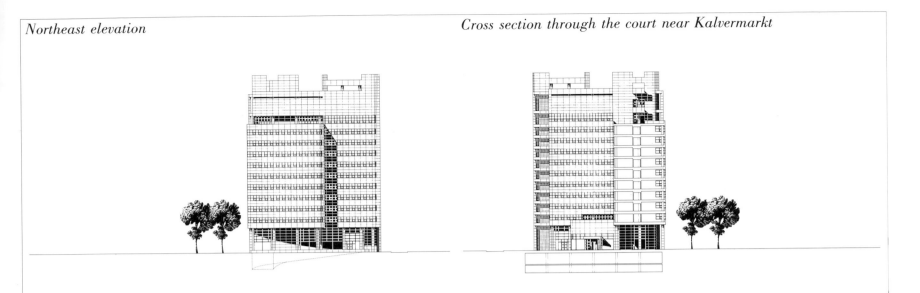

Northwest elevation

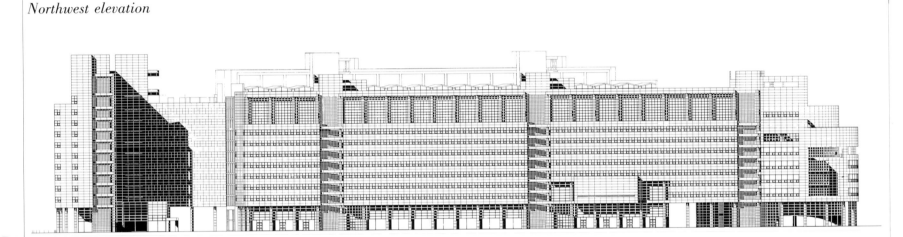

Cross section through the entrance square facing the atrium   Cross section through City Hall and atrium

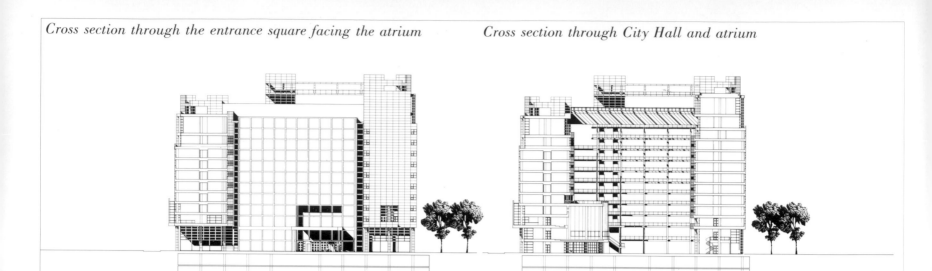

Longitudinal section through the entrance square, atrium and court at Kalvermarkt

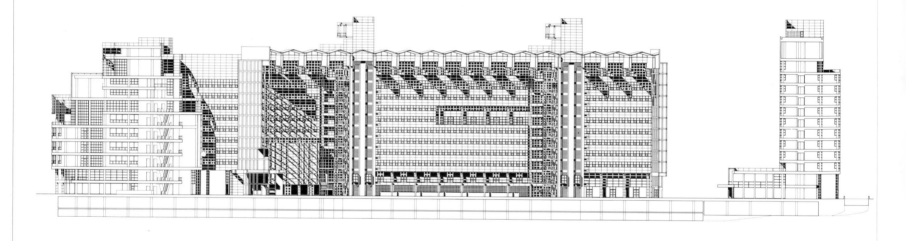

5 10   20   40

Study of the library atrium

Study of City Hall atrium facing the wedding stairway

Perspective view of the atrium

For American architects building in Europe, an awareness of that region's political complexities is important. Understanding the political climate and cultivating support is critical to the realization of any work of architecture. Winning a competition is only the beginning of a war in which many battles are won and lost. Architects who mingle personality with politics often lose the battle of aesthetics and design.

In the Hague, Alderman Adri Duivesteijn waged the strongest campaign in the City Council for the building of the new city hall. The political fight to realize this building cost him his job as Deputy Mayor, but ultimately his dream, and mine, will come true.

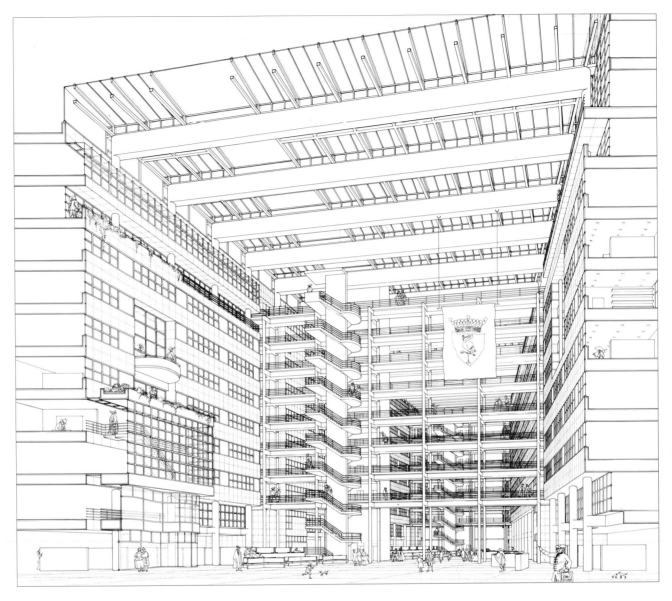

Perspective view of the atrium

208

209

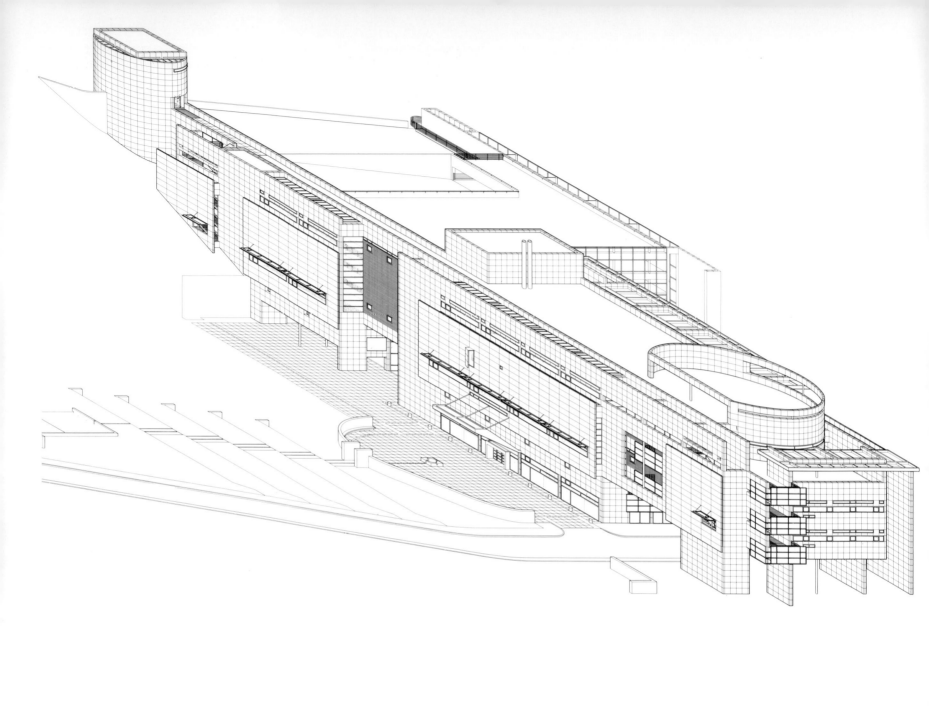

Eye Center for Oregon Health Sciences University

Portland, Oregon
1987

This structure is at the main entry to the university and spans two low hills. It was conceived as a portal to the campus, since vehicles would have to pass under it in order to enter the grounds.

The ophthalmic research/clinic on the lower floor accommodates the auditorium and library, and the laboratories and speaking rooms are on the floors above. A prominent feature of the composition is a cylinder stacked with operating rooms that passes through the upper four floors of this six-story section, and which also marks the vehicular entry to the campus.

The remainder of the complex is a large, 320-car, multilevel parking structure set into a slope at the north, and a central circulation core linked to the parking and all floors in the clinic. The building turns its back to the main approach, but a stepped, park promenade links the main pedestrian entry to the rest of the campus.

The bulk of the building is faced in metal panel, and the parking structure is covered on the side with a steel grid that screens the garage wall and the open escape stair running up the hill.

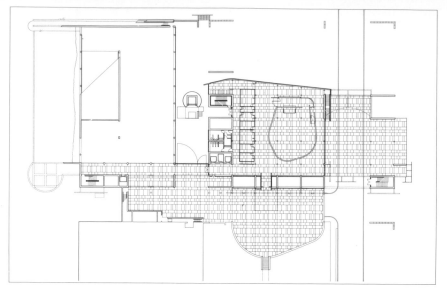

Ground floor plan

The history of architecture is filled with tales of aborted buildings, projects which have been designed by an architect and then wasted by a committee. A landscape of skeletons could inhabit any city, and Portland could very well be that city.

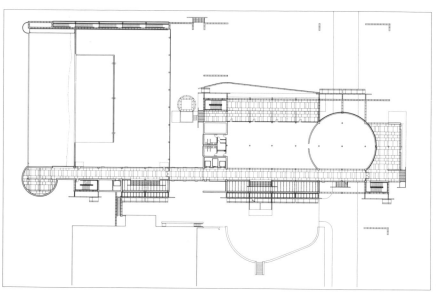

Third floor plan

Geometry

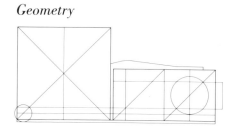

Structure

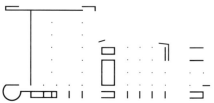

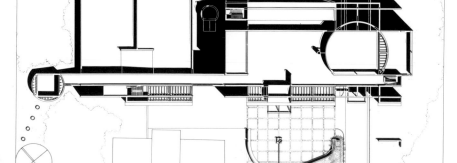

Site plan

Circulation

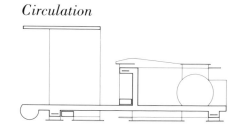

Enclosure

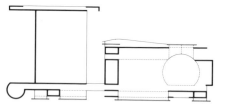

20 40   80   160

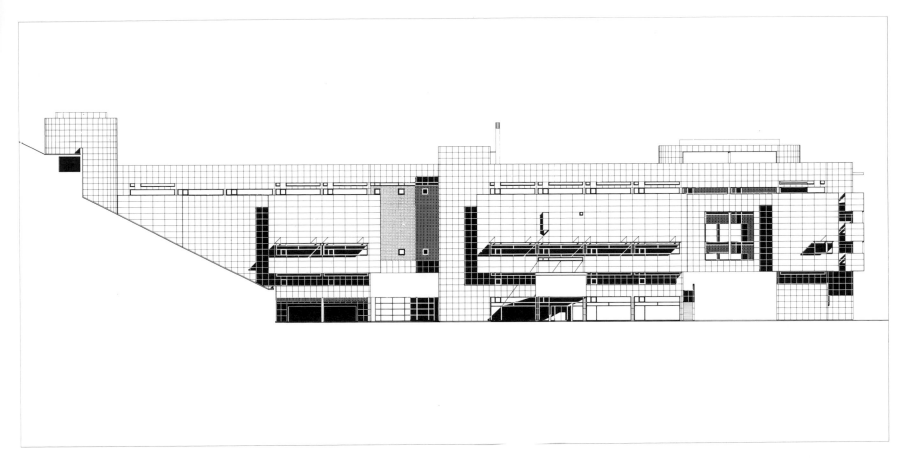

West elevation

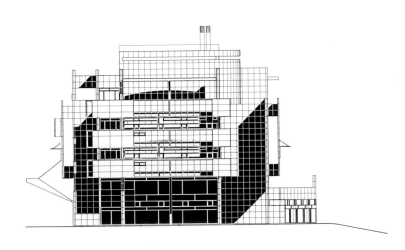

South elevation

| 10 | 20 | | 40 | | 80 |

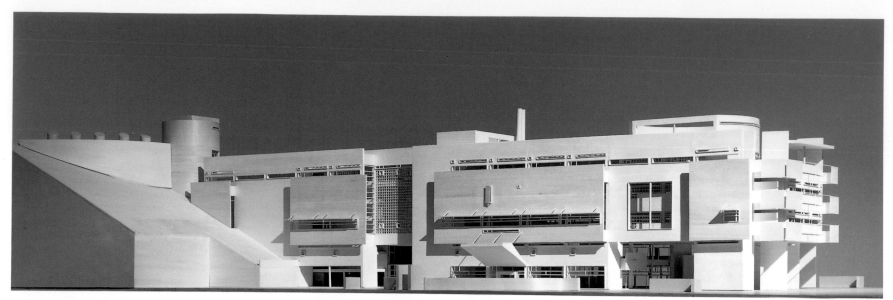

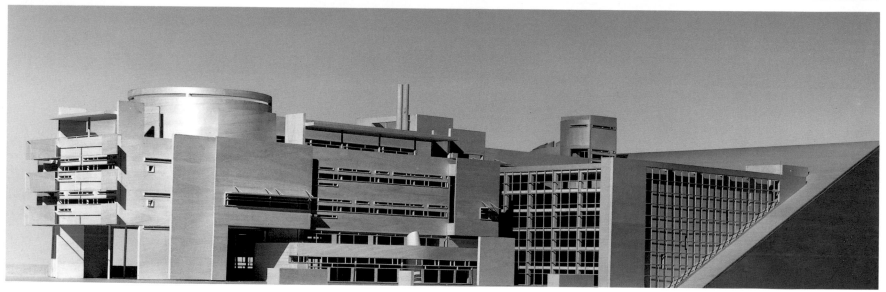

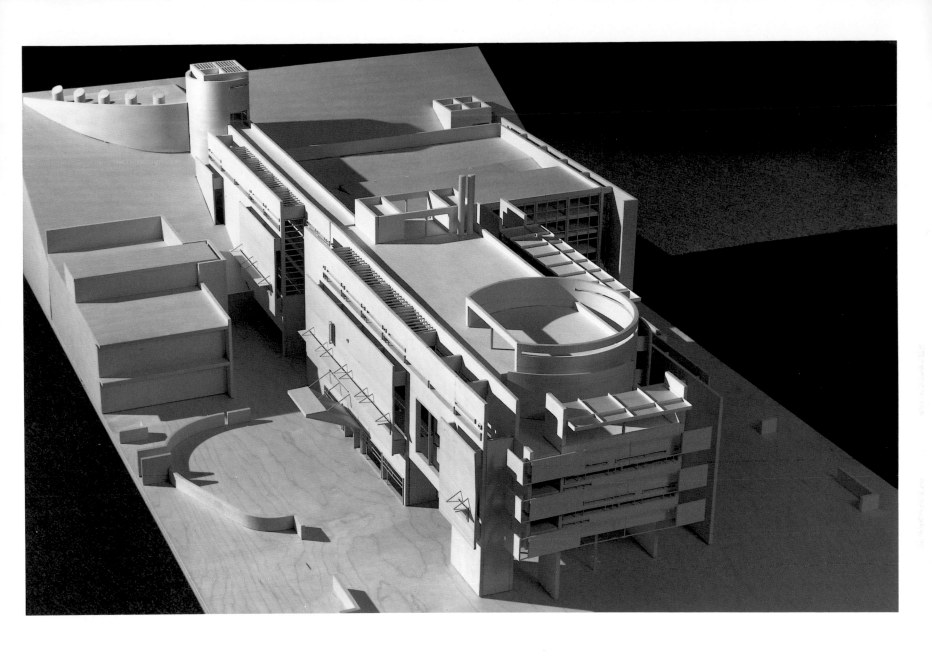

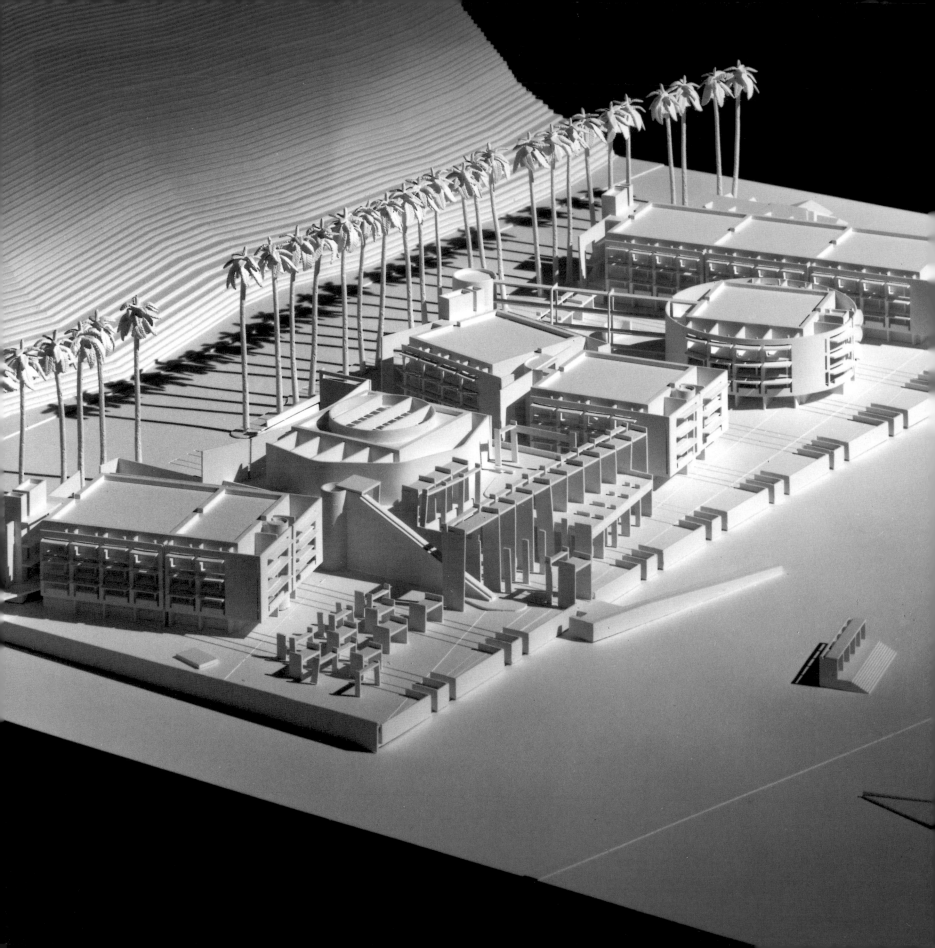

Santa Monica Beach Hotel

Santa Monica, California
1987

This competition for a luxury hotel called for a series of loosely arranged buildings on a podium overlooking a beach. The project mediates between two dramatic forces: the relentless grid of the city, which is abruptly cut off by a 200-foot cliff, and a magnificent view of the Pacific Ocean. The buildings form part of an ordered composition based on a series of overlapping grids. The podium is built over a parking garage, and both are defined by the beach, which acts as a datum line. The garage has public parking in addition to 500 spaces for the use of the hotel.

The hotel distributes 216 rooms in over four buildings, with the restaurant and other dining and recreational amenities in a fifth, central building. They are connected by a canopy-covered walkway.

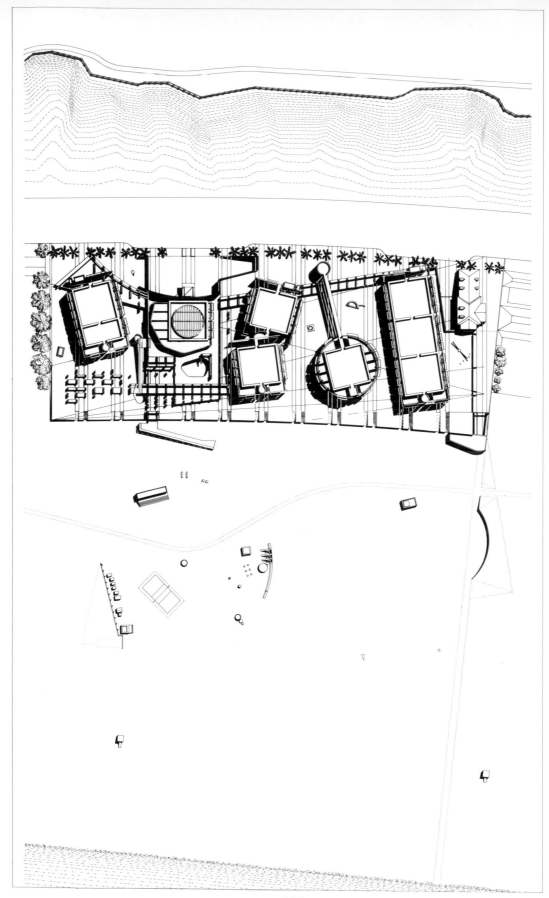

Ground level plan

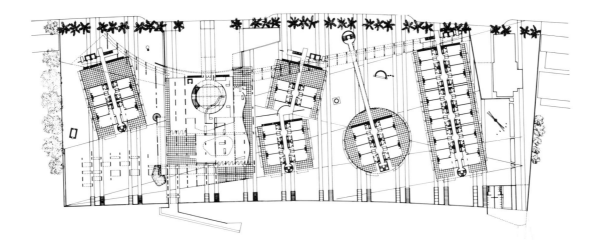

Organizing geometries

25 50   100   200

Madison Square Garden
Site Redevelopment

New York, New York
1987

The program for this competition called for the redevelopment of the present Madison Square Garden site (on the site of McKim, Mead and White's former Pennsylvania Station) into 4.4 million square feet of office space, including trading floors.

The influences on the site include the future growth expected to its west, beyond the full-block Main Post Office. The proximity of One Penn Plaza and the way in which people move under and through it to enter the site, plus the grid of Manhattan, influenced the organization of the project and the basic decision to subdivide it into three interrelated towers. By aligning each tower with the outer boundaries of the block, the street grid is respected. Siting the 72-story South Tower slightly in from Eighth Avenue enhances preferred views and provides greater sun penetration into the plaza. The lower 38-story East Tower responds to the random low-scale nature of its surroundings.

The entire project is on a podium above the large trading floors, which is lined with shops and restaurants reached by a series of stairs and ramps. The major approach is by a gradual slope in the podium down to Eighth Avenue.

Metal panels with punched windows on the rectilinear edges of the building express the core and structure, while glass and glass-panel banding, projecting balconies, and *brise-soleil* articulate the more freely expressive sides.

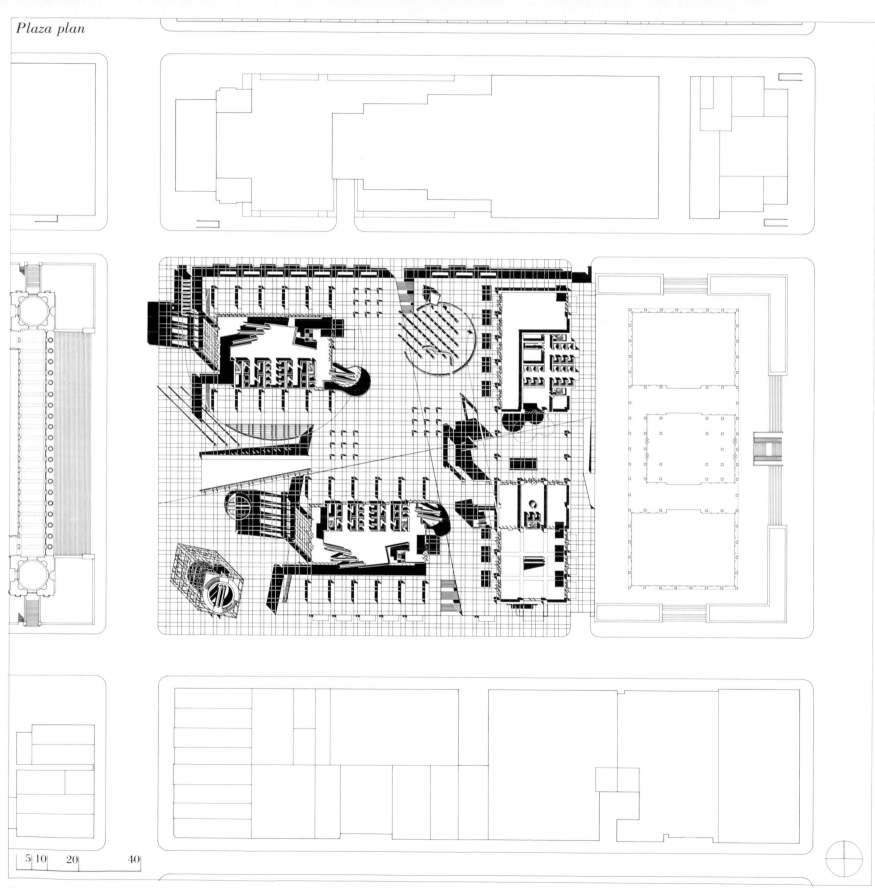

Plaza plan

5 10 20 40

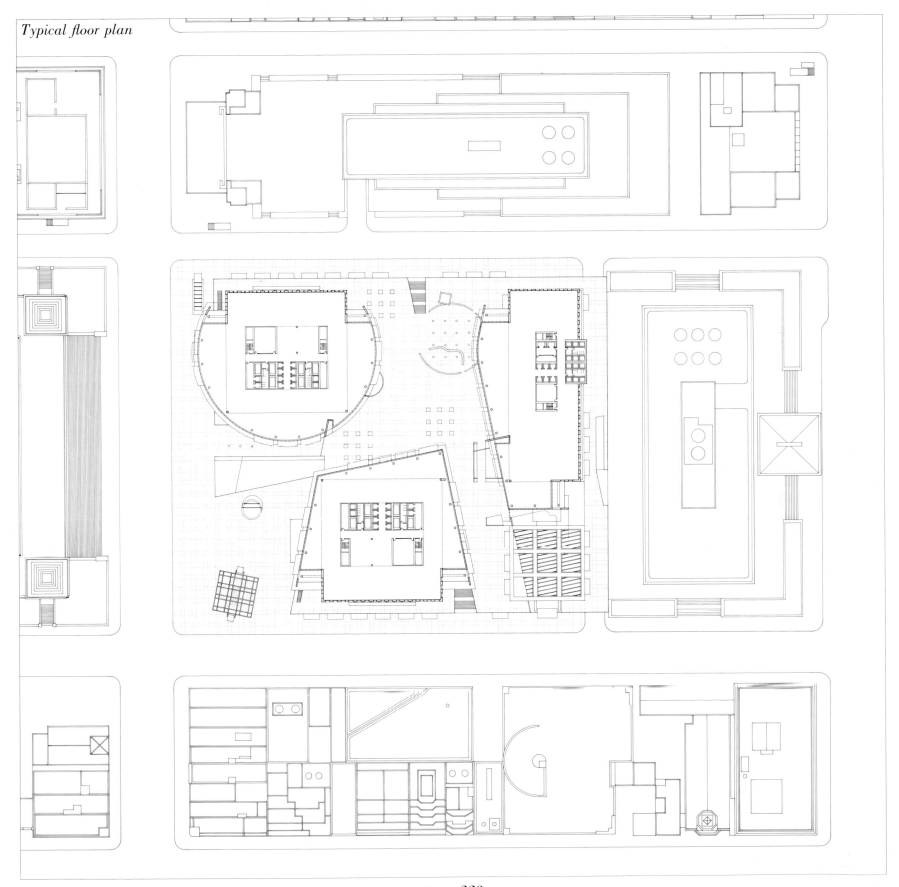

Typical floor plan

223

5| 10| 20| 40|

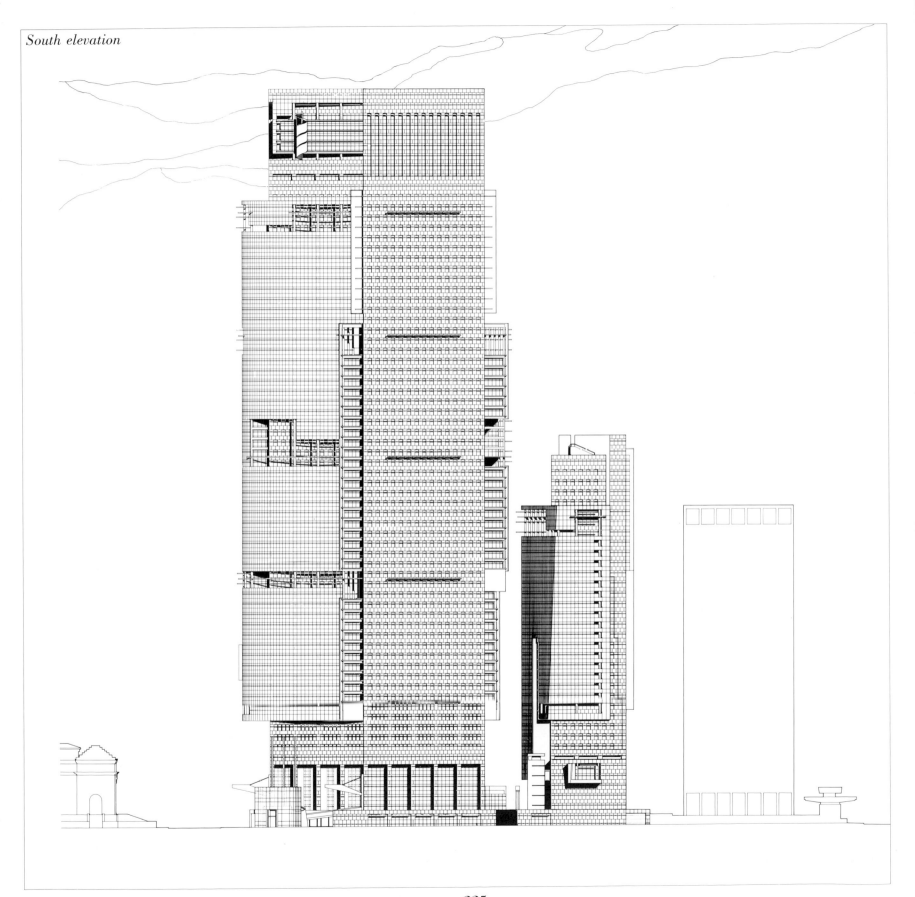

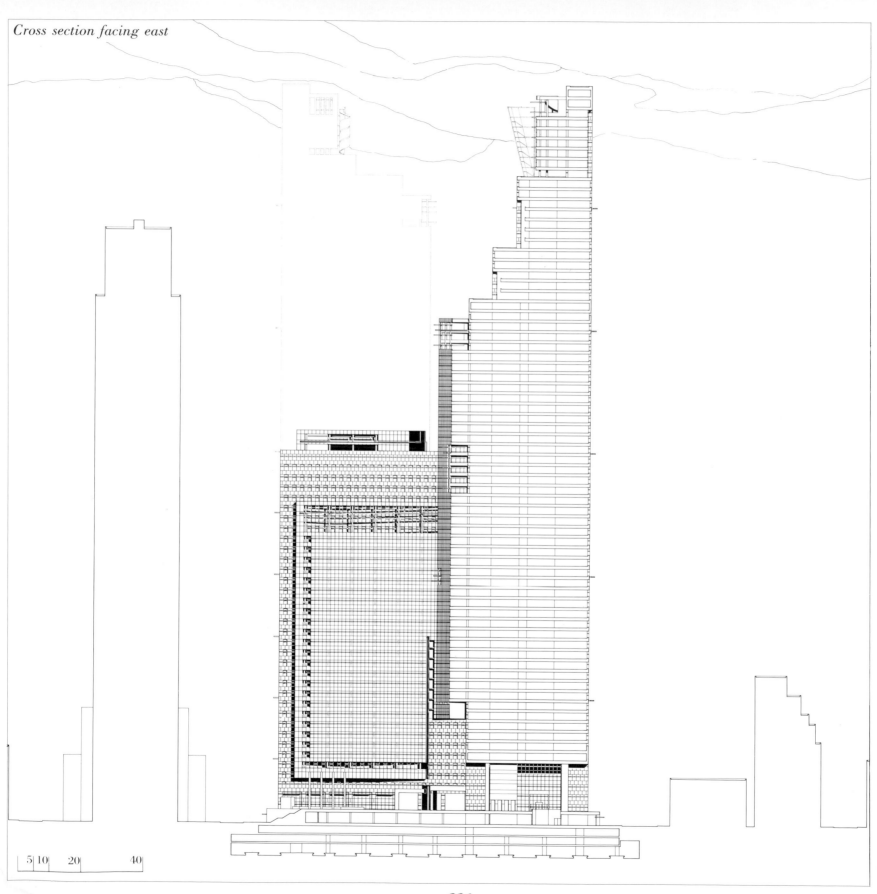

Cross section facing east

5 10 20 40

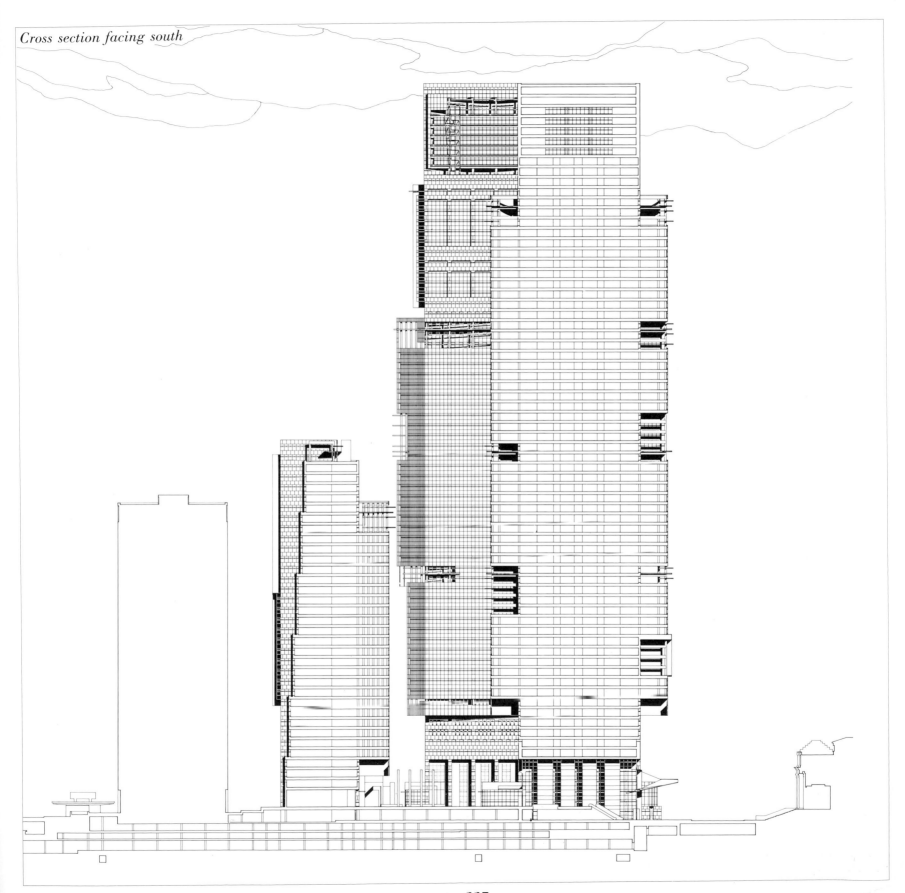

Cross section facing south

229

Weishaupt Forum

Schwendi, Germany
1987–1992

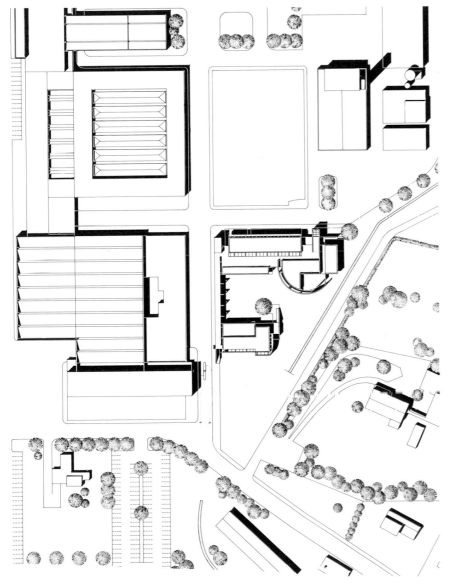

This two-story gateway complex for an industrial boiler manufacturer is flanked by meadowland in the remote and beautiful Swabian countryside on the edge of a small town. It provides ancillary uses, including exhibition spaces, a lecture hall, a dining facility, and a training center, within a U-shaped plan of two wings linked by a loggia.

The smaller wing, opposite the main entrance, has a product display area and a fifty-seat auditorium on the ground floor, and a private gallery for art of late-twentieth-century masters above. It is linked to the dining/training wing by a covered walkway that forms the third side of a cloistered garden and gives access to guest dining rooms and a two-story worker's cafeteria next to the kitchen at grade level, above which are two classrooms and a teaching laboratory. The large, 260-seat staff dining hall is entered at the northeast corner of this wing. The two-story space facing a small greensward to the south is in a monumental, half-cylindrical, top-lit volume that is a focus, unifying all the factory sheds that make up the complex. Four site entrances and two outside access stairs serve all the activities within.

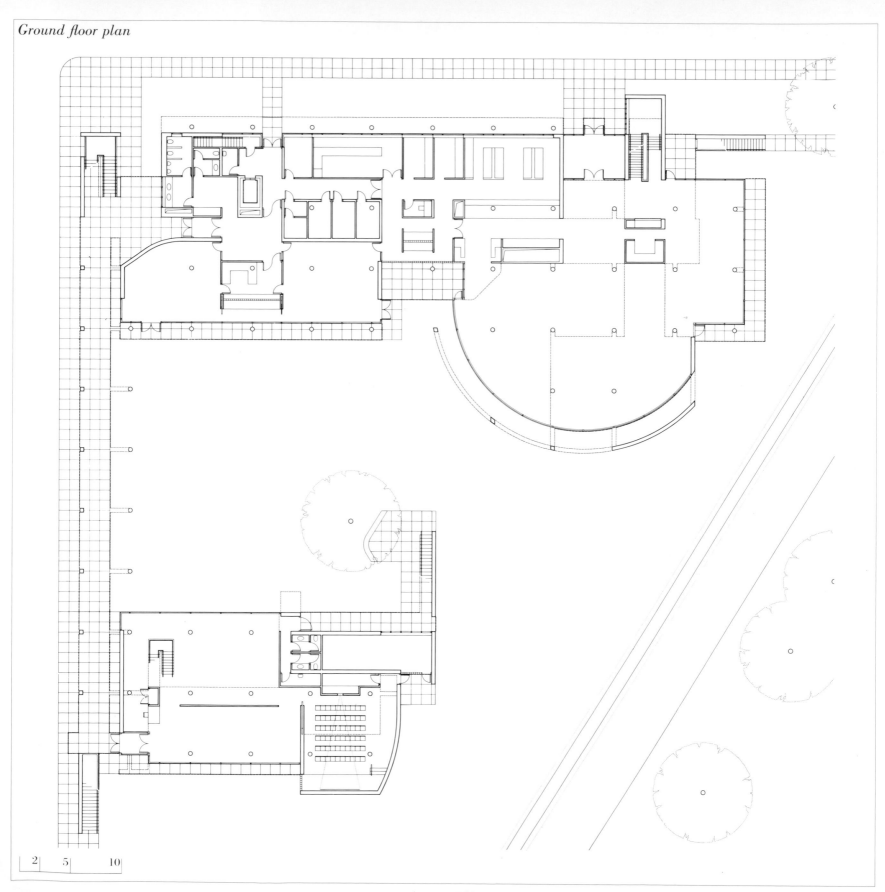

2   5   10

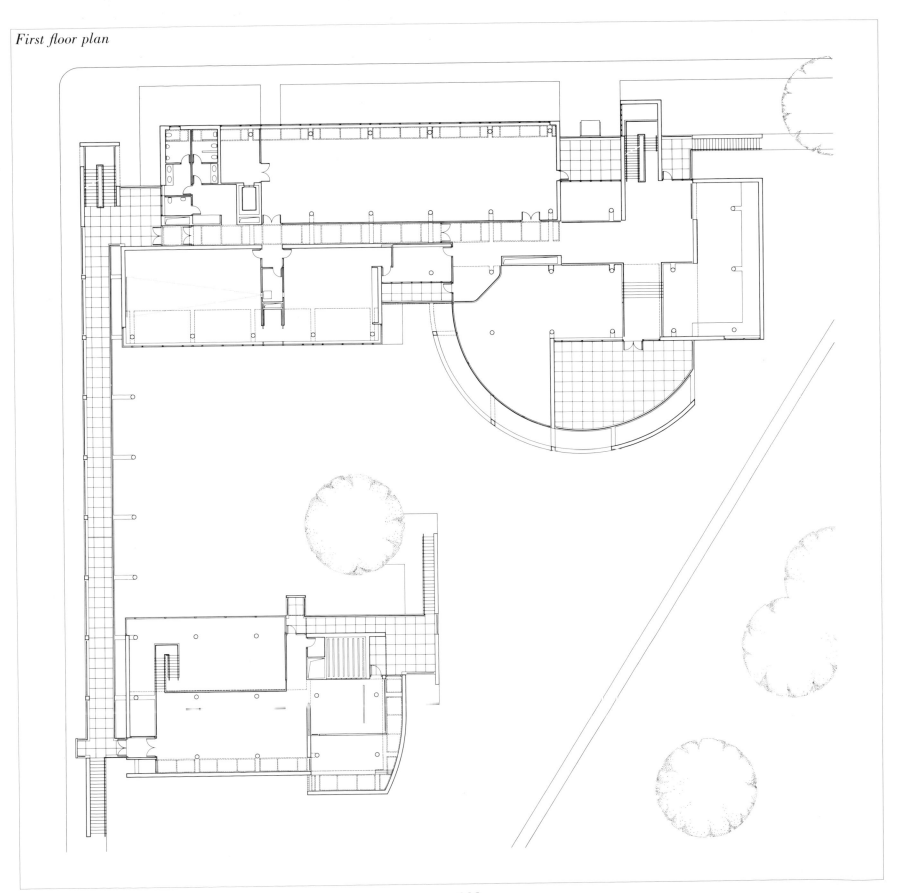

First floor plan

Southeast elevation

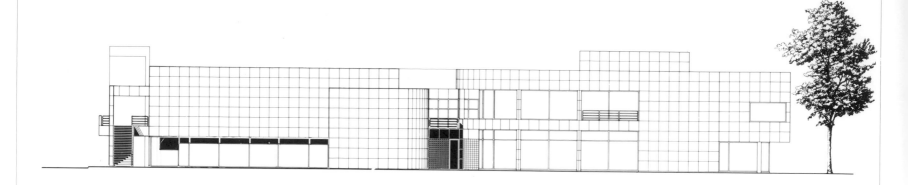

Southeast elevation of interior court

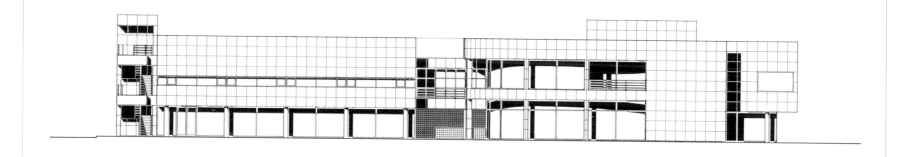

Northwest elevation

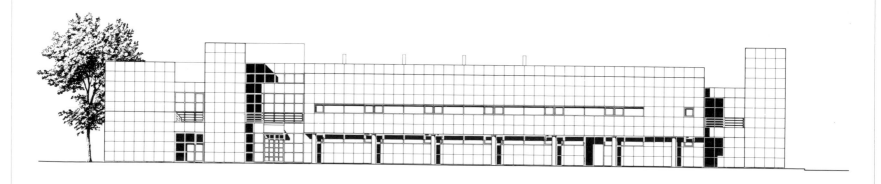

2 5 10

234

Northwest elevation of interior court

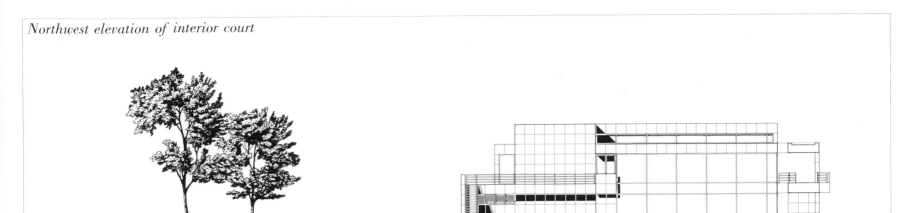

Northeast elevation

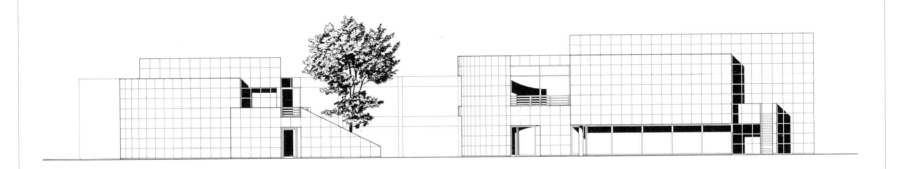

Southwest elevation

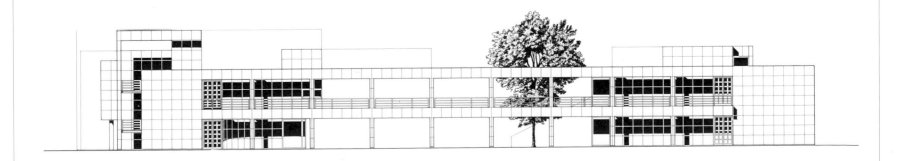

Cross section facing northeast

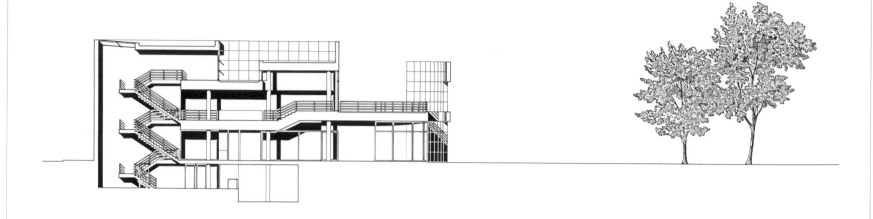

Cross section facing northeast

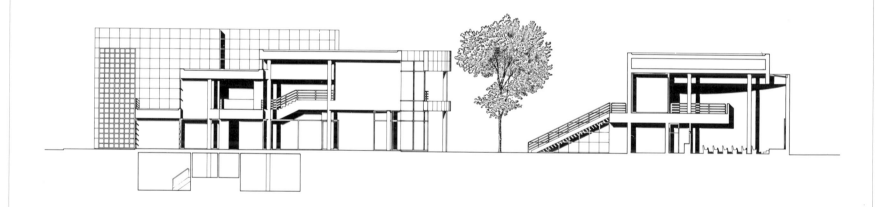

Cross section facing northeast

2   5   10

Cross section facing northeast

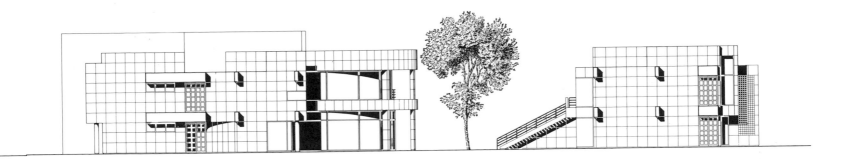

Cross section facing northwest

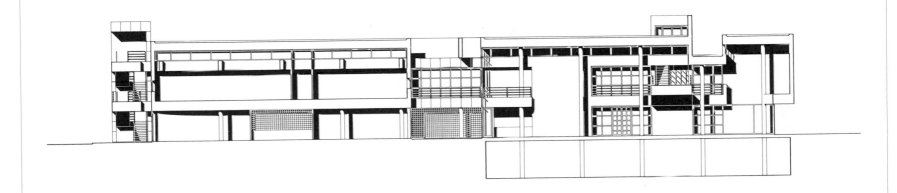

Cross section facing northwest

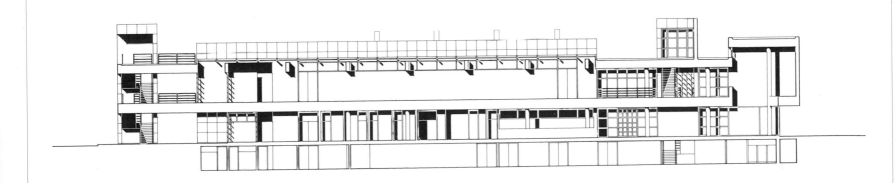

When Siegfried Weishaupt
asked me to be the architect for
his small museum and workers
cafeteria located at his factory
in Schwendi, he did so as a
leap of faith, for his needs were
not well defined. Miraculously,
what he wanted and what he
got was a work of architecture.
What is impossible to see in the
drawings is the changing
quality of light that illuminates
the building's spatial interplay.
Architecture, above all, is to be
experienced with all of the
senses.

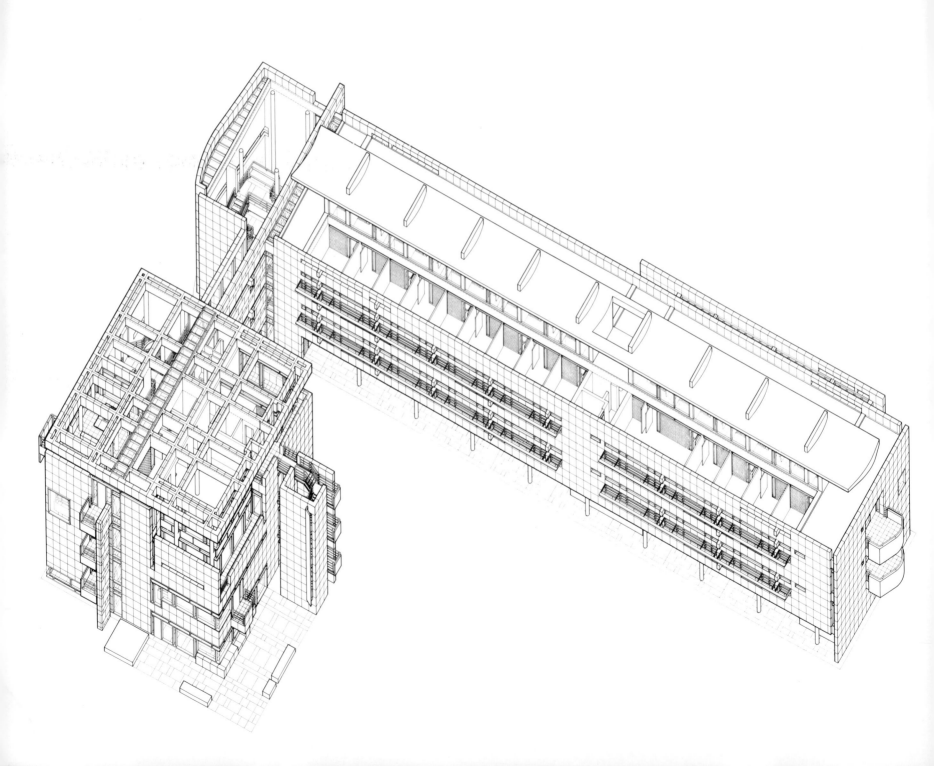

Royal Dutch Paper Mills Headquarters

Hilversum, The Netherlands
1987–1992

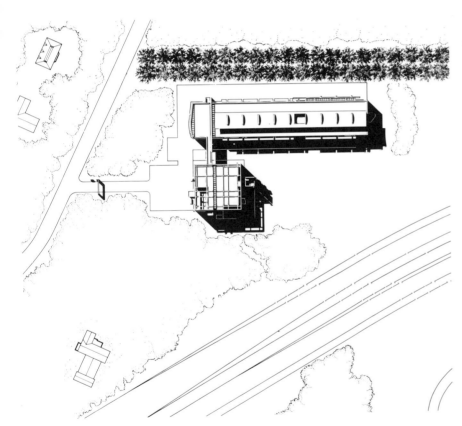

This headquarters for a prominent international paper company is designed for a pre-existing clearing in a densely wooded area. It consists of two linked structures: a four-story cubic reception building and a two-story office slab elevated above the greensward on piloti.

The reception building has dining facilities on the lower two floors, with the staff's in the double-height ground floor volume and three private ones on a mezzanine that look down into it. The largest private dining suite opens to the southwest and has an outdoor terrace. There are guest offices and meeting rooms on the second floor, and a 60-seat lecture hall and conference room at the top.

The building is organized volumetrically about two intersecting service slots, with the elevator/mechanical core in one running northeast-southwest, and the intermediate waiting/service zone on the opposite axis. This area is flanked by a four-story-high stone-faced wall that parallels an enclosed bridge on the first and second floors which connects the reception areas of the two buildings.

The office slab has two principle entrances: one at the northeastern end with a honorific stair, echoing a similar feature in the reception building; and another at mid-point with an elevator/stair core for the executive offices in the southwestern half of the slab. Both the executive and the staff offices are off a top-lit, double-height, double-loaded corridor with continuous access on one side and bridges to offices in pairs on the other. The office slab is based on syncopated counterpoint between the main structural bay, which is evident in the forms of flying beams and a secondary support system carrying the ridges and the monitor lights above.

241

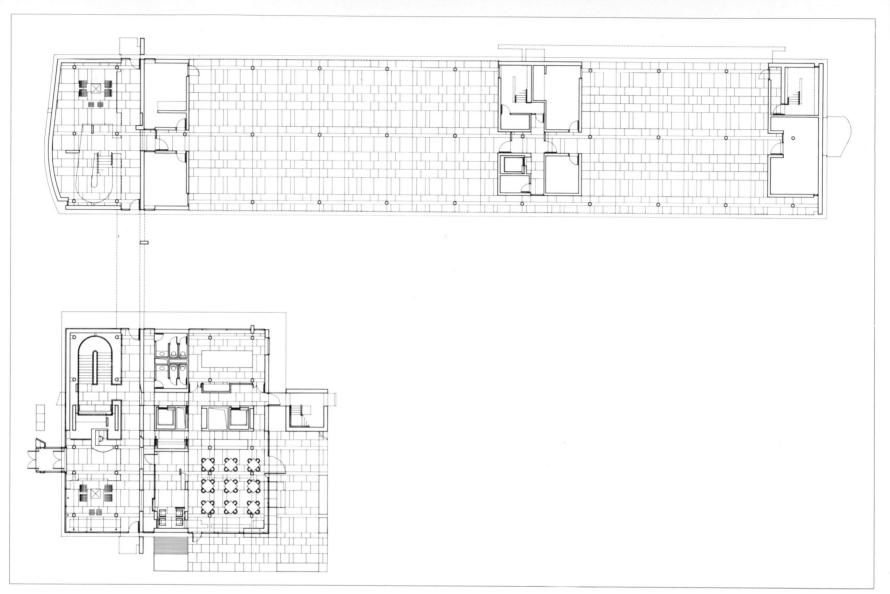

Ground level plan

Geometry
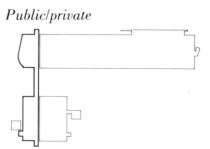

Public/private
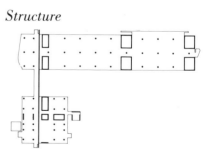

Structure

2   5   10

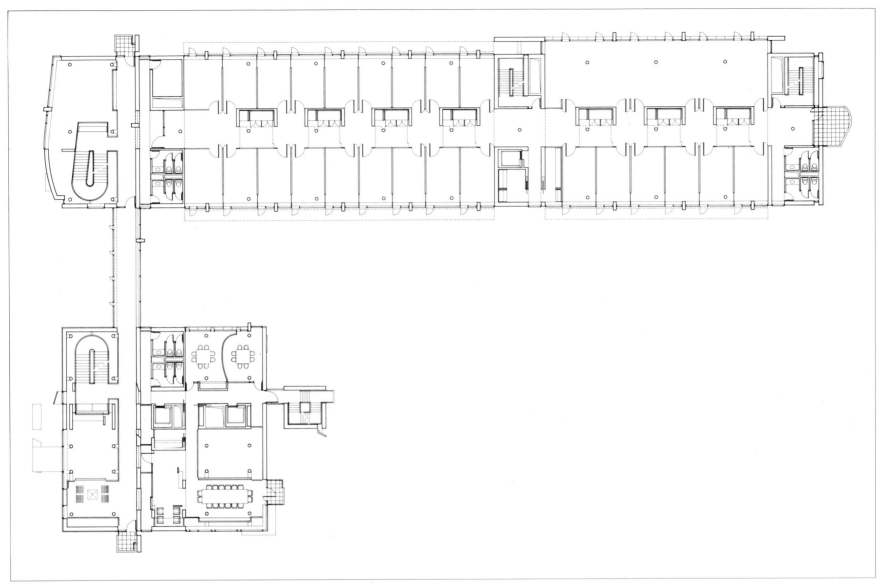

First level plan

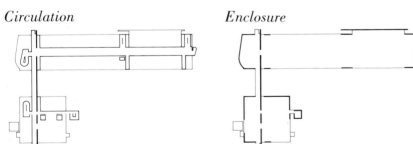

Circulation

Enclosure

Southwest elevation

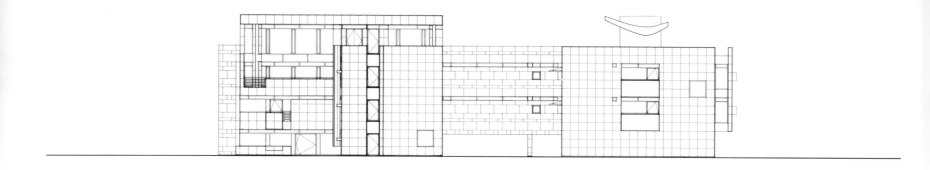

Northeast elevation

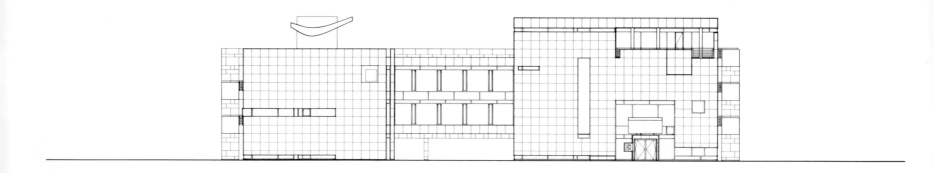

Cross section facing northeast

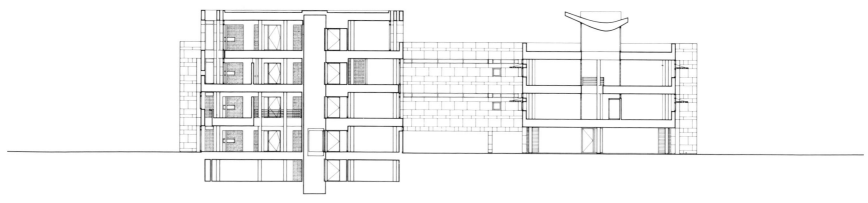

2 5   10

244

This suburban-scaled office
block is being built in a lovely
wooded site near the town hall
W. M. Dudok built in the
1930s. This building is a
simple foot soldier in the grand
army of architectural
movements in which Dudok was
a general.

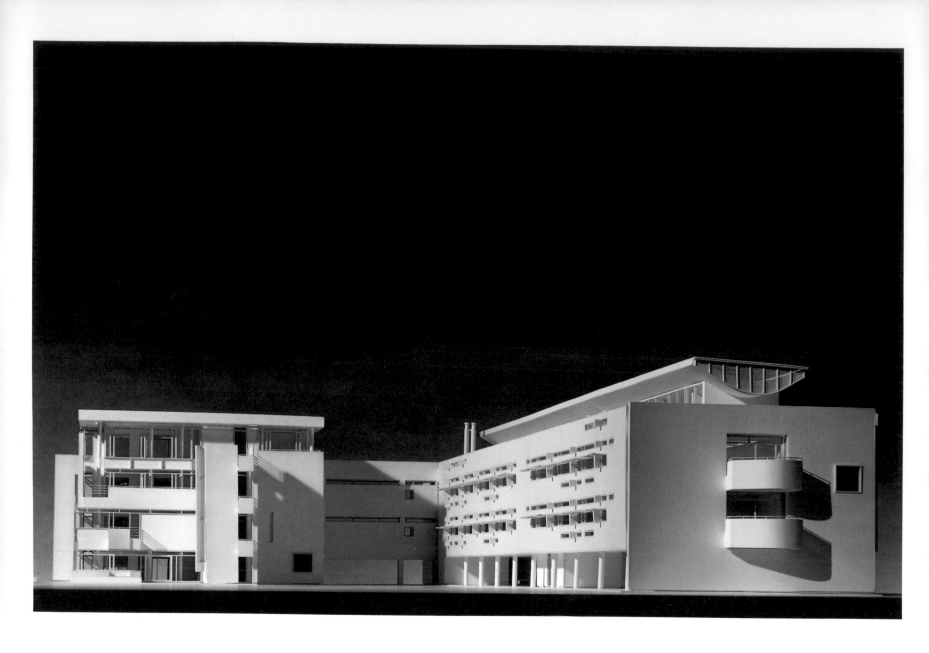

The growing awareness in Europe of the importance of commercial architecture has presented a great many opportunities to bring to Europe a building genre that has reached its apex in the United States. Fortunately, the scale of building in Europe demands a more human proportion and a more habitable workplace.

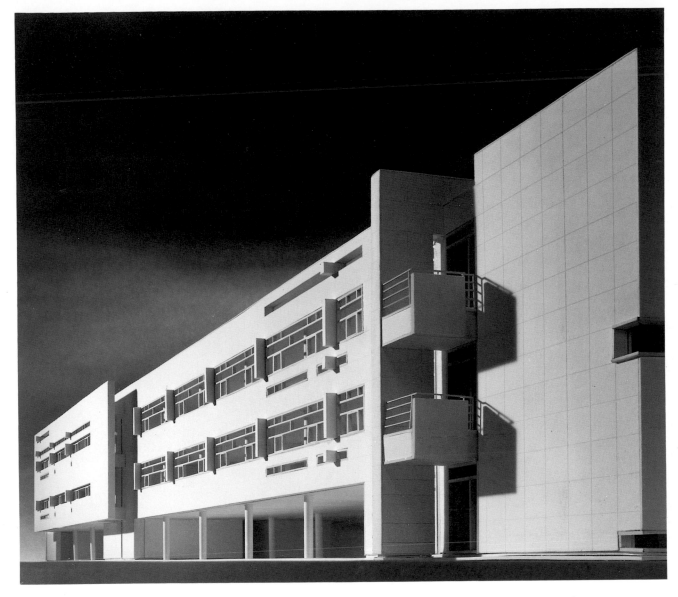

Cornell University Alumni and Admission Center

Ithaca, New York
1988

This is a terrific project. The site is magnificent and the scheme is dramatically beautiful. Each building hugs the site's gorge and refuses to let go. The architecture heightens this natural spectacle. No university that I know of has such a passionate landscape. To see this place is to be captured by it. The architecture attempts to equal its setting.

This double-headed complex on opposite sides of Falls Creek at the northern end of the original campus includes a four-story reception building on the northern face of the gorge and a four-story administrative wing on the opposite bank.

The first structure governs the main public approach to the campus from the north and east and accommodates undergraduate admissions offices, and seminar rooms and a cafeteria grouped around a nine-square, four-story-high monumental Great Hall that looks south over the falls towards the administrative wing and a pre-existing, stone-faced, hydraulics laboratory let into the gorge. Conceived as a propyleum, the reception building is topographically related to particular features around it: to the greensward in front of Balch Hall, to Beebe Lake to which it is connected by a service building and a boat house, and lastly, to the gorge itself by a pedestrian passerelle linking the two buildings, and by a stepped promenade leading down to a belvedere facing the falls. This inflected play with outbuildings is concluded with an eight-story campanile at the northwest corner of the reception building that ties the whole complex back to the Triphammer Bridge, which is one of the main vehicular approaches to the campus.

The new administrative building is treated as a linear foil to the cubic mass of the reception building. It houses the central administration, alumni, development, and university council offices. For obvious compositional considerations, both new buildings are ordered on an identical, twenty-five-foot structural module.

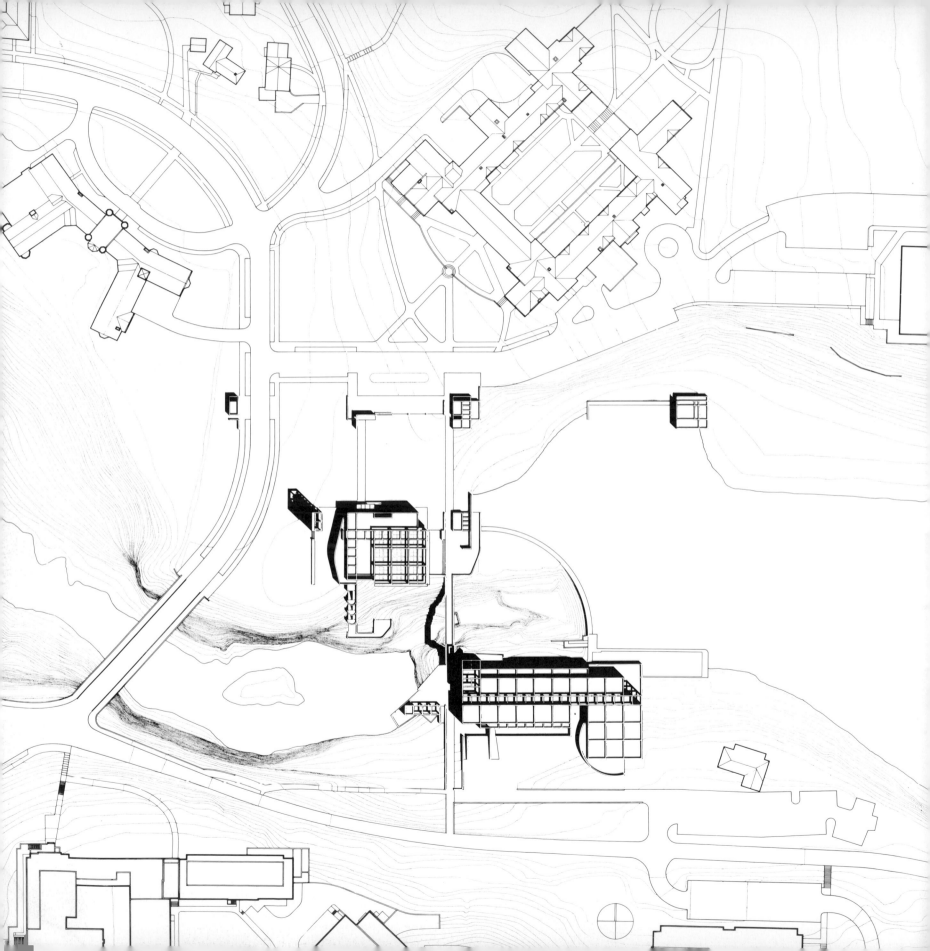

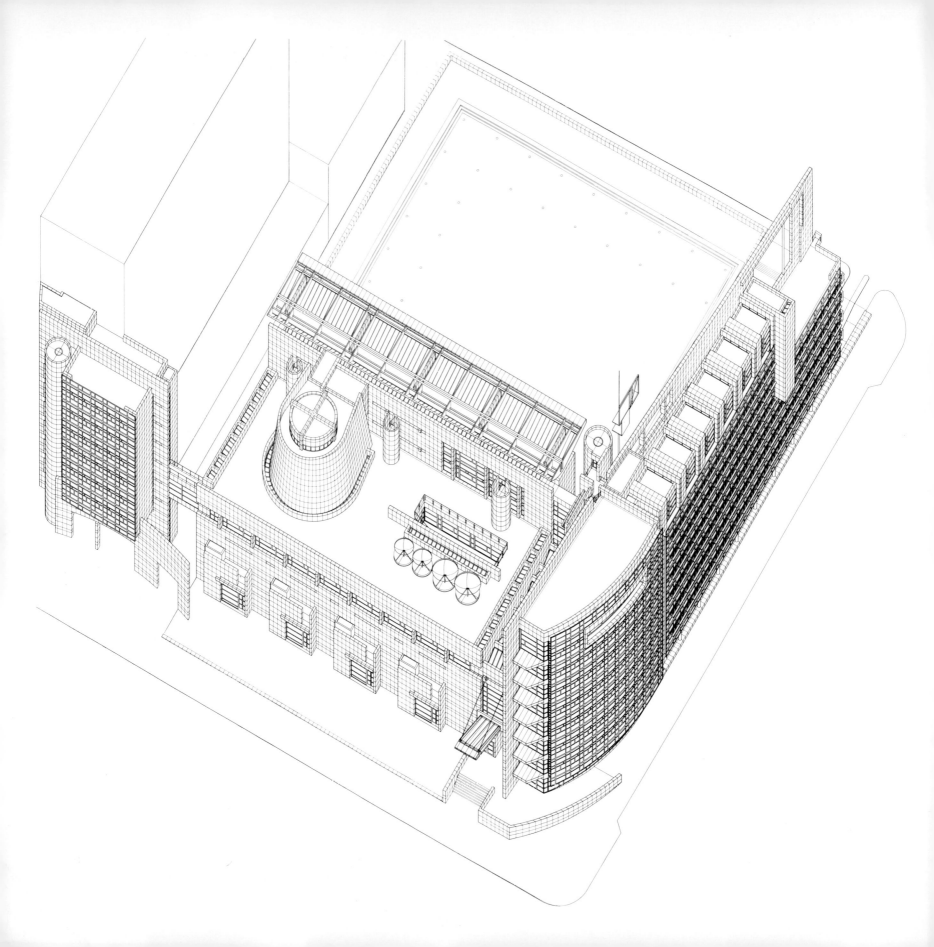

Canal + Headquarters

Paris, France
1988–1991

Building on the Seine in Paris demands an architecture of heroic urban stature. The Paris of President Mitterrand has a climate of tremendous artistic freedom. Andre Rousselet, the president of Canal+, is in perfect concert with this visionary time in Paris. How fortunate it is for all of those architects who have had a hand in this brilliant continuum in which the art of architecture is treated as a sacred trust.

The new headquarters and production facilities for the Canal+ television company, on the left bank of the Seine just west of the Pont Mirabeau, is divided into a western wing for administration facing the Seine, and a wide, eastern wing mainly for audio-visual production.

The general organization derives from the overall context and some fairly severe site restrictions. The thin, tapering plan of the administration wing is a result of the northeast and northwest boundaries of the L-shaped site, which define two adjacent sides of a square park occupying the best part of the block.

Conceptually, Canal+ depends on a series of delicately tessellated membranes. Of primary importance is the combination of clear, translucent, and opaque white glass that make up the curtain wall on the river facade, in conjunction with the projecting, lightweight aluminum *brise soleil* along its entire length. A similar curtain wall is on the southern facade of the audiovisual wing facing the park.

All offices in the western wing face the river, and the building is backed by a metal-paneled spine facing the park behind. Three large, four-story television studios determine the basic shape and mass of the eastern wing, which has been partially sunken to comply with the zoning envelope. Between the wings is a three-story, sky-lit, glass entry hall that provides access to the studio floors.

It is hoped that the aerodynamic thrust of the office-wing wall opening to the river, and the broad, contrasting mass of the studios will bring new life and a sense of civic destiny to this somewhat moribund and "wasted" quarter of the city.

255

I like to think of this building as Parisian in feeling, intellectual yet sensual, and beautiful in its rationality. Spatially it is simple, but technically it is complex. The building's sheer wall becomes the placard both for Canal+ and its urban presence. Its image from the Seine is of a great ship whose only movement is the changing light.

Geometry

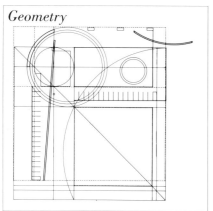

Structure

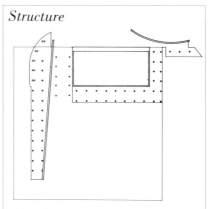

Elements

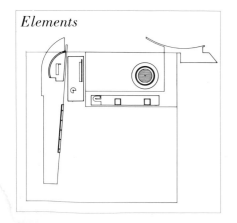

Circulation

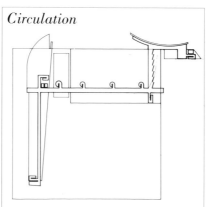

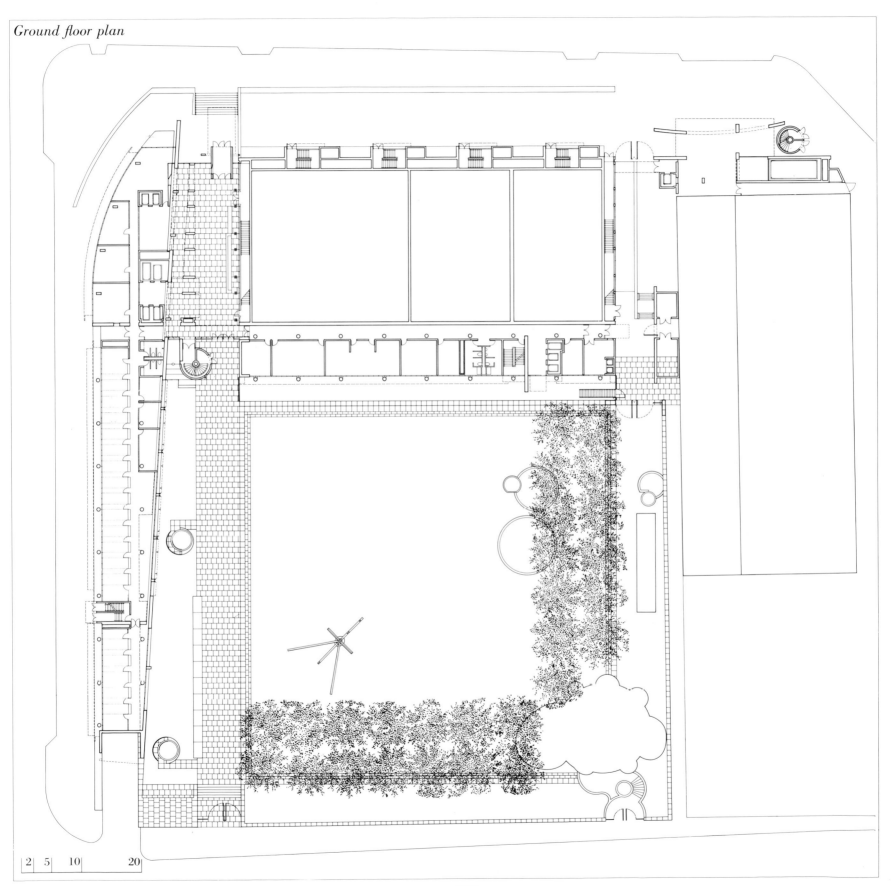

2 5   10   20

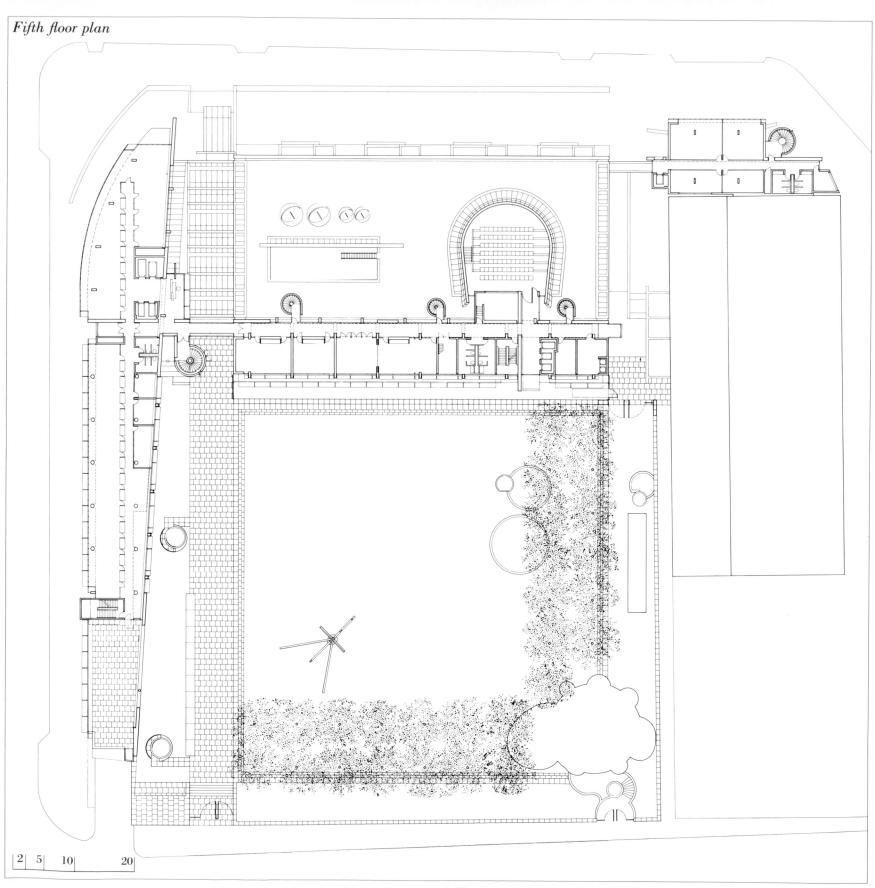

2 5 10 20

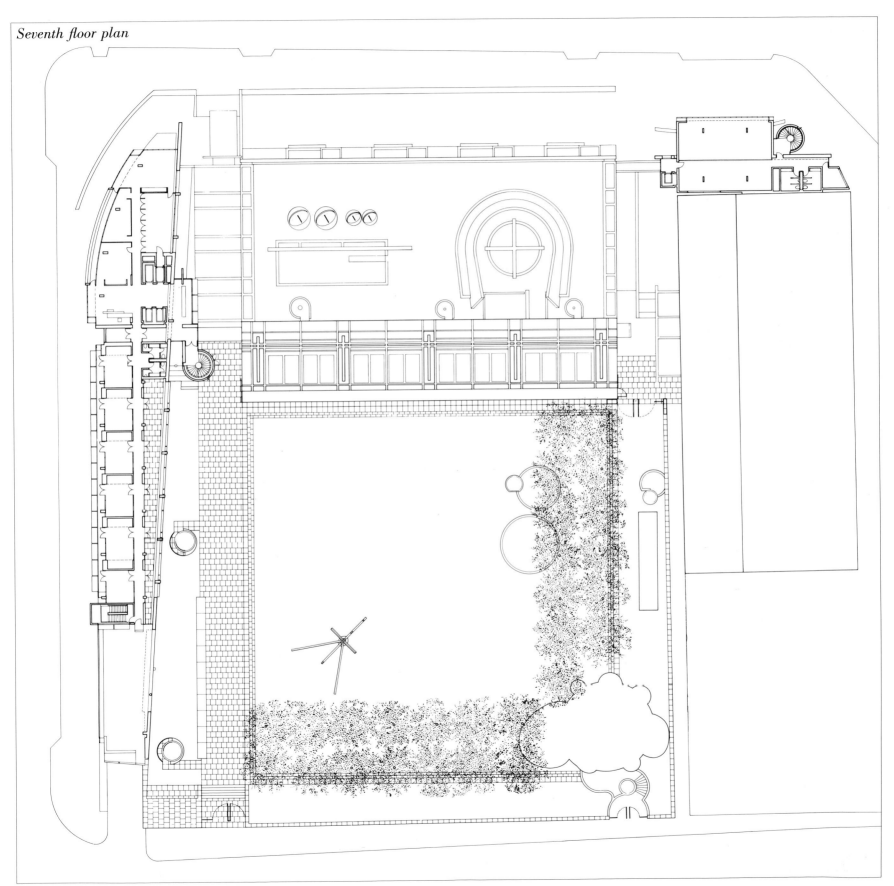

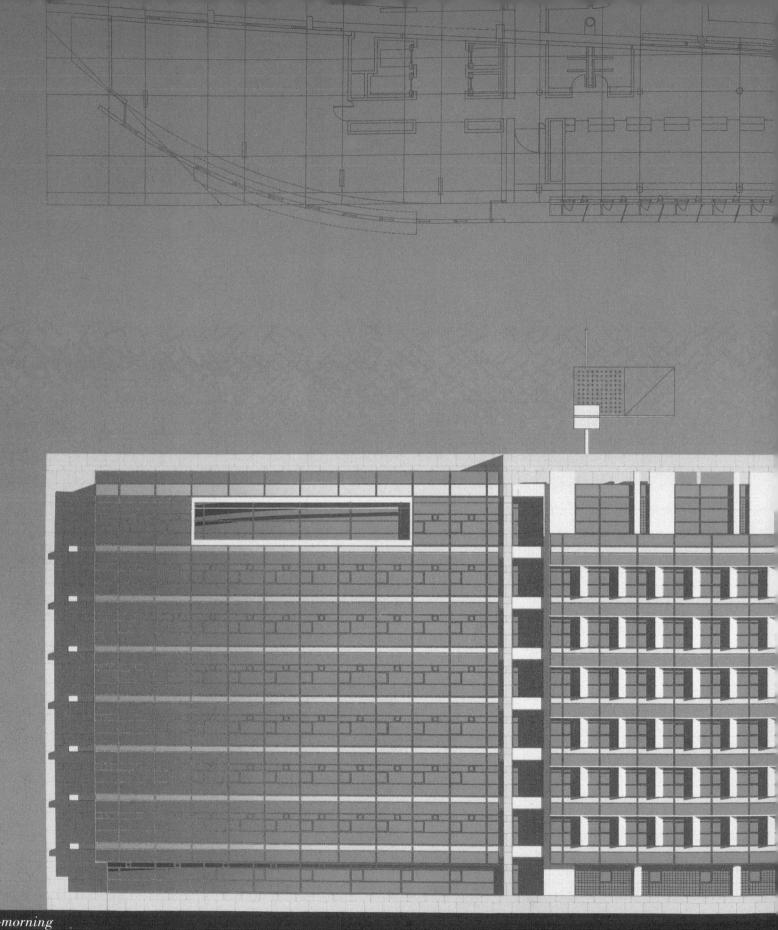

Northeast elevation—morning

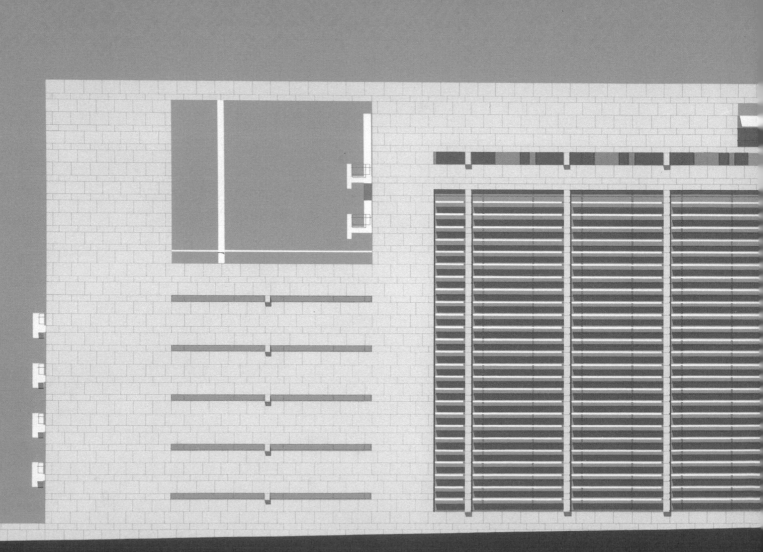

Southeast elevation—noon

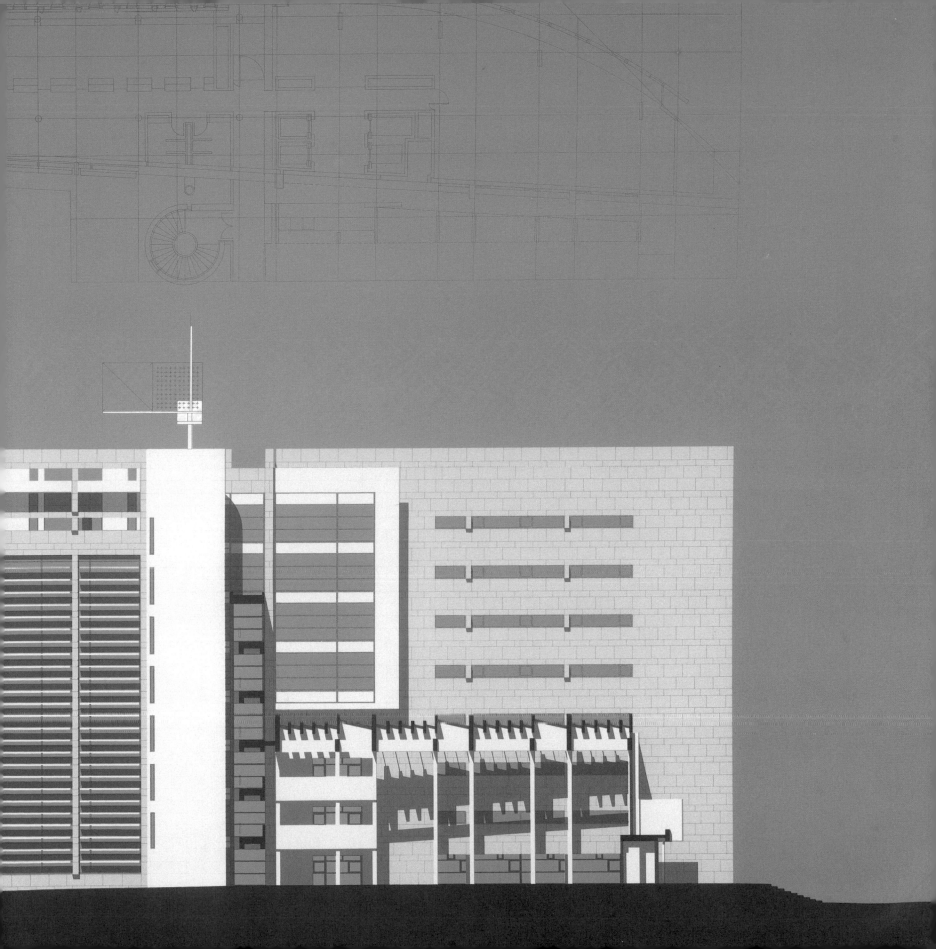

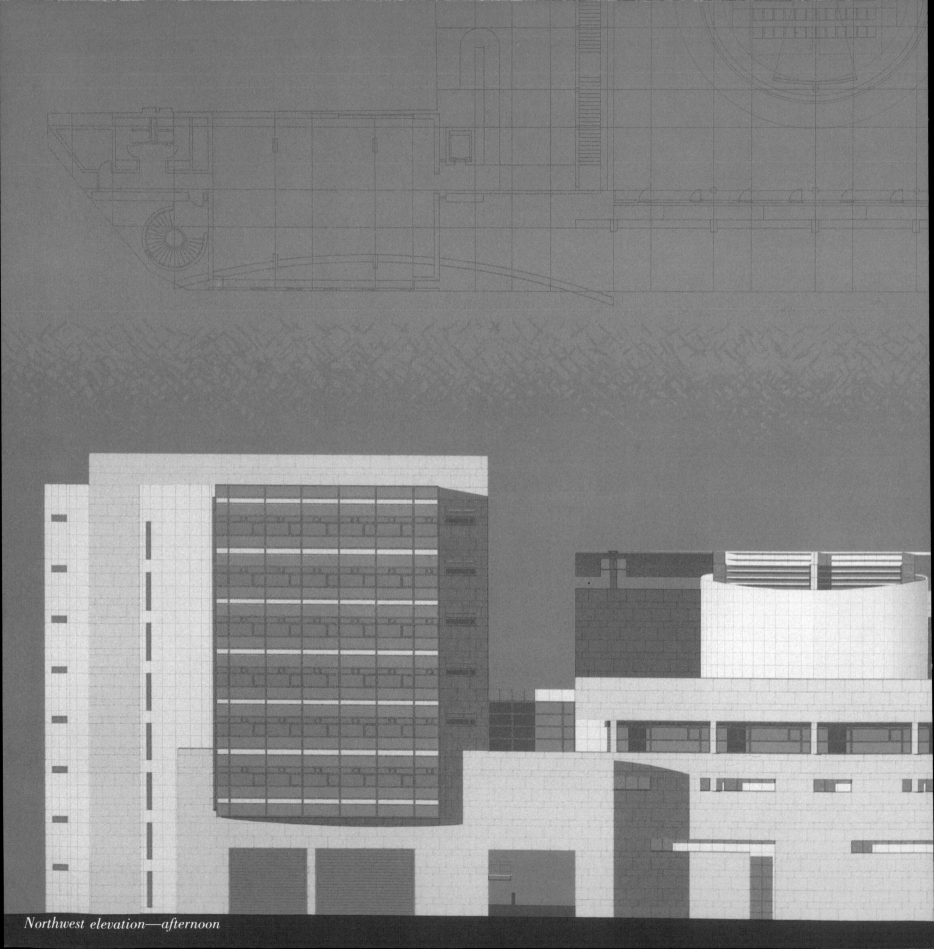

Northwest elevation—afternoon

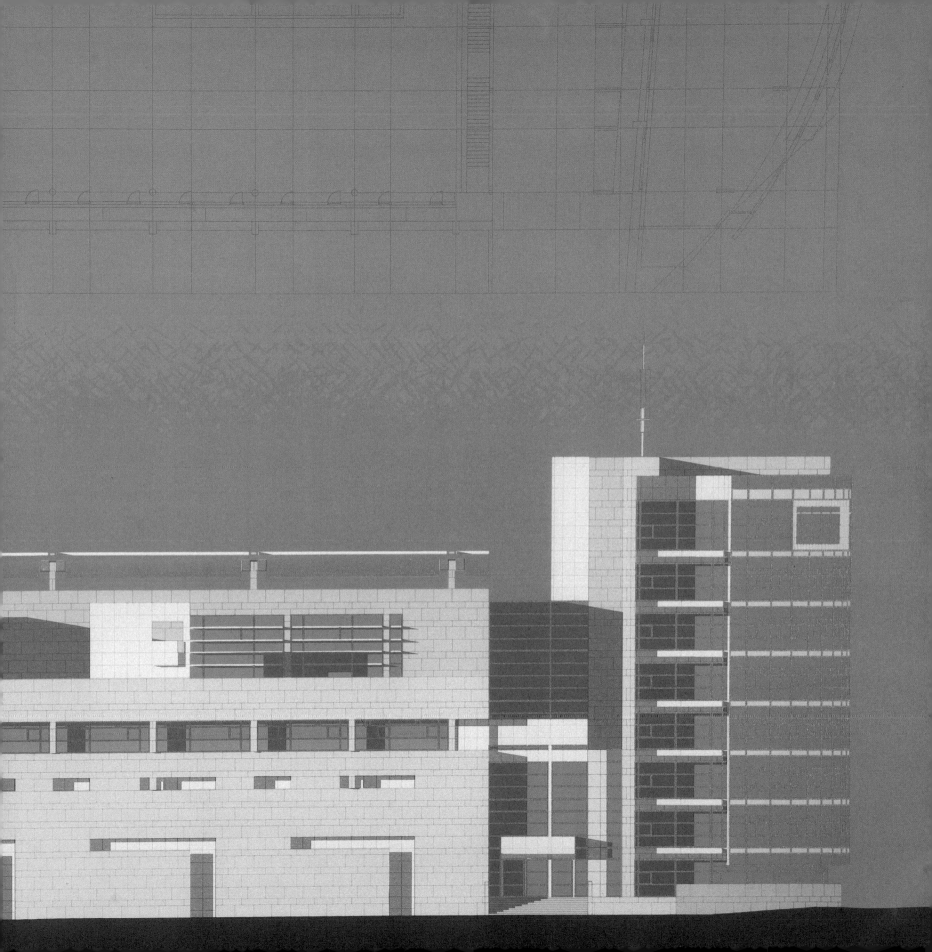

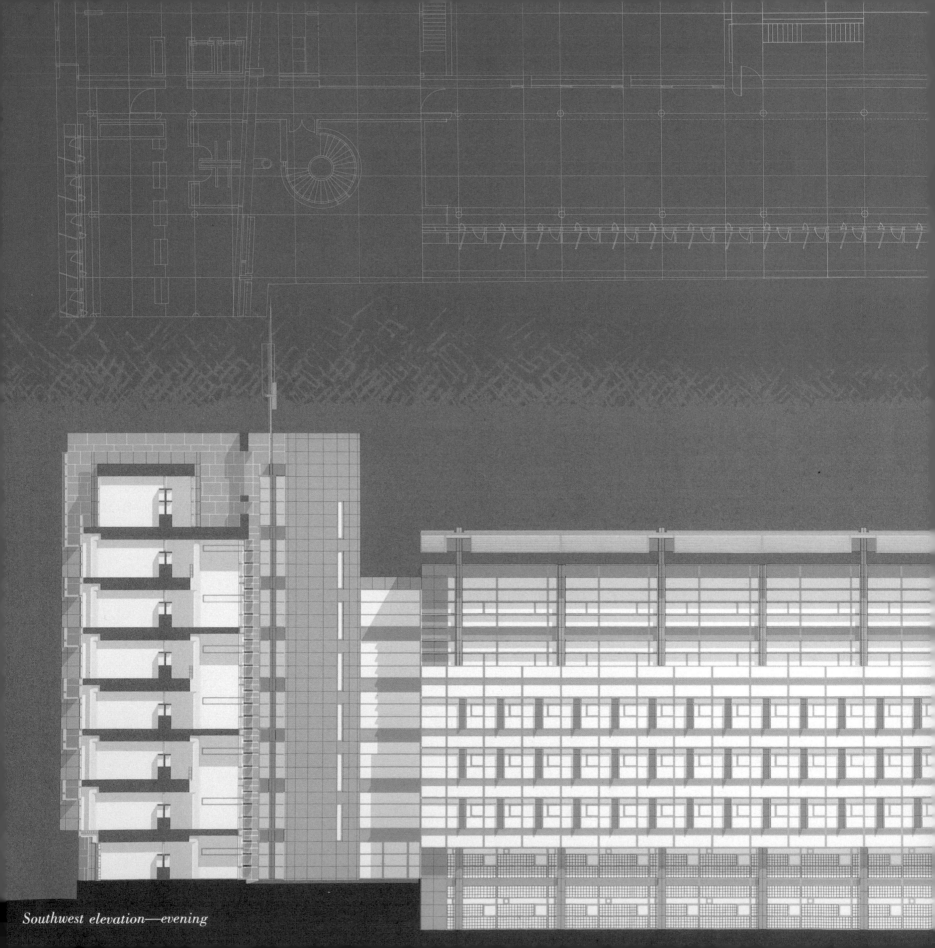

Southwest elevation—evening

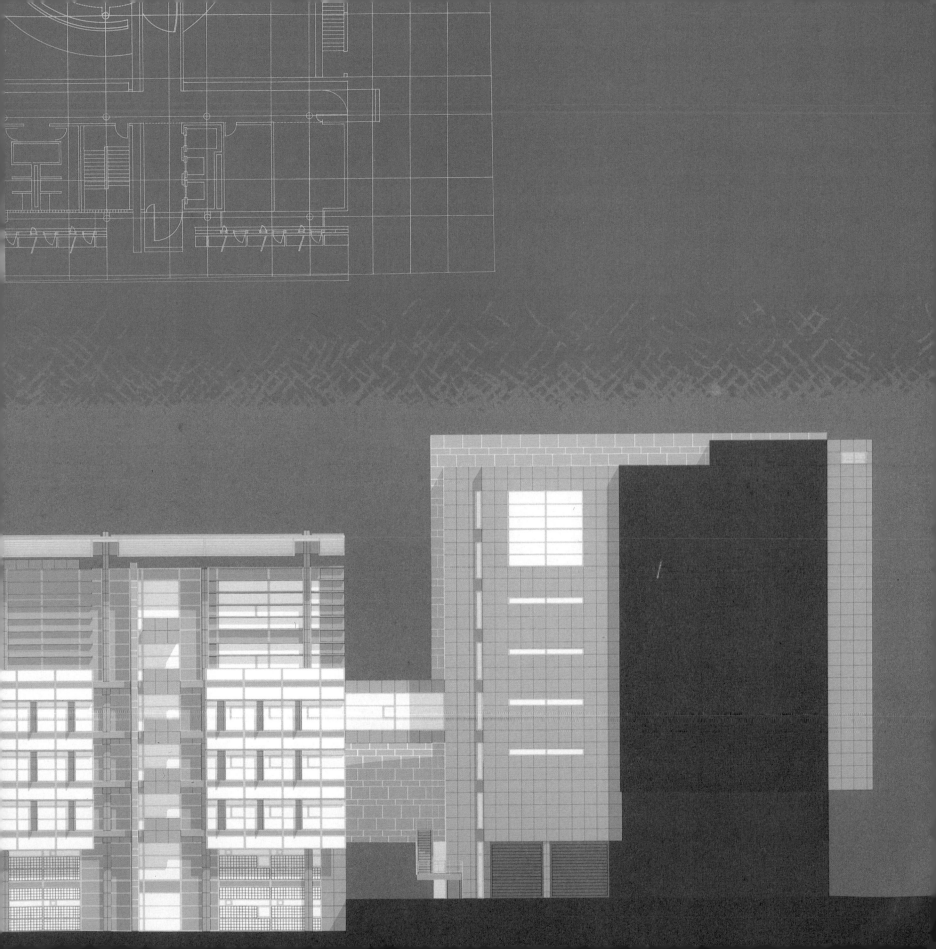

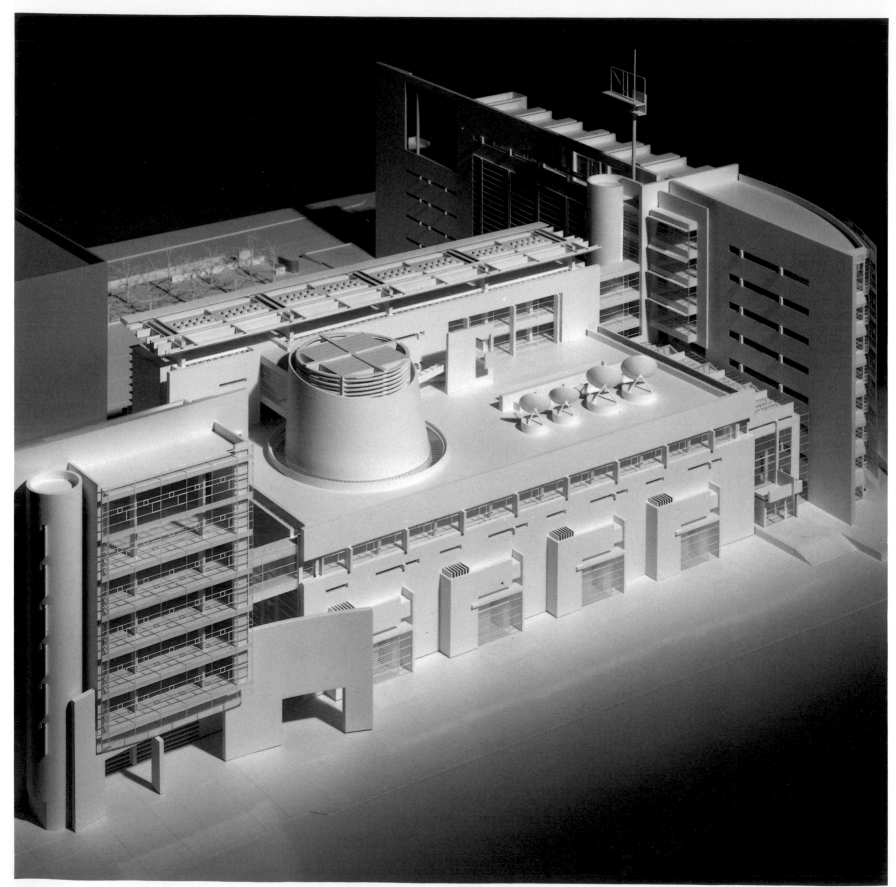

269

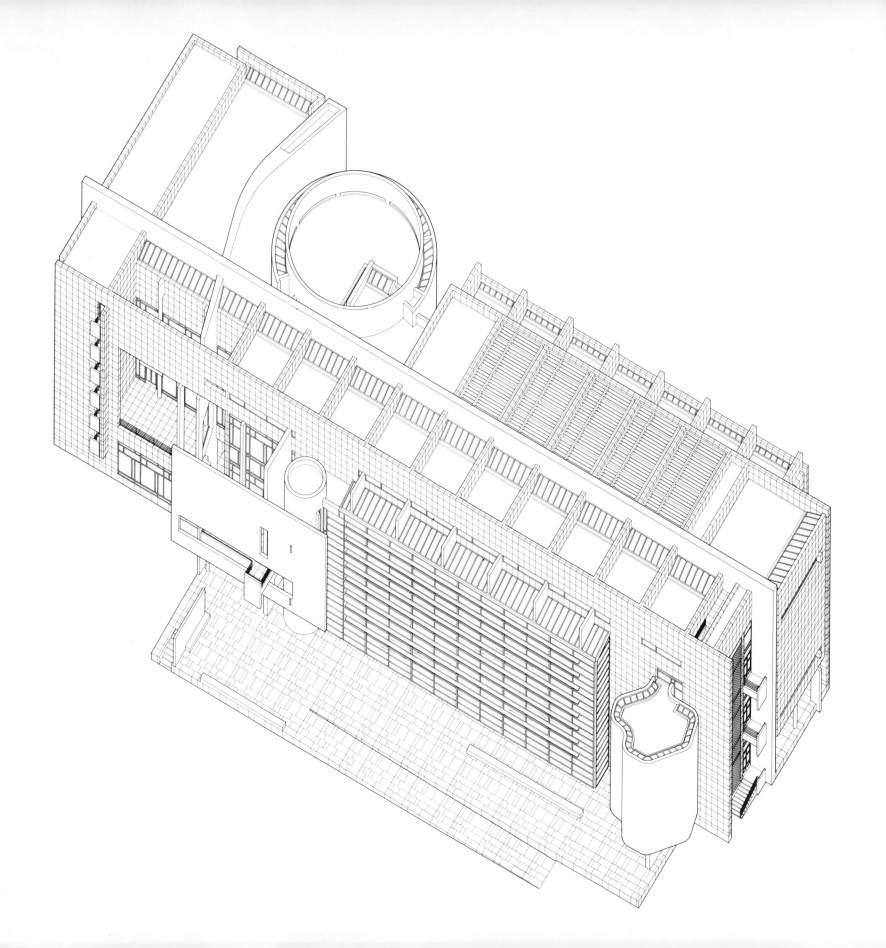

Museum of Contemporary Art

Barcelona, Spain
1987–1992

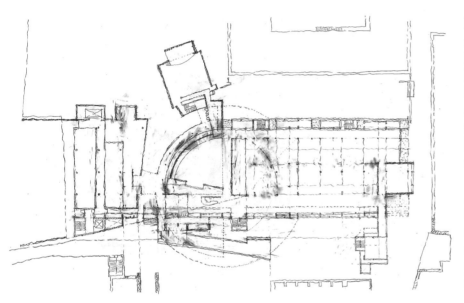

Located in the area of the Casa de la Caritat, a previous monastic enclave, this museum creates a dialogue between the historic forms of its context and the contemporary art within. The labyrinthine nature of its surroundings is reflected in the building's organization. This is perhaps most evident in the main entry, which is paralleled by a passage for pedestrians between the museum's back garden and a newly created plaza to be known as the Plaça dels Angels. This *paseo* will join a pedestrian network running throughout the old city.

A ramp leads to the main entry, which is raised one meter above the plaza. Once past this portico, visitors enter a cylindrical reception area where they have a view over the *paseo*. From here, a ramp in a triple-height hall looks onto the galleries and the plaza, thus serving as an orientation device. The louvered hall also helps to filter natural light entering from the south.

The principal gallery spaces are close to the entry and parallel, in their bulk and placement, the general mass of the Casa de la Caritat behind the museum. They are large, open, loftlike spaces that can accommodate sizable art works.

Possibly the most striking feature of this exhibition sequence is the layering of space from the ramp hall to the double-height gallery running the full length of the northeastern facade. Visitors must cross over full-height light "slots," complete with glass-lensed floors, in order to enter the main galleries or to pass from these to the viewing balconies.

With its low profile and contextual harmony, the light patterns of this museum will bestow a totally new rhythm of movement and energy upon the medieval core.

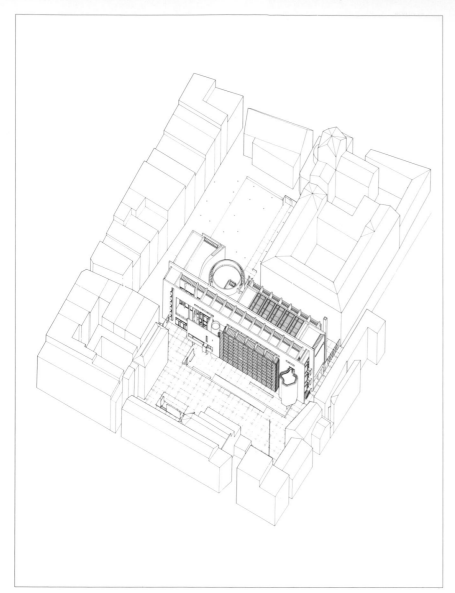

Axonometric in context

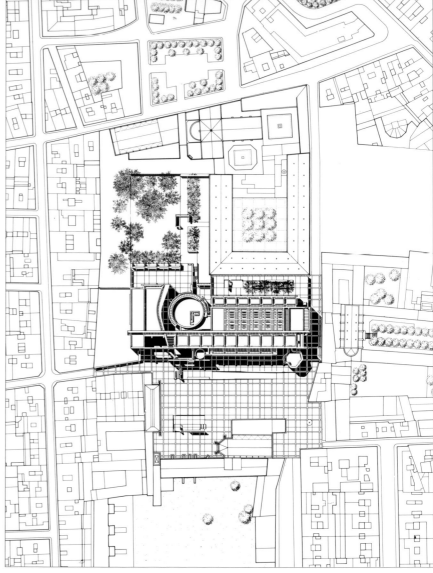

Site plan

272

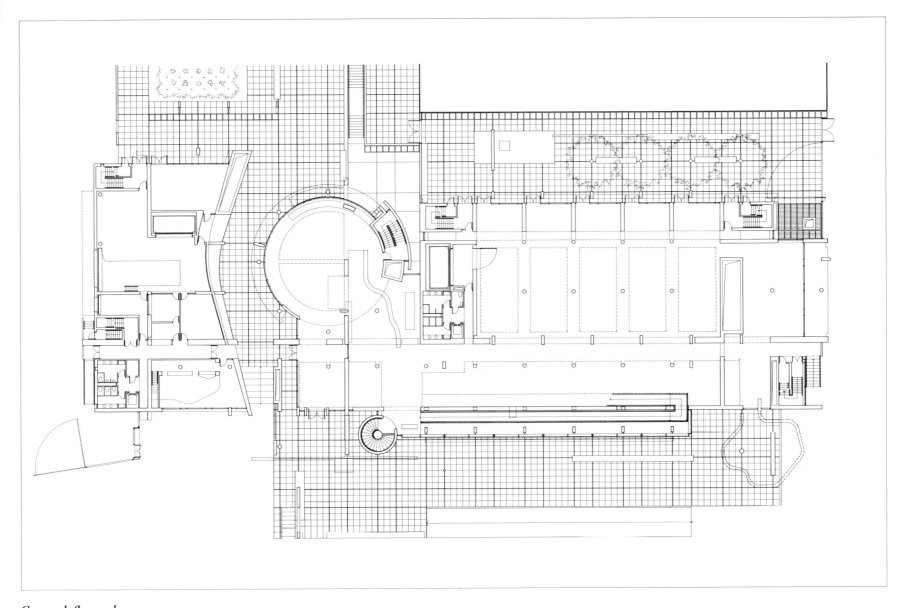

Ground floor plan

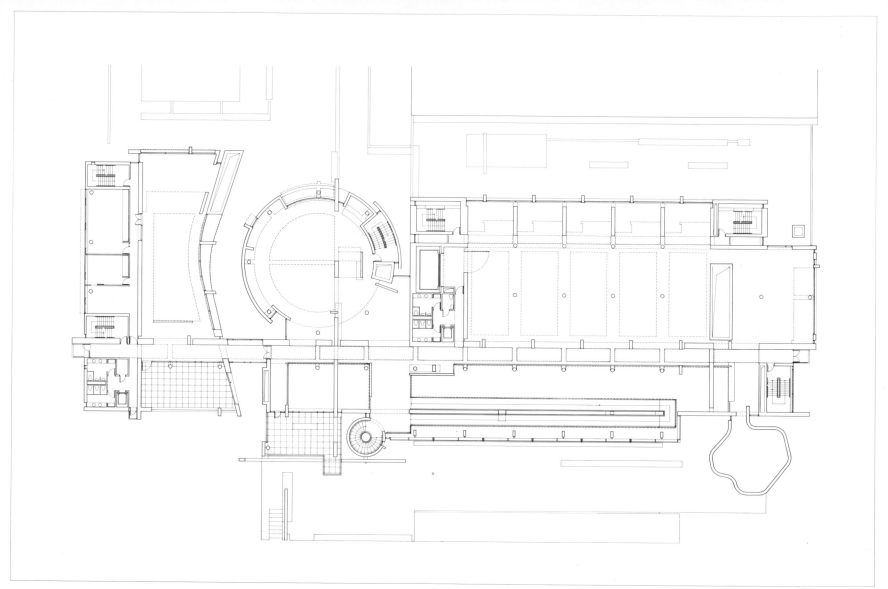

First floor plan

Geometry

Program

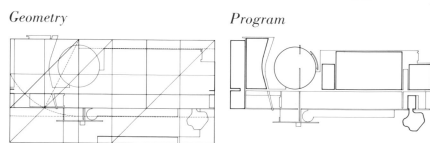

2 5 10 20

274

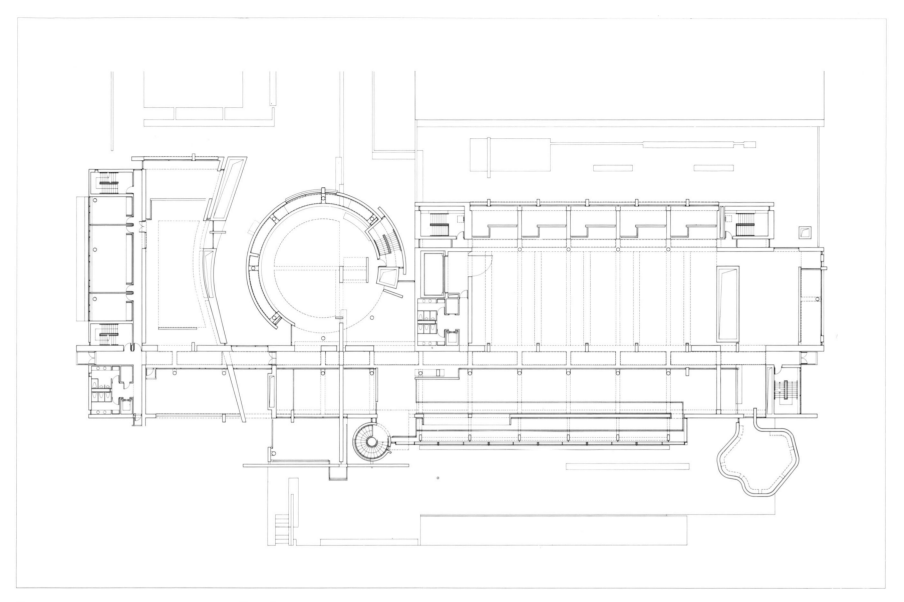

Structure   Circulation   *Second floor plan*

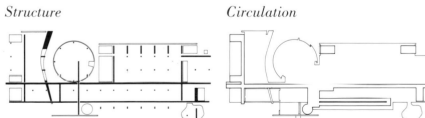

South elevation

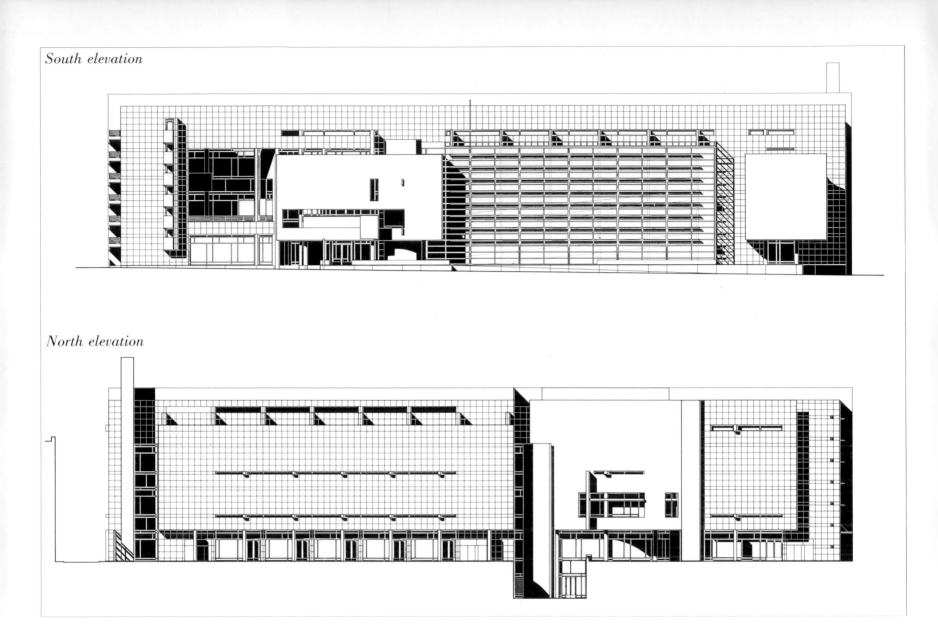

North elevation

2 5 10   20

West elevation

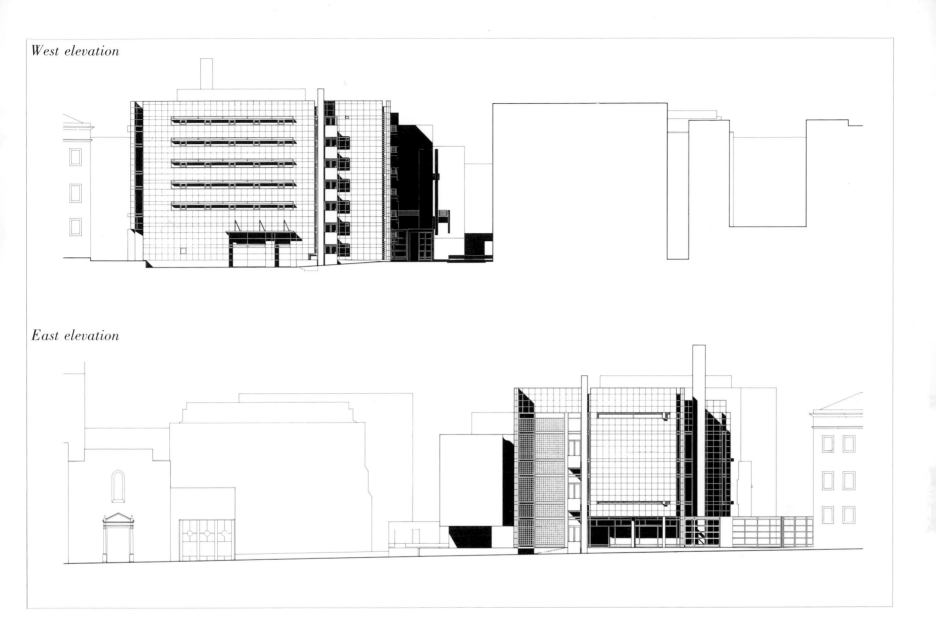

East elevation

At a dinner one night in New York a few years ago I met Mayor Pasqual Maragall of Barcelona, who was the guest of honor. He asked me what type of building I would like to do in Barcelona. My answer was simple, a museum.

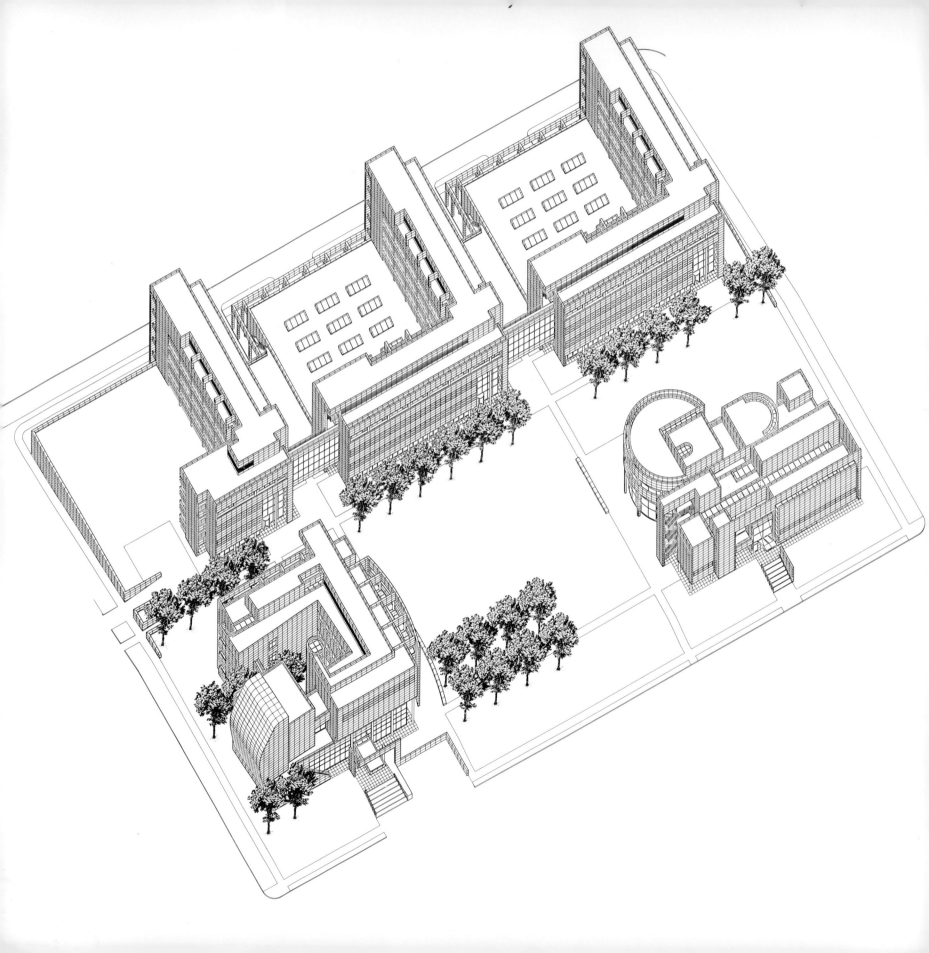

Research Center for Daimler-Benz AG

Ulm, Germany
1989–1993

These new laboratory/research facilities for Daimler-Benz in a pastoral setting in Ulm are the partial realization of a master plan for an eventual research campus about eight times as large as the present one. The repetitive grid of the office/laboratory units is focused on a Jeffersonian greensward in the center of the campus. This lawn, with two central semipublic buildings, also doubles as a kind of assembly between the older research facilities on the northeast and the new laboratory planned for continuous expansion toward the south and northwest.

The basic, L-shaped, office/laboratory module can be readily adjusted to accommodate specific conditions. In general, offices are on the external perimeter and laboratories line the interior and look over a green inner court. Two of the L-shaped research modules of the first phase share a large, open, below-grade workspace for the fabrication of oversized components, which is lit by skylights in a turf-covered roof. A service road ringing this area is depressed to preserve unobstructed views over the city and to the open country.

While security clearance is needed to enter the compound, all circulation is basically on foot. Employees and visitors enter a central parking lot at the northern edge of the present phase by a single, internal access road on the southeastern edge of the greensward. The main "public" structures are close to this road and include, first, a central building for executive offices, lecture rooms, display, and an auditorium, and second, a cafeteria building with various dining and lounge facilities and a small central reference/research library.

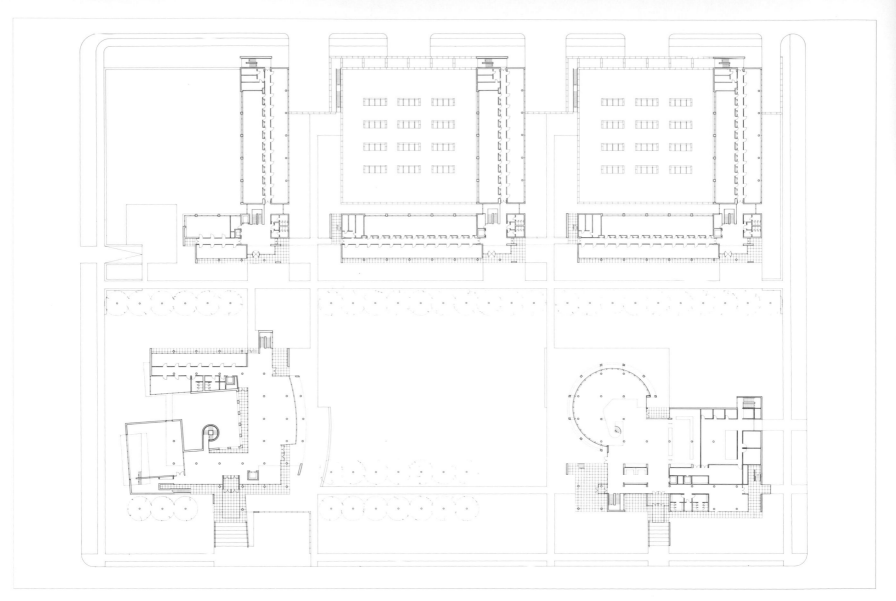

Ground level plan

Master plan

5|10   20   40

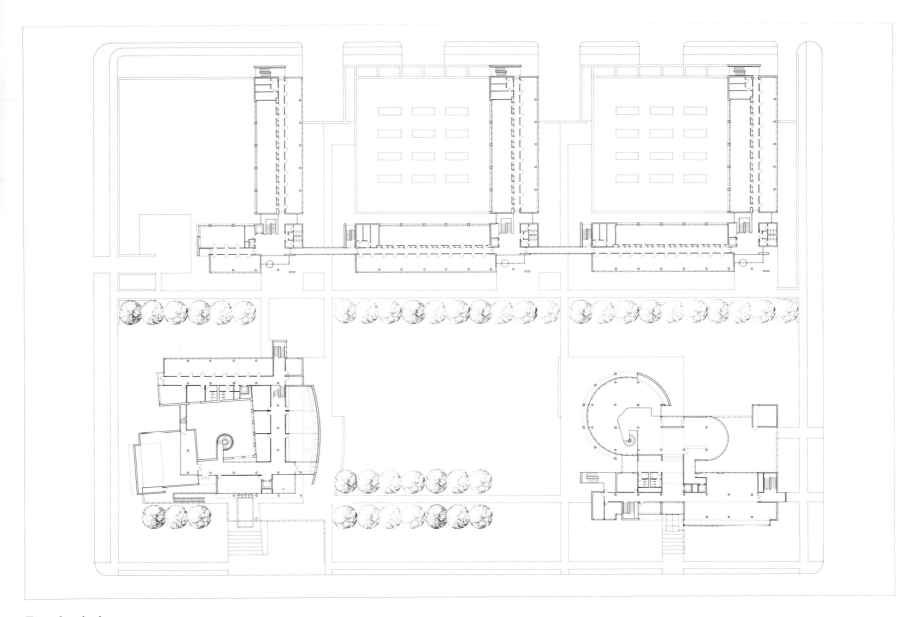

First level plan

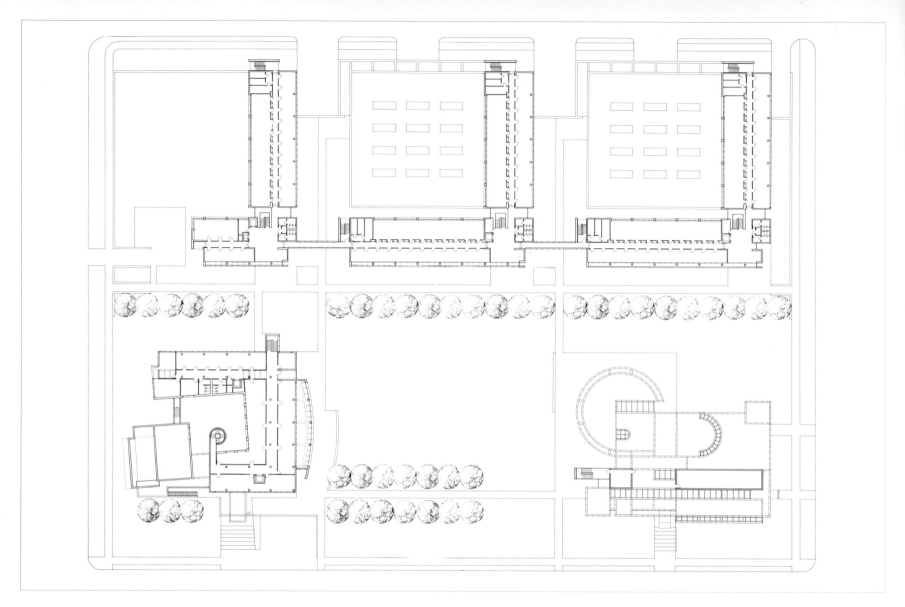

Second level plan

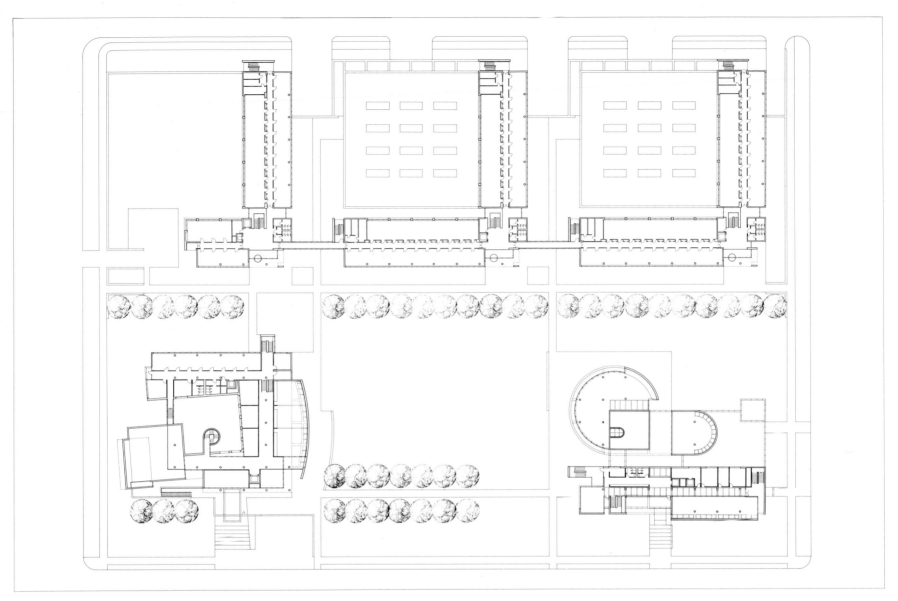

Third level plan

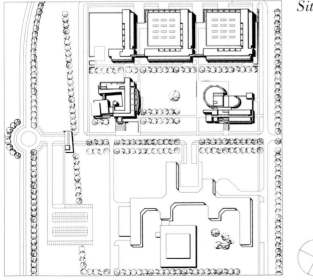

Site plan

Cross section facing southwest

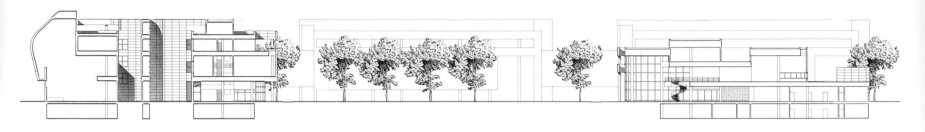

Cross section facing northwest

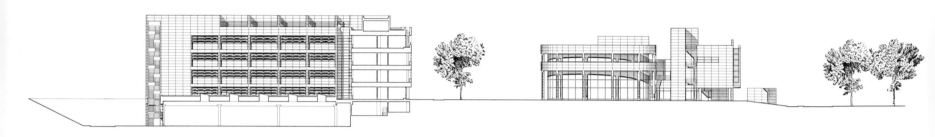

Cross section facing northwest

Cross section facing northwest

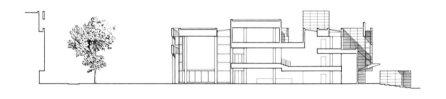

5| 10| 20| 40|

Northeast elevation

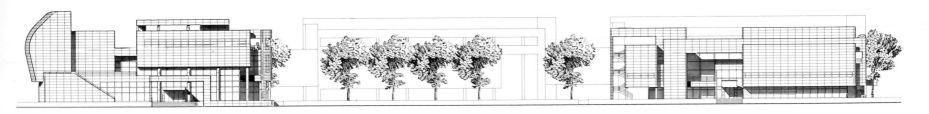

Northwest elevation

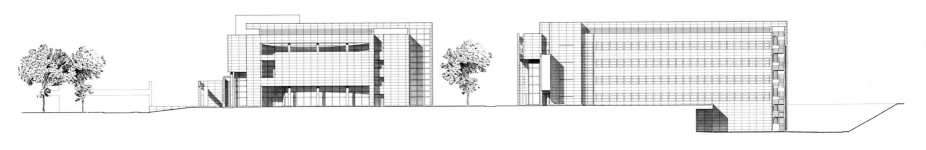

Southwest elevation

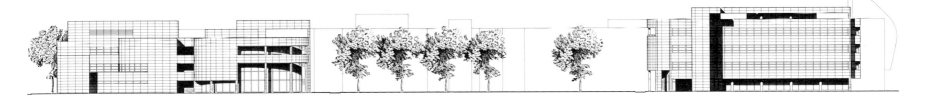

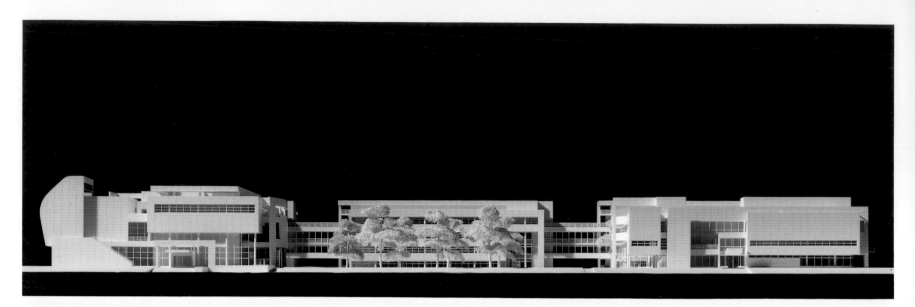

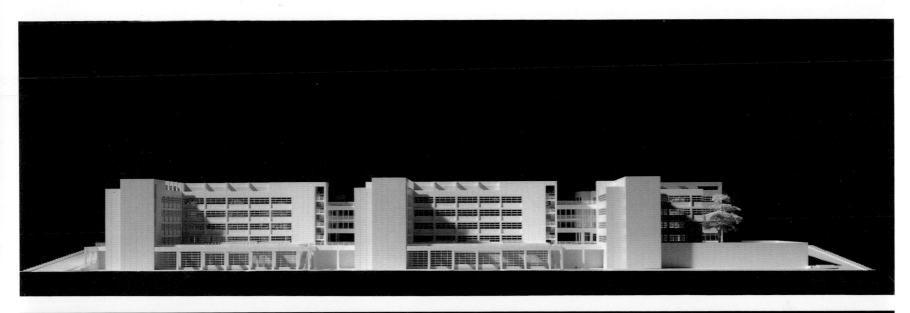

I have been fortunate to have been able to build so much in Germany. The arena of Architecture has become worldwide. German architects have gained commissions in Chicago; Italian, Spanish, and French architects build in Japan. Japanese architects work in Los Angeles and New York— everyone is everywhere. It gives one a great sense of freedom and richness to be able to think across borders and cultures in the universal language of architecture. Beyond regionalism, architects have become players on a world stage, a stage on which opportunities to build occur more frequently far afield than at home. The script of the drama or comedy, as the case may be, is full of cross-cultural references that must enrich not only the experience but the architecture. The scenes are ever shifting from one forward-looking society to another. Who knows where we will next meet.

*The Daimler-Benz Research
Center focuses on the impact of
the automotive industry on the
environment. The design of the
complex contains the spatial
hierarchy of a small university,
for it depends upon information
and interaction. The formal
organization of this
forward-looking institution
reflects these dual interests.*

Library of France

Paris, France
1989

This project for the new French national library is related to the city by a megascale achieved through a number of decisive features. First, a vertical office tower would have proclaimed the presence and position of the library through the long vistas that are a traditional part of the Parisian skyline. Second, the building would have been directly related to the river by footbridges to the Parc de Bercy on the opposite bank. Finally, it would have visual connection to the historic center through a panoramic window in the principal research library at the western end of the main reading room.

Conceived for a limited site facing north onto the Seine, this design followed the competition conditions to the letter by breaking the overall building form into the seven parts: entrance/ exhibition space, restaurant/colloquium space, film and music library, recent acquisitions, main reading room, research library, and administration tower.

The main pedestrian approaches were perceived as coming from three main directions: from the RER station to the southeast, close to the eastern boundary along the rue de Donremy; from the metro station on the Boulevard Vincent Auriol two blocks to the west; and from the footbridges leading to Parc de Bercy.

Primary to the organization of this vast complex was the positioning of the entire book storage and processing facility in a two-story podium between the 35-meter, 100-year flood plain and 42.20 meter datum of the podium plaza. Thus, in approaching from the west and south, the public enters over the collection itself. Books circulate from this memory bank along a series of north-south axes to the reading room and the six-story main library stack parallel to the river, which is divided into five reference sections according to specific categories.

The main entrance hall at the east end includes a large exhibition hall/foyer flanked by shops to the south and a children's library to the east. Below, immediately to the south, is a top-lit podium area for a restaurant and meeting facilities. In the middle of the entry area is a cone-shaped elevator tower that provides controlled entry to the library. From here, bridges connect to the recent-acquisitions area, where books are accommodated on orthogonal "trays" suspended within the outer cylindrical form of the library, and to the music and film libraries.

One of the primary considerations of this *parti* was the creation of a monumental reading room facing the Seine. As in Henri Labrouste's Bibliothèque Nationale of 1868, this room was conceived as a kind of internal outdoor space under a tented roof. In this instance the nomadic metaphor translates into a fully glazed double roof sustained by a 10-meter truss tapered to assume an aerofoil section. This roof not only functions as a multiple light source, flooding the interior during the day and glowing outwardly at night with artificial light, but it also doubles as an insulating void that can be freely ventilated in hot weather and hermetically closed in winter to provide a blanket of warm air above the reading room.

Organized by the golden section, this building is a tour de force in reticulated form with multiple light filters in every plan—not only in the podium and restaurant roofs, but also in the saw-tooth monitor lights of the entrance hall and in the double-glazed, seven-story-high window wall of the reading room. In many instances these lightweight, thick walls are filled with passerelles and platforms that hold some of the innumerable carrels distributed throughout the structure. These slots are thought of as "inhabited" filters that are as much activated by human movement as they are by changes in the patterns of natural light.

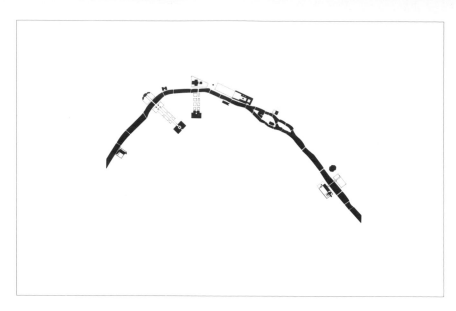

Site location in the city of Paris

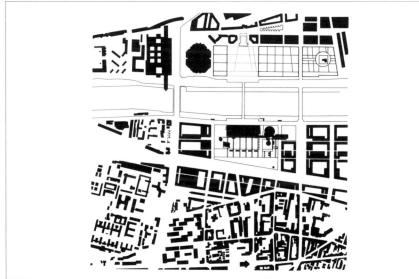

Urban relationship

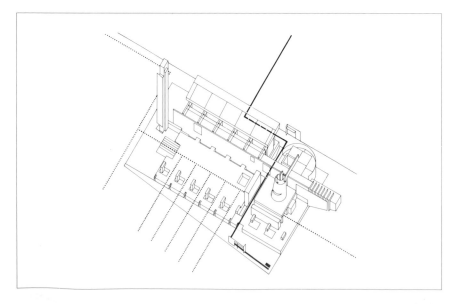

Public access

294

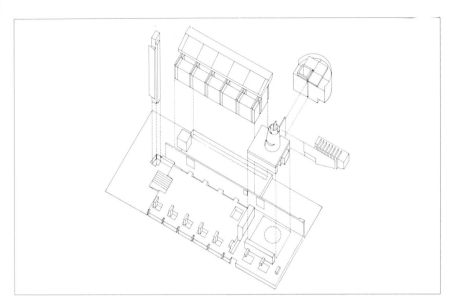

Program

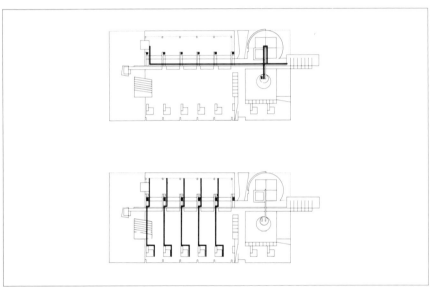

Public circulation/stack system

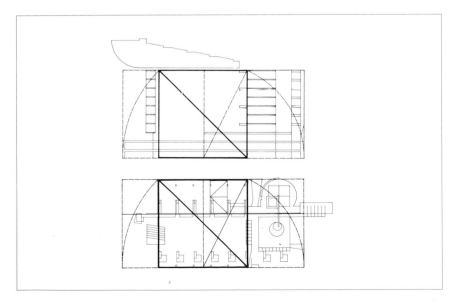

Geometric analysis

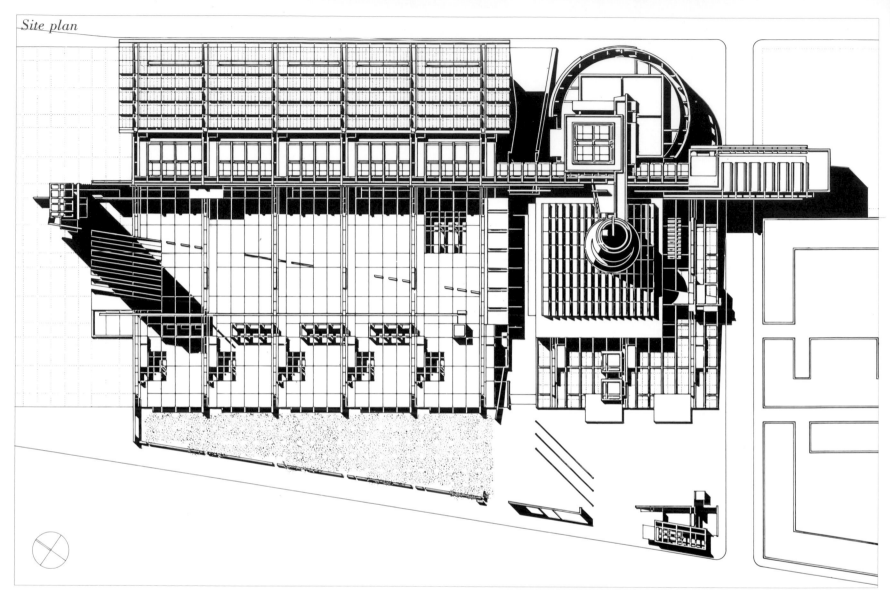

Site plan

10 20 40 80

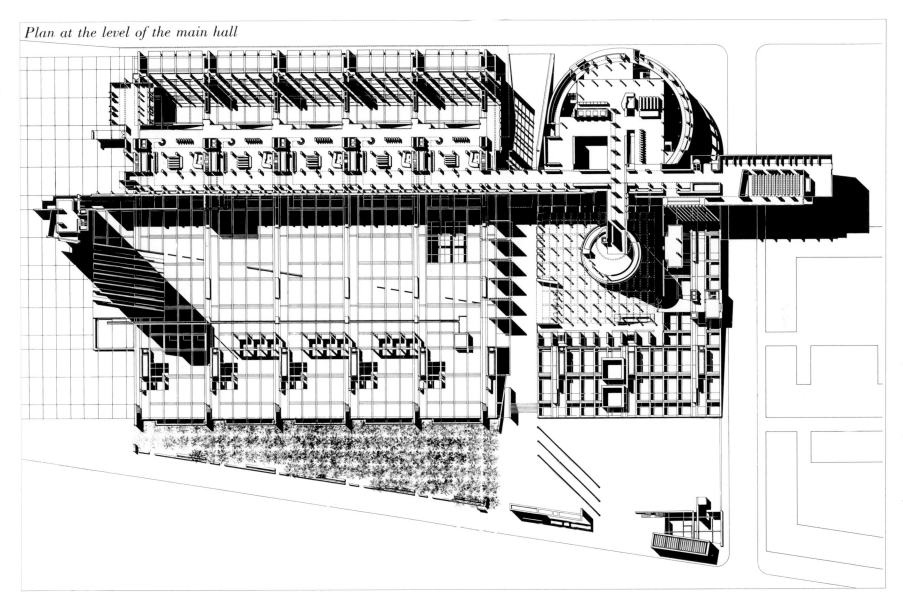

The Grand Projects of President Mitterrand in Paris have fostered a new hope for the architecture of France. How could one refuse the opportunity to be the architect of the grandest of the Grand Projects. The disappointment in losing the competition equalled the enthusiasm with which we approached the chance to succeed Henri Labrouste. In that spirit, this project was to be filled with light and the radiance of knowledge.

Schematic section facing northeast

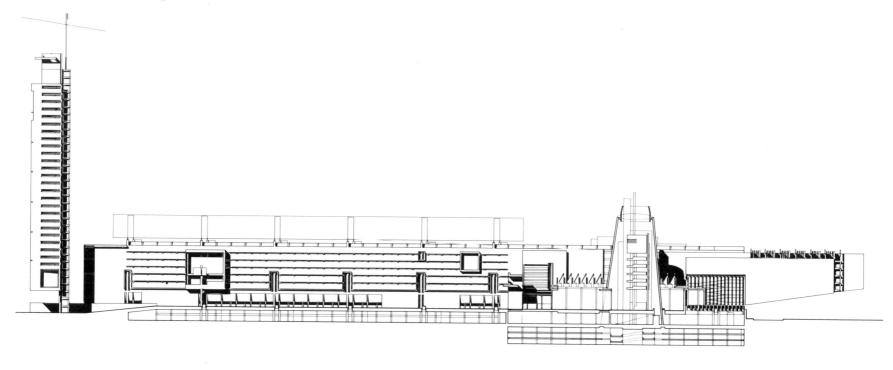

Northeast elevation

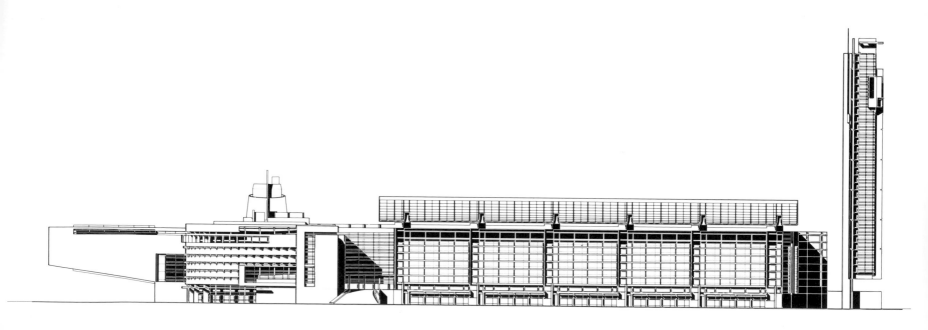

|10| 20| 40| 80|

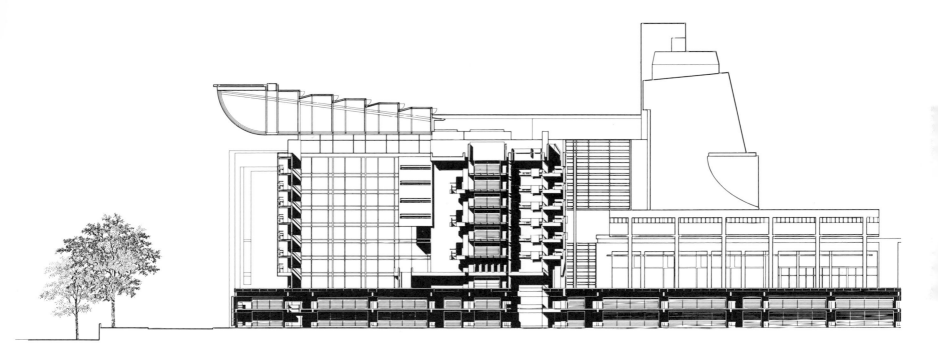

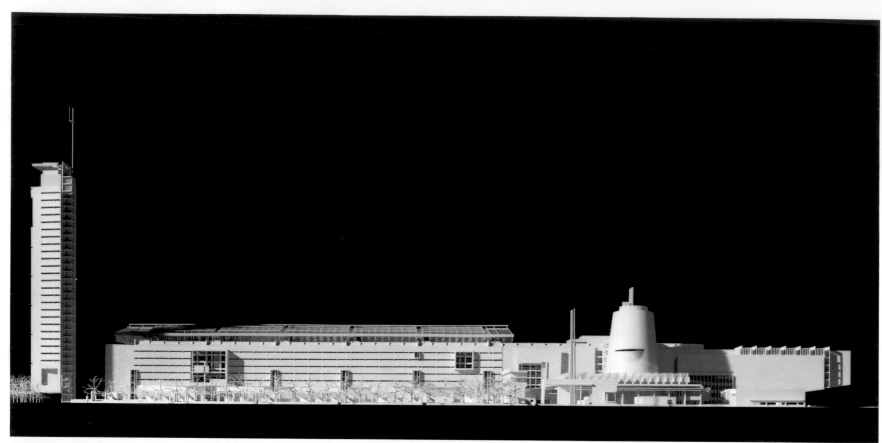

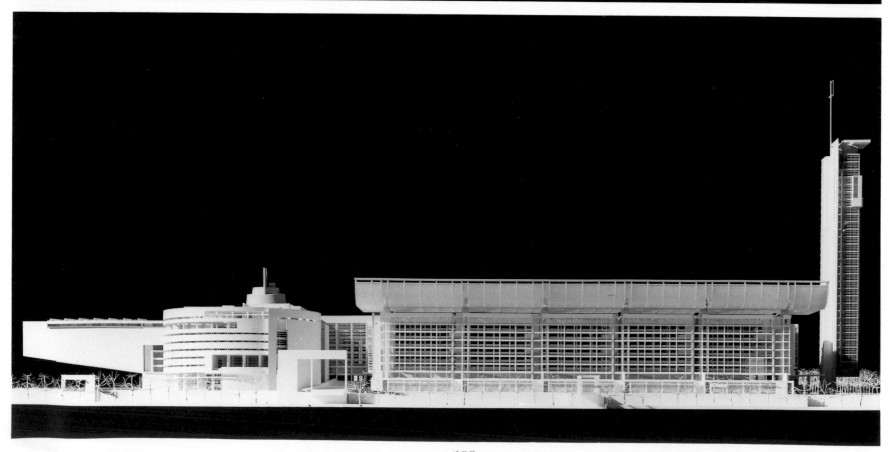

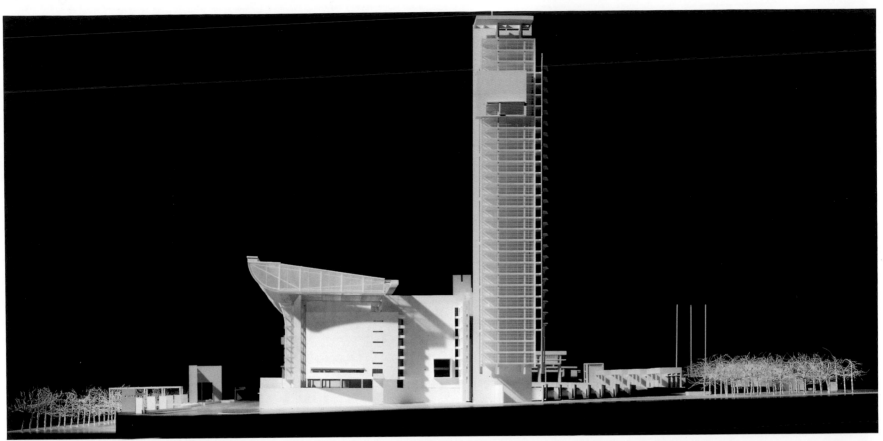

Museum of Ethnology

Frankfurt am Main, Germany
1989–1994

Site

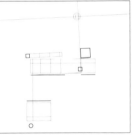

Geometry

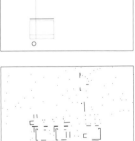

Structure

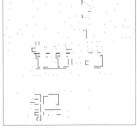

Circulation

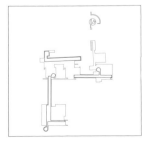

The organization of this building arises from a need to preserve as many trees as possible while respecting the scale and the height of the adjacent villas. Conceived as a kind of "conservatory-museum," this latest addition to the *Museumsufer*, a line of museums along the river Main, is organized about a long, glazed ramp hall that opens onto a park and provides views to the Schaumainkai and to Meier's Museum for Decorative Arts.

In contrast to the standard, encyclopedic presentation typical of earlier collections, this museum exhibits its holdings as series of set pieces housed in top-lit and side-lit galleries. Extra care was taken to screen out direct sunlight by shielded monitors for the inward-oriented, top-lit upper galleries, while, in contrast, the lower floors open out for indirect light and lateral views over the court. The museum's curatorial policy is to represent ethnology as a "unified diversity," first through a series of independent but linked, top-lit cubic forms, and then through alternative itineraries afforded by the plan. In this respect, the formal strategies adopted for the Museum of Decorative Arts and this museum are complementary in that the first consists of prismatic masses with an inner cruciform circulation system, while the second consists of the ramp-hall backed up by cubic pavilions along the Metzlerstrasse.

To attract the casual visitor as well as to gratify the habitual museum goer, large, dramatic exhibits, such as boats and a ceremonial house have been placed adjacent to the entrance hall. Following these, the ramp leads along and then across Metzlerstrasse to the American collection on the *piano nobile*, and then to the African collection on the ground floor. This sequence extends into the open-air court, where African statues and a clay Massai hut will be displayed. The Oceanic collection will be on the top floor.

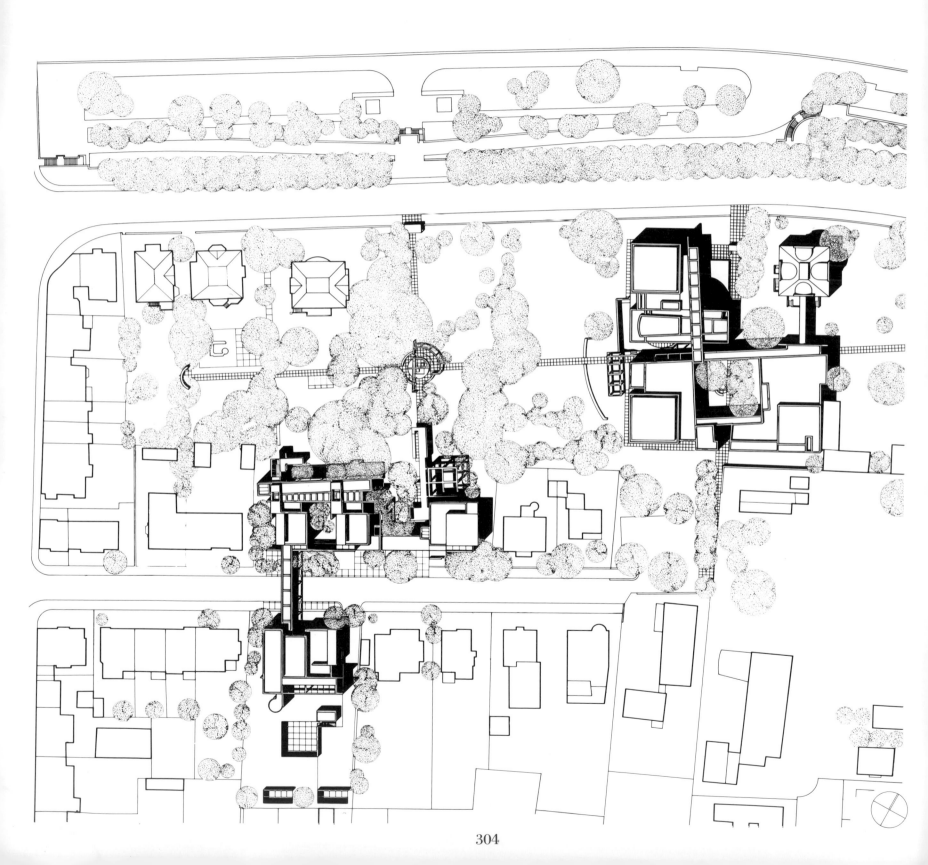

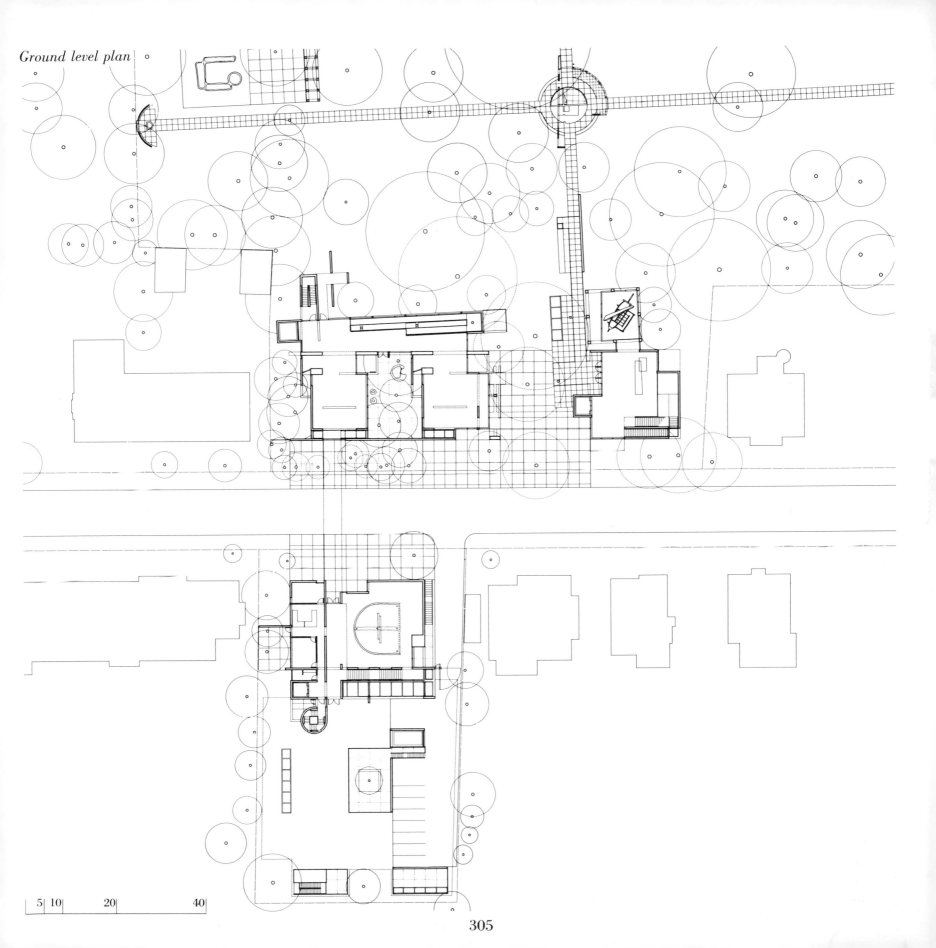

Ground level plan

5| 10| 20| 40|

305

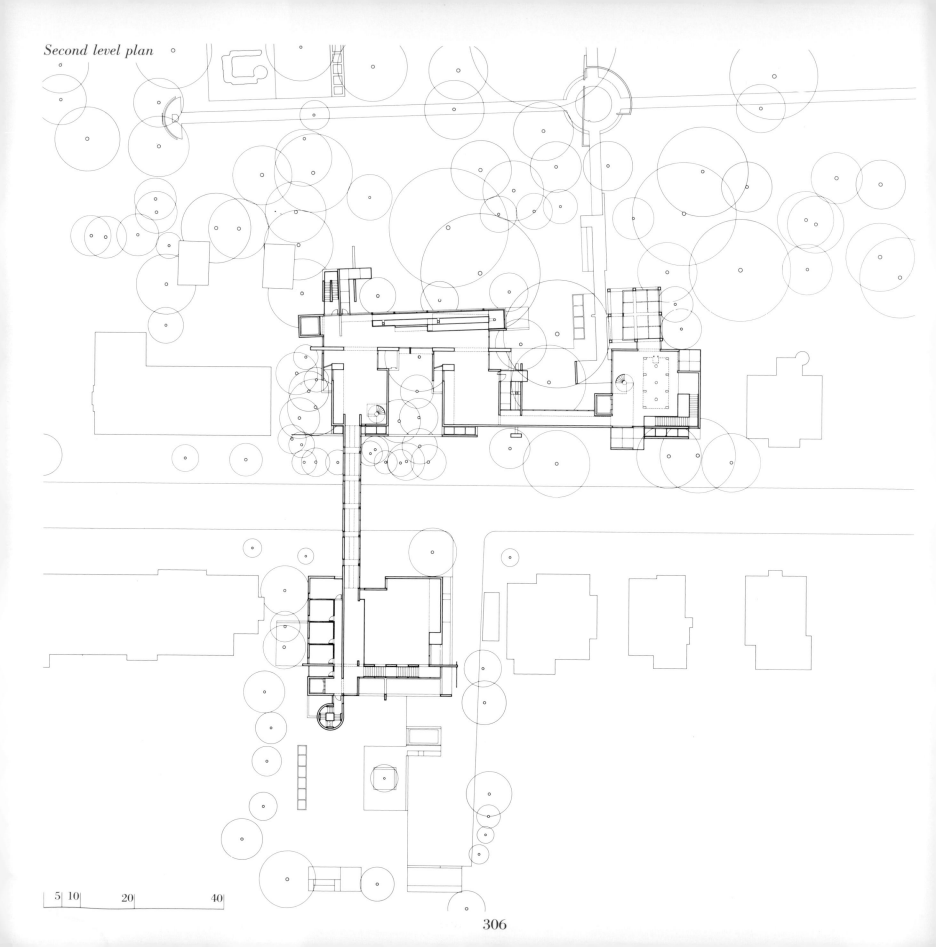

Second level plan

5 10   20   40

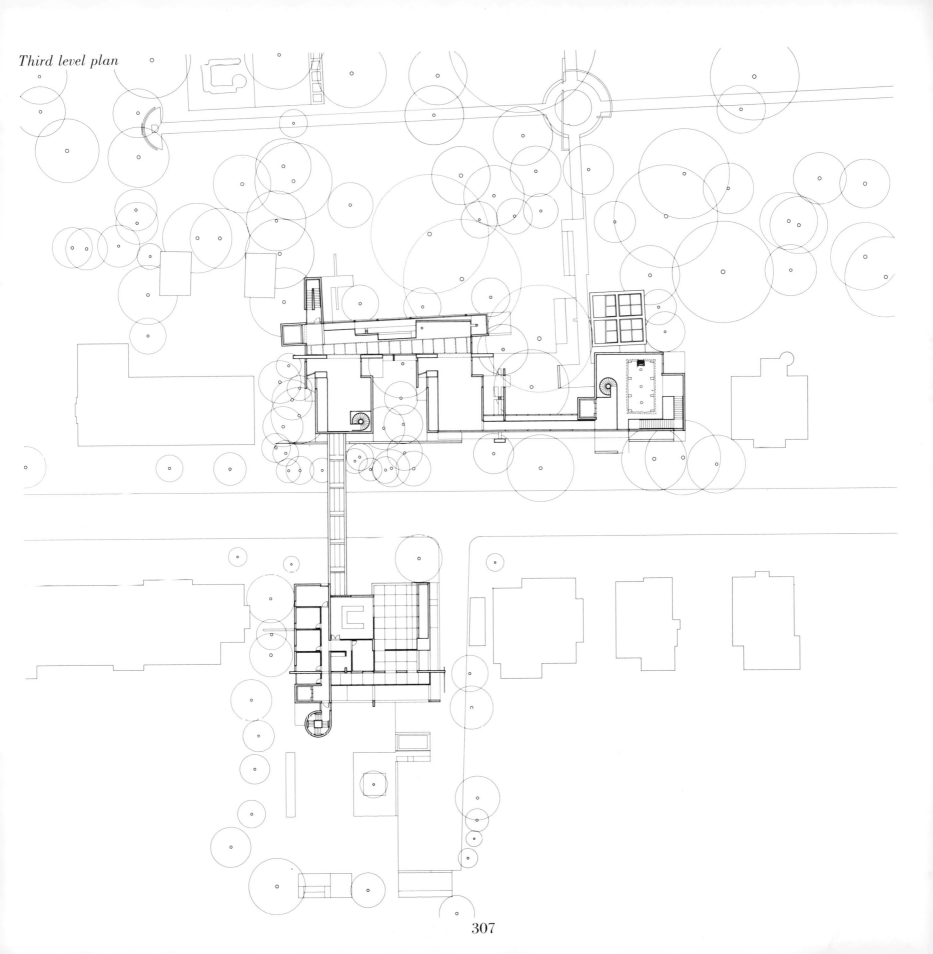

Third level plan

307

Northwest elevation

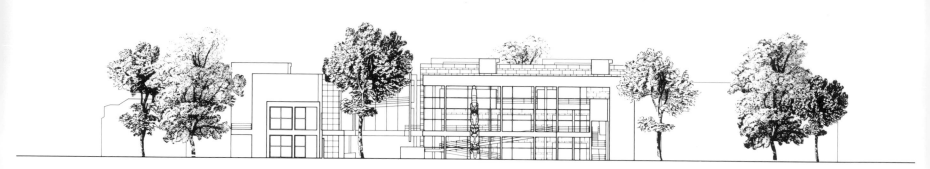

Southeast elevation

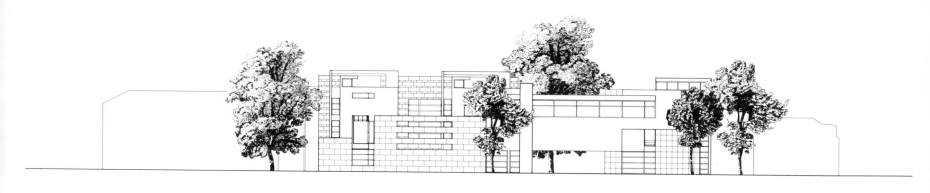

5| 10| 20|

Study of the northwest sectional elevation

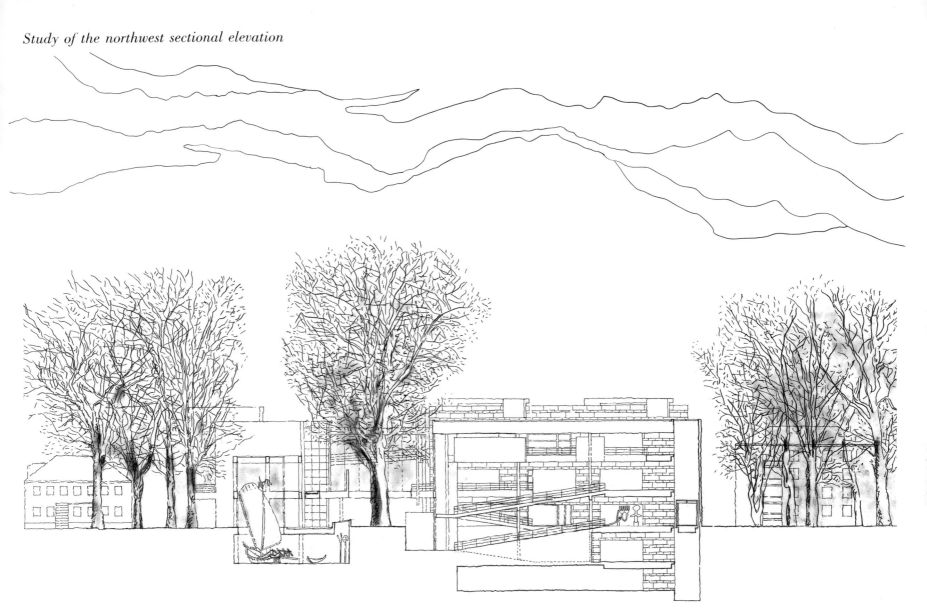

In Germany, before World War II, there was an intellectual atmosphere that manifested itself in all the arts; the avant-garde flourished in music, film, theater, literature, painting, and architecture. The intellectual and cultural destruction wrought by the Nazi period had a profound affect on me and many of my generation. Now, with more than fifty years passed, it is deeply meaningful to me to have the opportunity to bridge that gap, to build with the influence and the remembrance of those great German architects, men of brilliance, such as Ernst May, Erich Mendelsohn, Otto Haelser, Martin Wagner, Bruno Taut, and from Czechoslovakia, Otto Eisler.

Hypolux Bank Building

Luxembourg
1990–1993

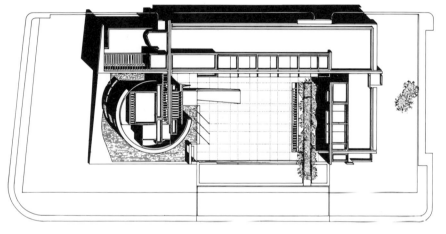

This complex is located at a crucial urban intersection on the outskirts of the city, where a sunken freeway rises to street level. Its cylindrical reception area and L-shaped office slab are on a podium slightly above the street. A planted formal court with an ornamental pool defines the surface of the podium and reflects the cylinder, to which a short ramp rises, from the court, and leads to the main lobby suspended above the pool. Here, in the symbolic center of the bank, a glass lens in the floor indicates the presence of the vault beneath.

The L-shaped slab parallel to rue Alphonse Weicker has modular offices for most of its length. The southeastern end adjacent to the cylinder houses semipublic bank functions, a cafeteria, lounges, and waiting rooms, while the opposite end has rental space with its own entrance. This adjunct slab has been planned, in accordance with the competition brief, so that it could be eventually absorbed by the bank. Between the two are the general administrative offices.

Through the adoption of a 90-centimeter planning module and a minimum office width of 2.70 meters, the offices have been planned to provide a high degree of flexibility and efficiency while affording some individuality to each space through a syncopated window pattern. Such generous space standards reflect the social traditions of the institution, while the high quality principal facing materials, namely dressed stone and metal fenestration, are meant to evoke the progressive reputation of the bank.

The entire complex is modulated by *brise soleil* and screen walls, respectively on the slab and cylinder, while the rhythm of the whole is based on a double square, and tree planting is intended to reinforce the rotating nature of the composition.

311

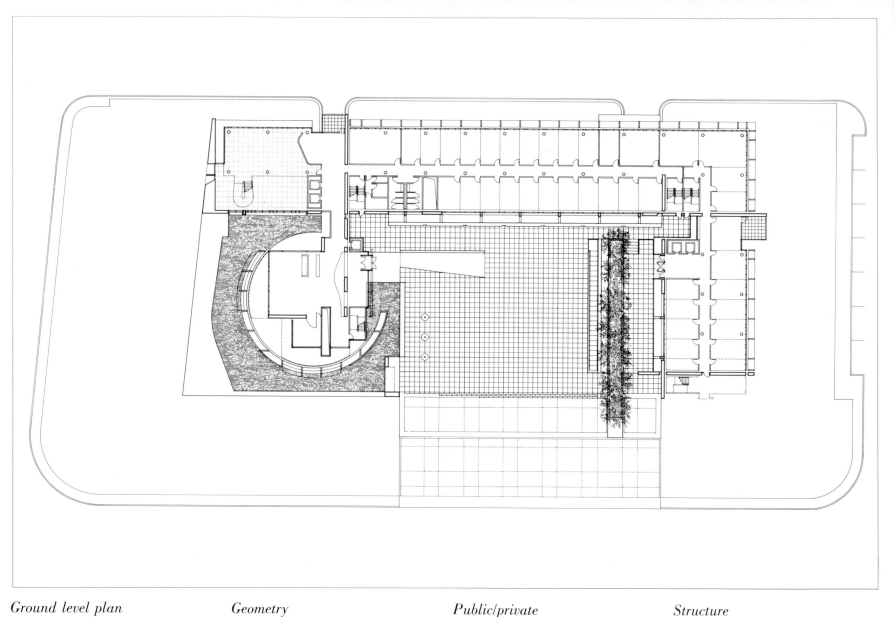

Ground level plan   *Geometry*   *Public/private*   *Structure*

Ground level plan

Geometry

Public/private

Structure

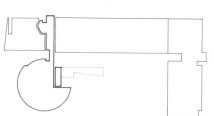

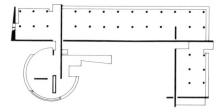

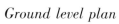

5   10   20

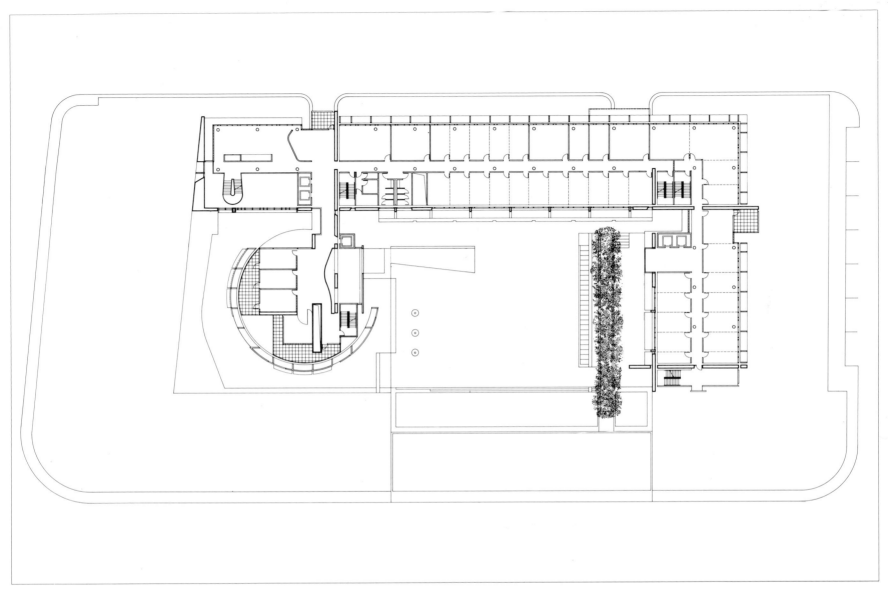

Entry　　　　　　　*Circulation*　　　　　　　*First level plan*

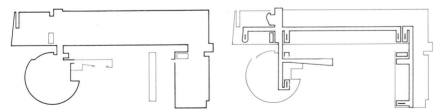

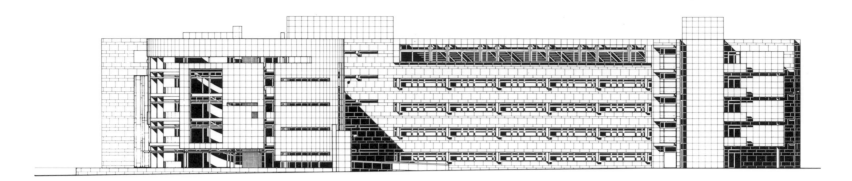

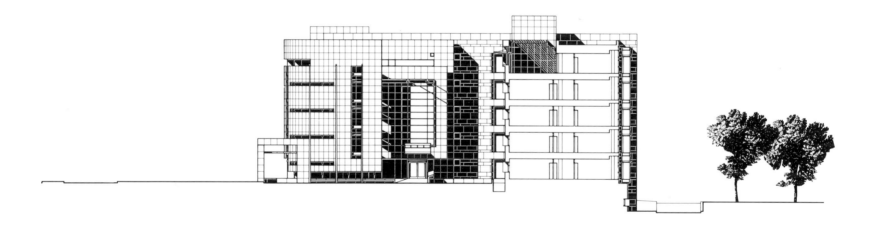

5 10 20

South elevation

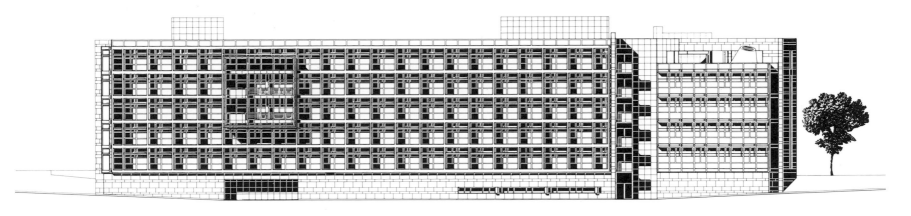

East elevation

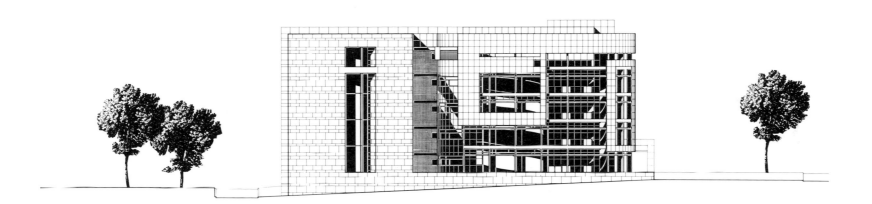

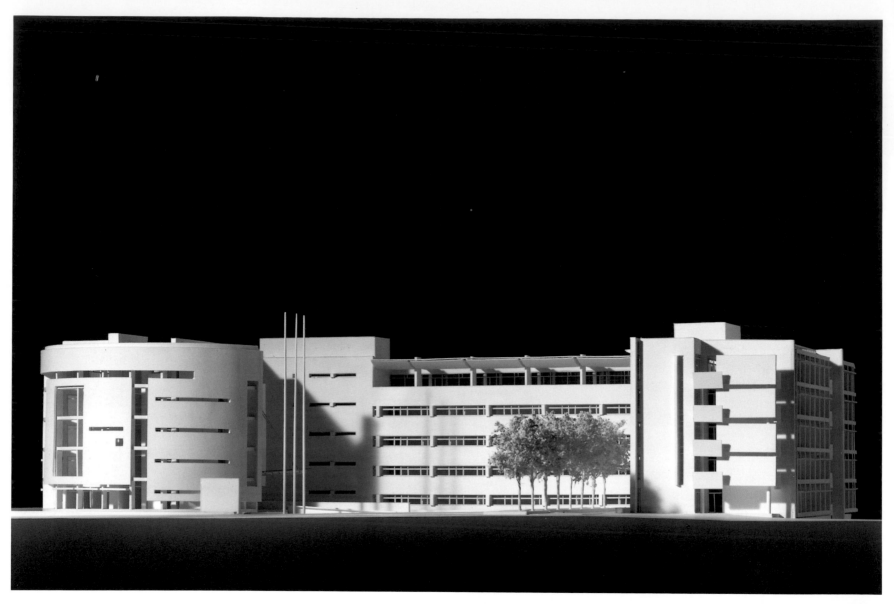

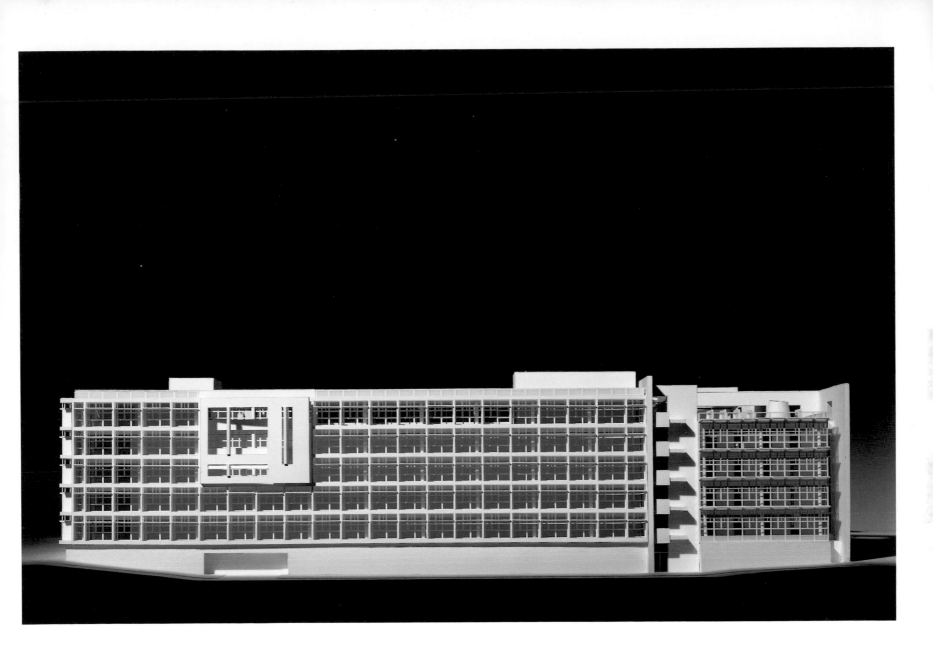

Office Building for Harald Quandt Holding

Frankfurt, Germany
1989

This fourteen-story office tower, conceived as "rond-point" building at a busy traffic intersection on the outskirts of Frankfurt, is largely given over to rental offices except for a double-height showroom/foyer at grade. The building is faced in white enamelled panelling, its pinwheel form articulated by two fenestration systems: a continuous strip of windows set in front of the structure on the curved northeast-to-northwest exposure, and pierced rectangular openings in the straight southern facade.

As one moves around this dynamic composition it continually changes and forms a conceptual spiral that, starting from the main entrance to the east, rises up the strip-glazed cylinder to culminate first in a leading right-angle corner to the northeast emphasized by a five-story superimposed grid above the seventh floor, and then in a cylindrical escape stair running up the full height of the block at the southeast corner. The spiraling movement is reinforced by the three-quarter cylindrical plan of the last three floors and by the blank service level on the roof.

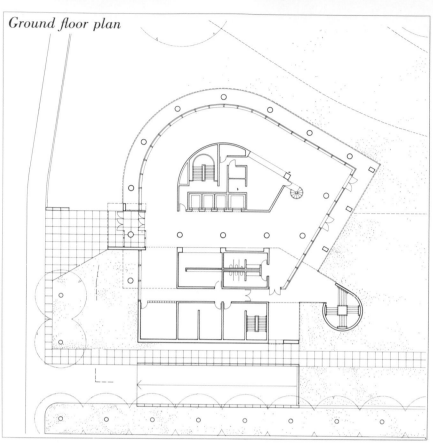

Ground floor plan

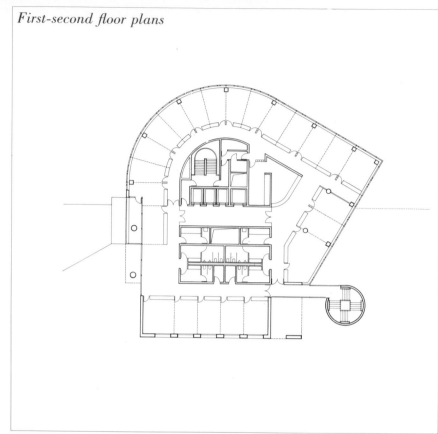

First-second floor plans

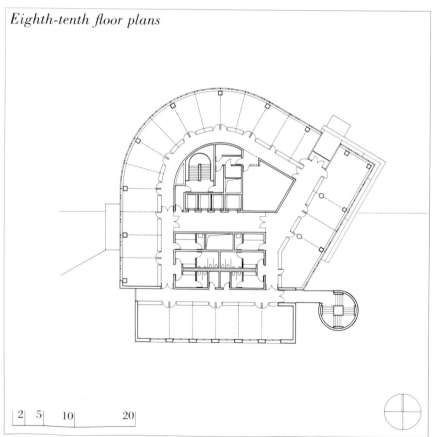

Eighth-tenth floor plans

| 2 | 5 | 10 | 20 |

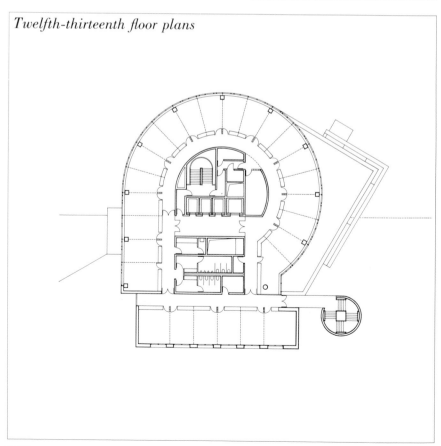

Twelfth-thirteenth floor plans

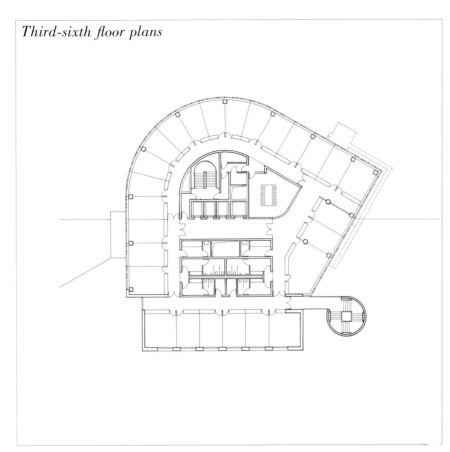

Third-sixth floor plans

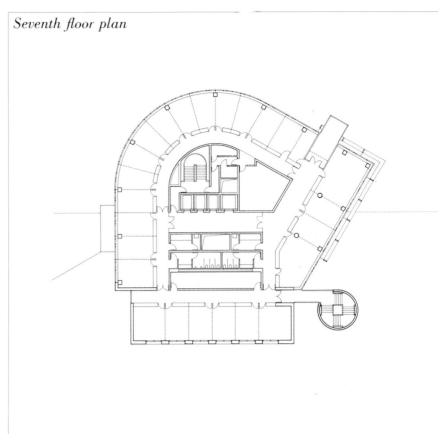

Seventh floor plan

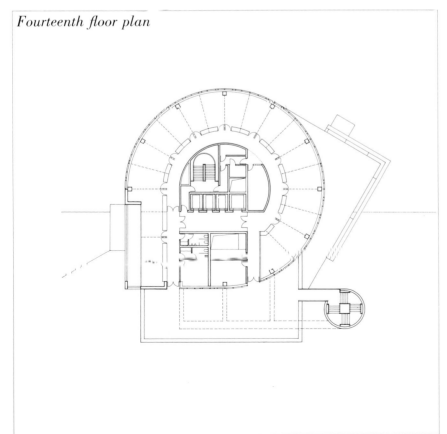

Fourteenth floor plan

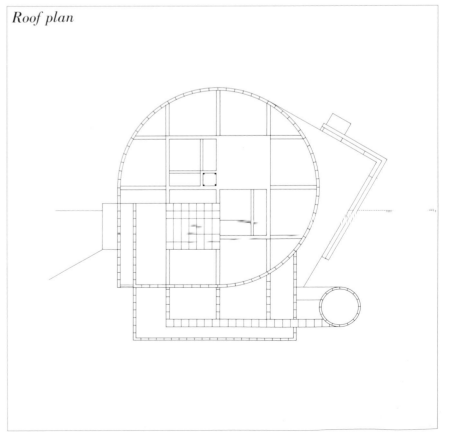

Roof plan

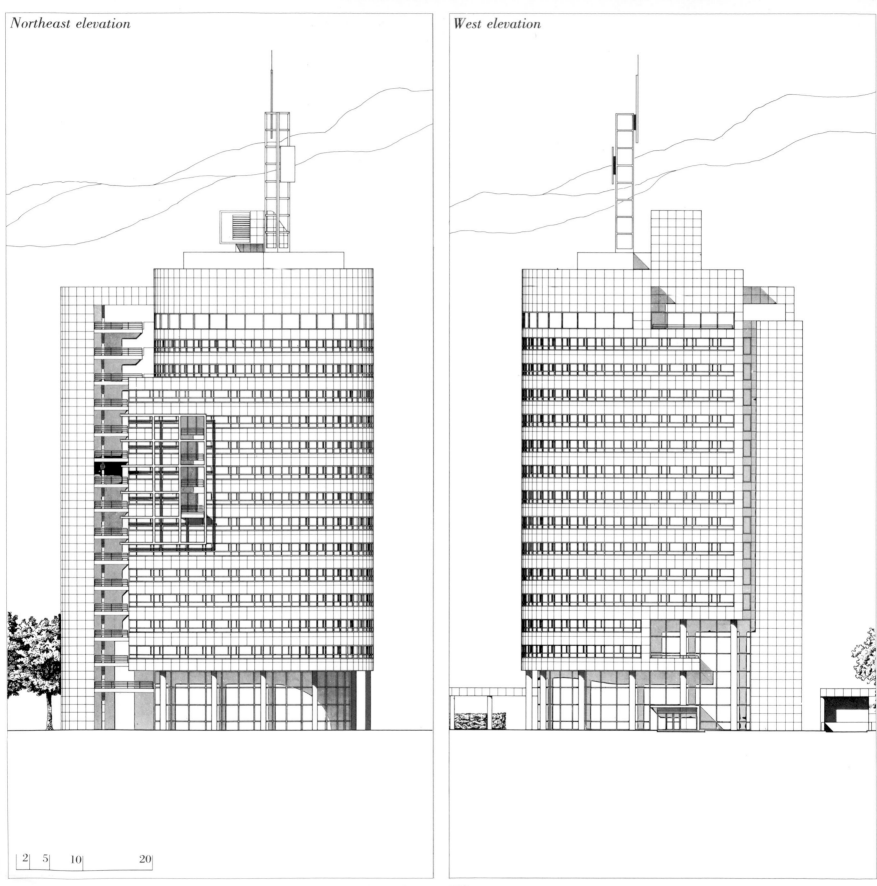

Northeast elevation

West elevation

2 5 10   20

324

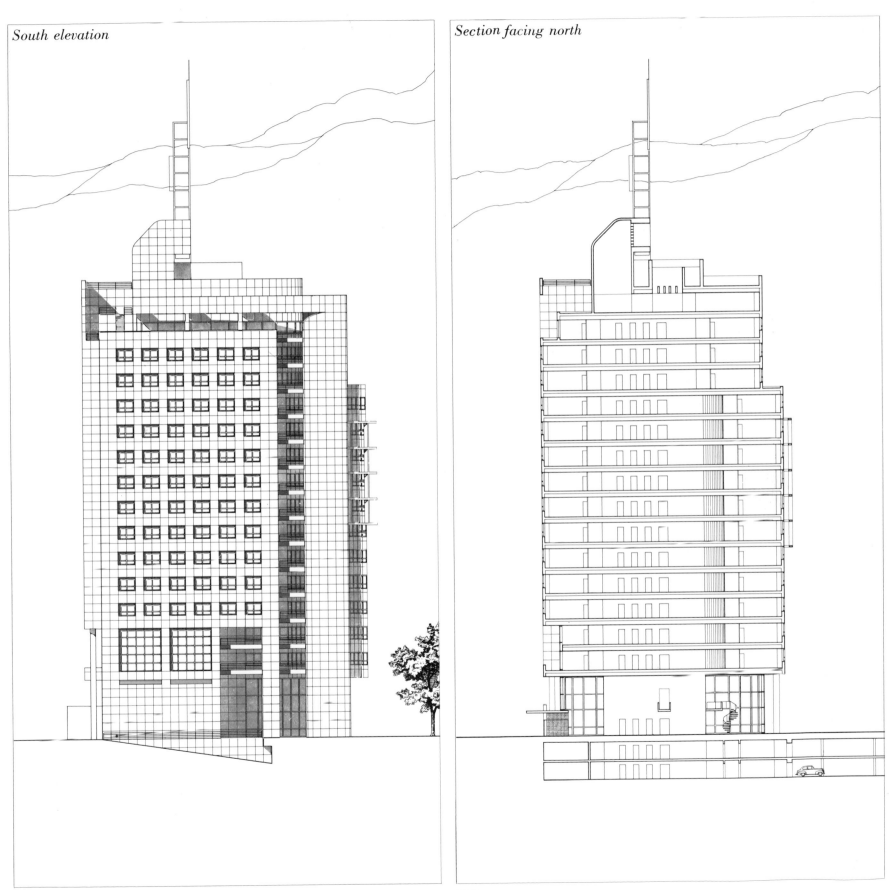

South elevation

Section facing north

325

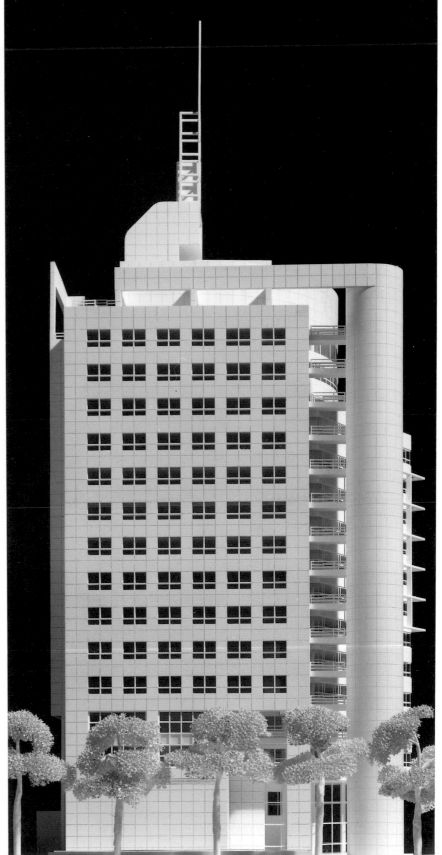

Study of the rotunda and the new casino

Sextius-Mirabeau Master Plan

Aix-en-Provence, France
1990

This master plan for the redevelopment of the old industrial area of Aix-en-Provence concentrates on the east/west extension of the Cours Mirabeau, between the old town and the new town to the southwest. Along this spine, new residential, commercial, and cultural facilities will be developed in the Sextius-Mirabeau area, including three new main activity centers, a convention center, a casino/hotel, and rail and bus station. The Cours Mirabeau extension begins at an existing, rotary entry plaza that has an ornamental foundation in the center surrounded by trees. It will be redefined by a circular pergola that will lead to the present post office and to a new casino-hotel.

At midpoint of the extended Cours Mirabeau will be a new multilevel circular plaza with access at grade and below to the new bus and train station. From here, the arc of the Cours Mirabeau continues, and finally terminates the extension in a plaza for the new convention center. A new promenade will be lined on its sunny side with shops and cafes and with offices on the shaded side.

The buildings for the extended Cours Mirabeau will be different types of low-rise housing providing perimeter block development to the north and low-rise courtyard housing in the southwest quadrant. New university administrative facilities are planned for the triangular area bounded on three sides by the present post office, the trajectory of the railway, and the sweep of the Cours itself.

The Convention Center at the western end of the site is expected to be an attraction for the promenade, and an important hub for the city. In addition to a hotel, it will provide meeting halls, performance spaces, sports, recreation, and other leisure facilities.

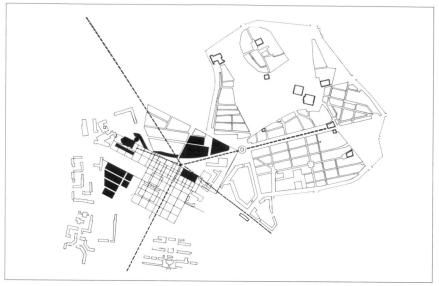

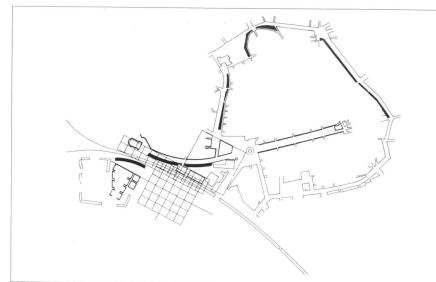

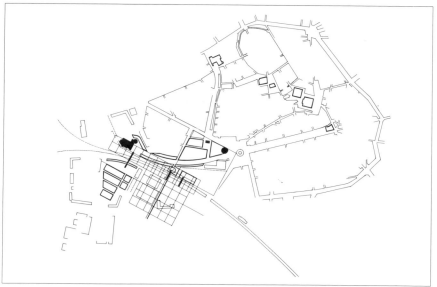

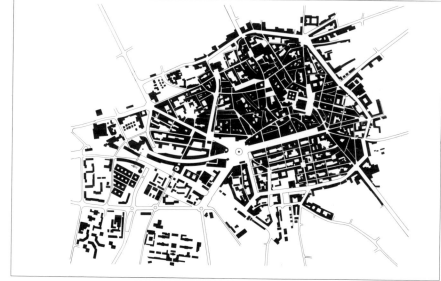

Urban structure/context

Urban spaces and connections

Definition of edges/borders

Urban fabric

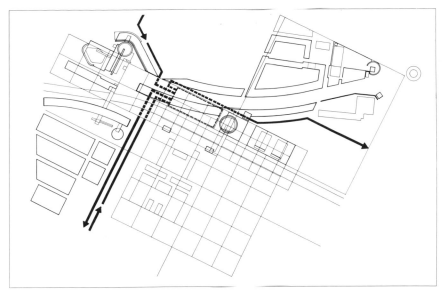

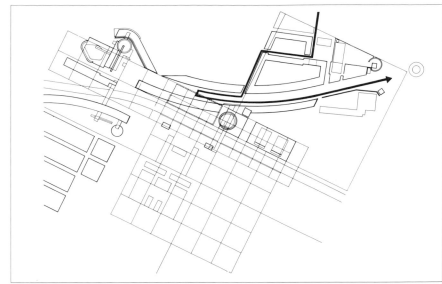

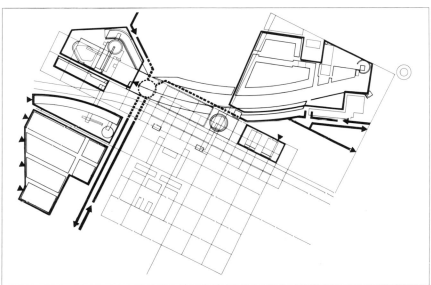

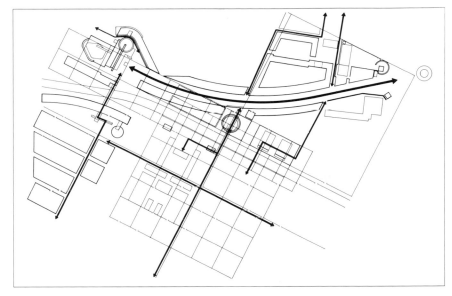

Inner-city buses and train circulation

Automobile circulation and parking

City bus circulation

Pedestrian circulation

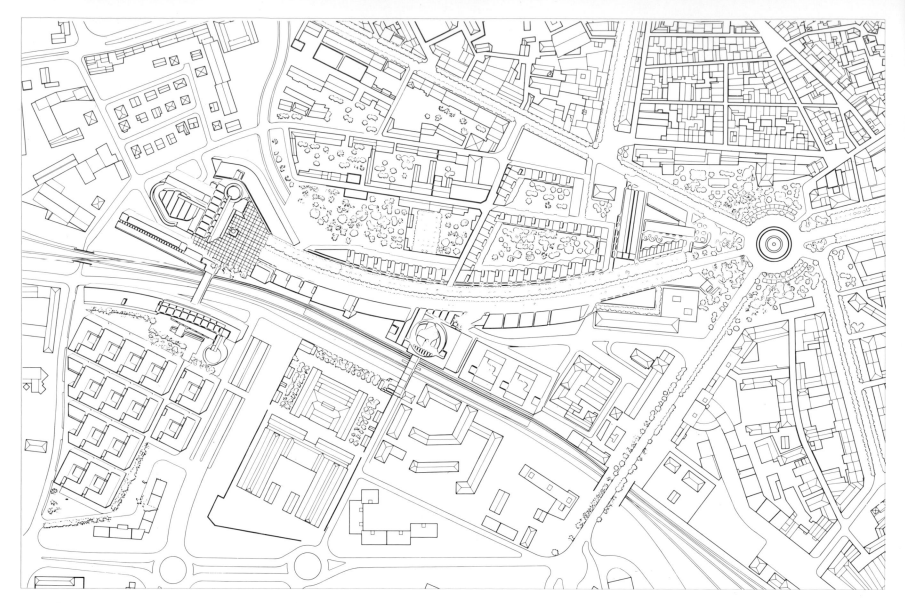

Site plan

25 50 100 200

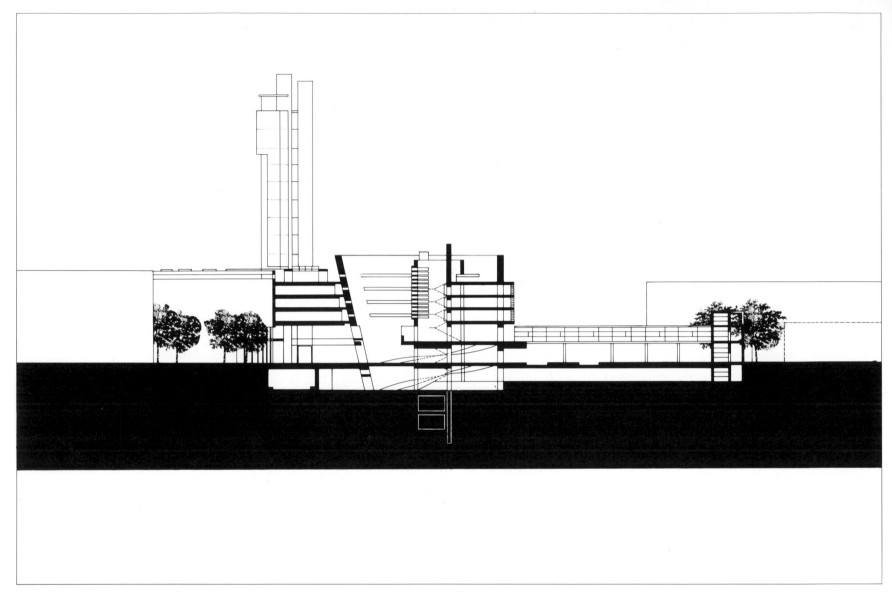

Section facing southeast

5 | 10 | 20

Study of a section through the extended Cours Mirabeau

Aix-en-Provence is the land of Cézanne, a town with a rich history whose linear center is the Cours Mirabeau. The power of this tree-lined avenue and the gracious light that filters into it served as the inspiration for this project.

Study of housing courtyard

Jean Arp Museum

Rolandswerth, Germany
1990–1993

The precise geometry of this museum's architecture is an informative counterpoint to the fluid grace of Arp's art. His amoebic forms are both personal and timeless, and the museum was designed to embody these same qualities.

Winged Being, Jean Arp, 1962, brushed graphite.

The main elevation of the Jean Arp Museum, set above the Rhein on foothills below the ruins of Roland's castle, follows the general course of the river. Its overall character responds to the surroundings through its siting, which is somewhat analogous to that of the many castles in the region.

Due to the steepness of the slope and the restrictive boundaries of the site, access to the museum has been limited to pedestrians, who approach along a drive. The only exceptions are for service vehicles and tour buses that can reach the forecourt for deliveries and reception. The few parking spaces are for the staff.

Much vegetation is preserved, and the building is integrated into the land in order to create open-air terraces for exhibiting bronzes. A glazed conservatory at the entry houses plaster casts, and a ramped pathway leads to sculpture terraces above.

The museum itself is cradled between a podium and a screen wall that act as background and foil to the primary, drum-shape mass of the building. A cubiform gallery, designed to double as an informal space for chamber concerts and covered by a curved screen wall, houses the bulk of the collection—sculptural and two-dimensional works by Jean Arp and works in various media by Sophie Tauber-Arp. A circulation spine/exhibition gallery adjacent to the screen wall links the main exhibition volume to a freestanding cube at the northern end that houses a double height, temporary exhibition space on the lower floors and small apartments for visiting artists above. Circulation for the whole, linear complex is by a stepped ramp and elevator close to the entry. The administration, research library, shipping, and storage are located one floor below, with direct access to the forecourt.

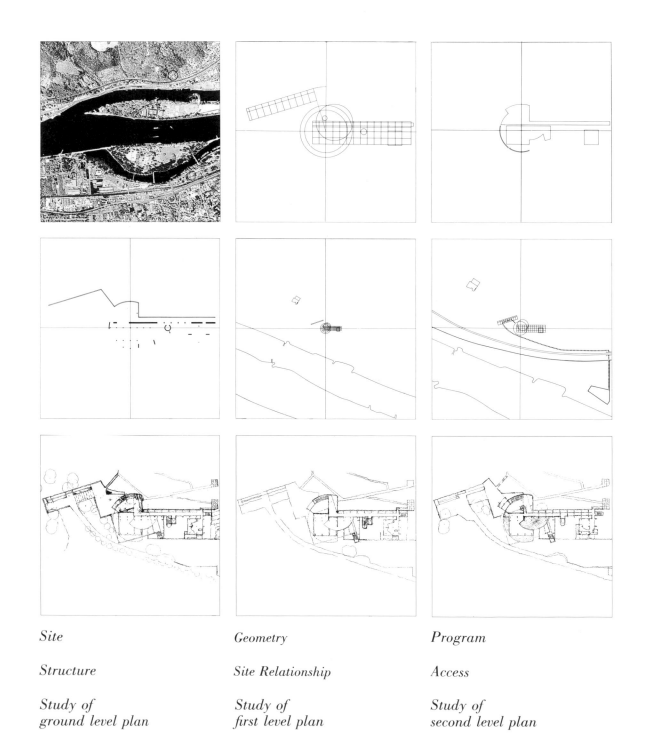

Site

Geometry

Program

Structure

Site Relationship

Access

Study of
ground level plan

Study of
first level plan

Study of
second level plan

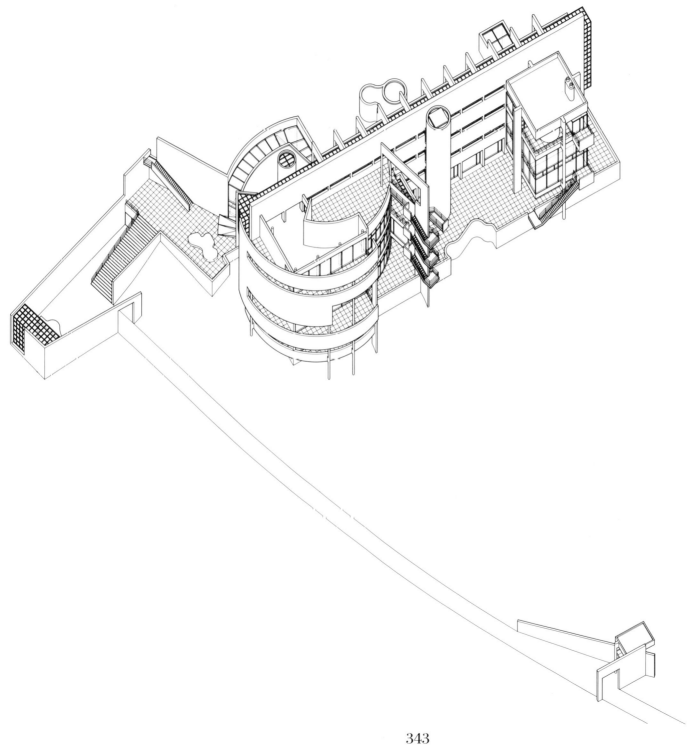

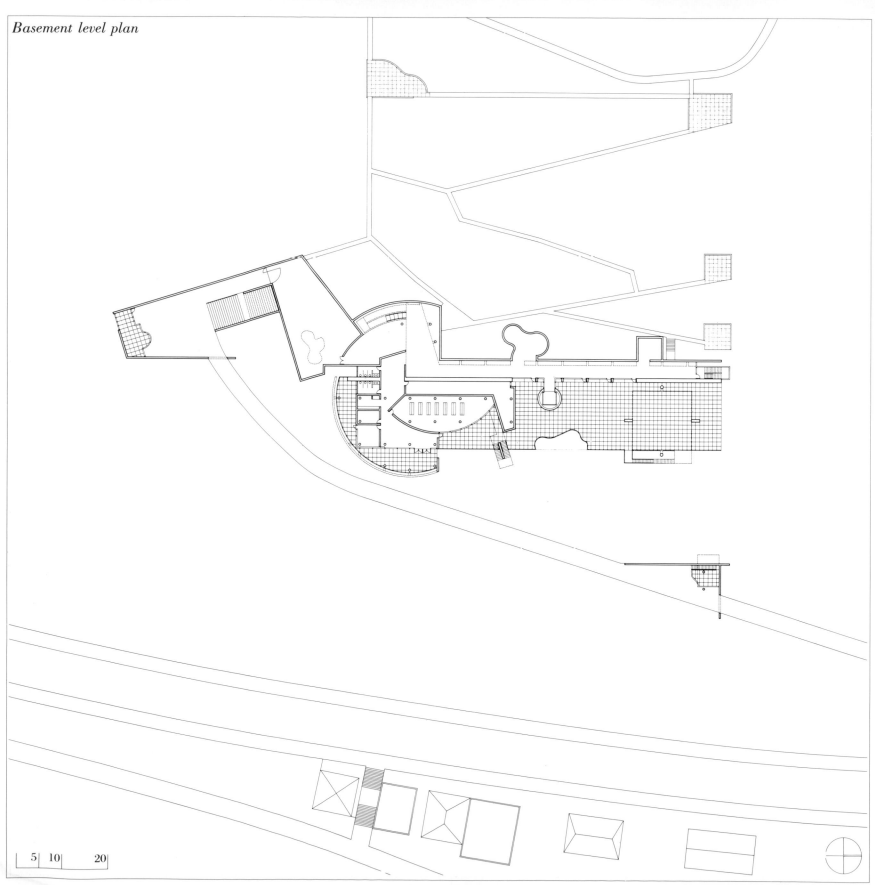

Basement level plan

`5 | 10 | 20`

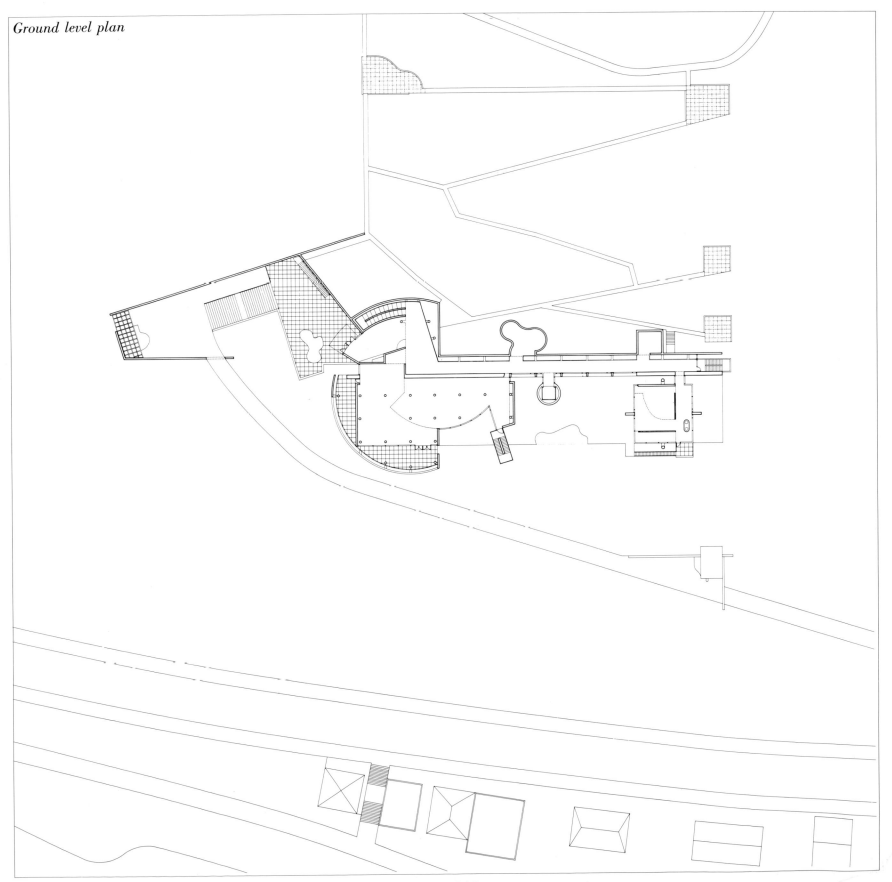

Ground level plan

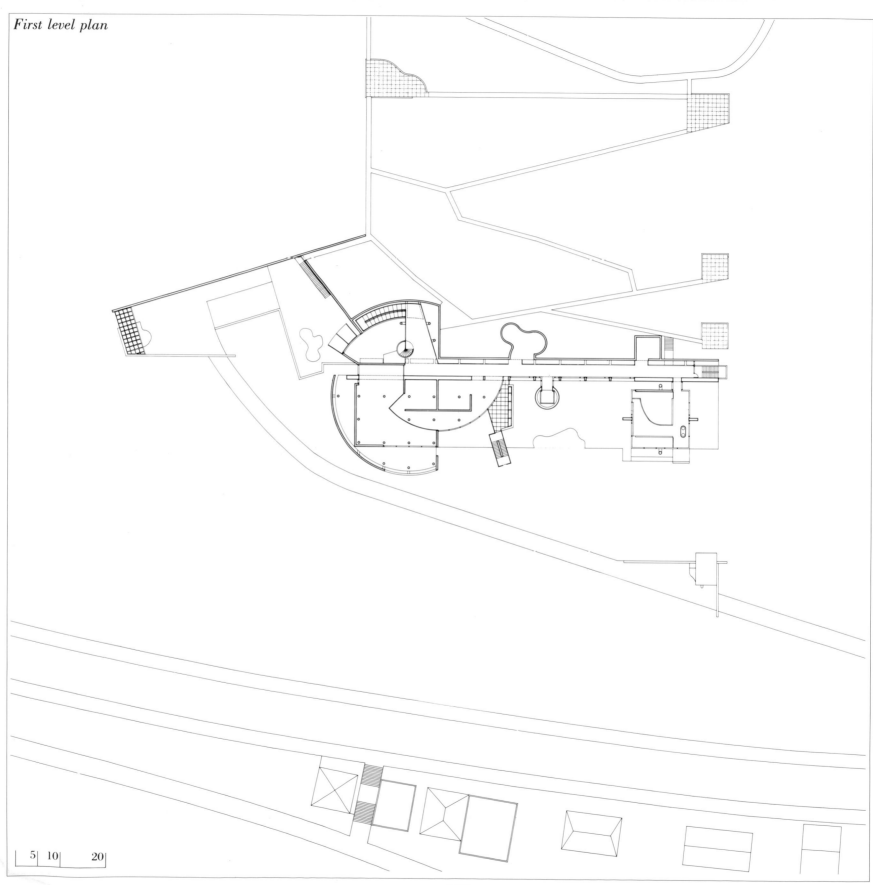

5 | 10 | 20 |

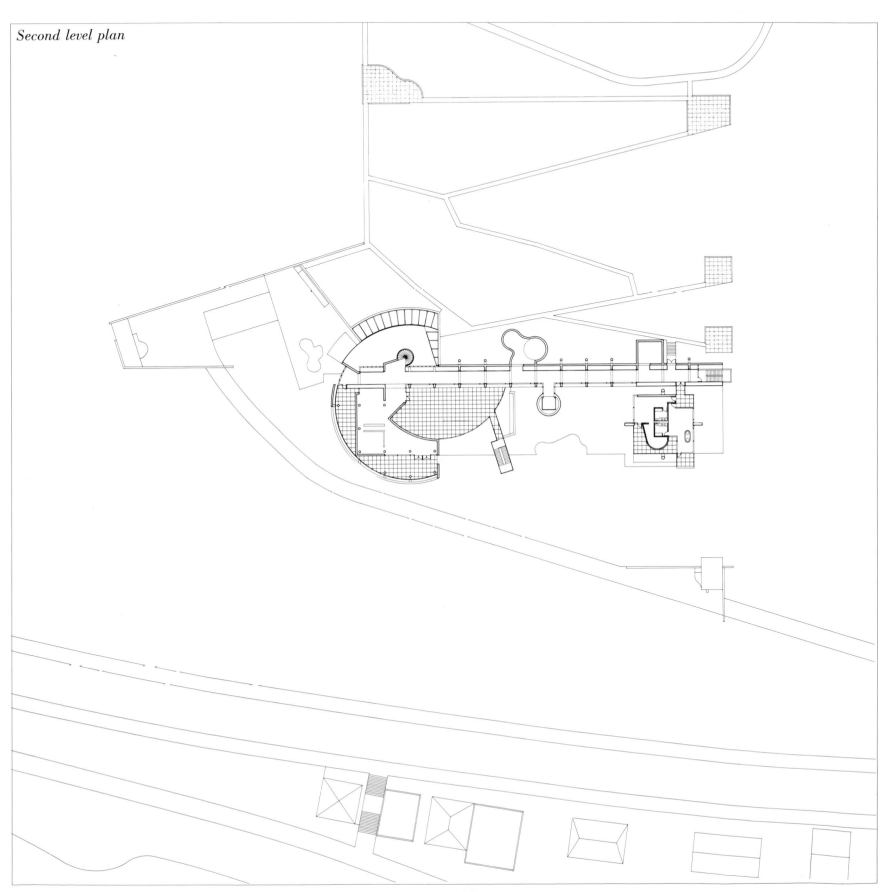

East elevation

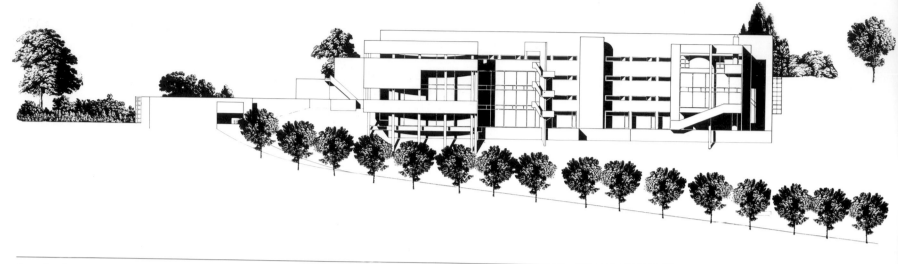

South elevation

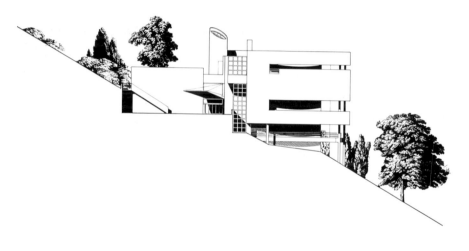

Cross section facing north

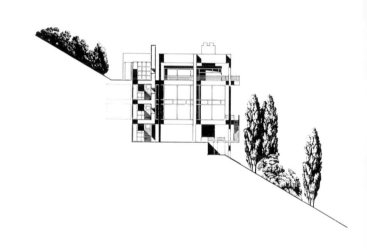

Cross section facing north

Cross section facing north

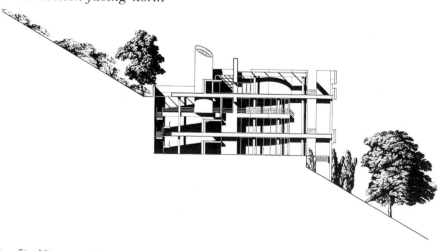

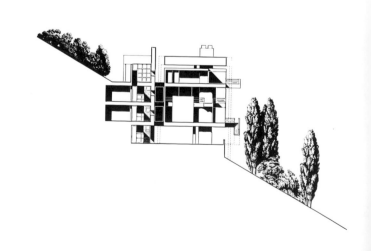

5 | 10 | 20 |

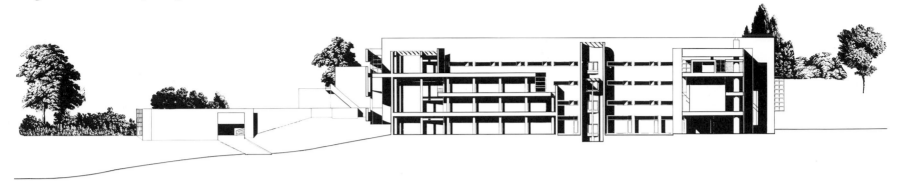

Longitudinal section facing west

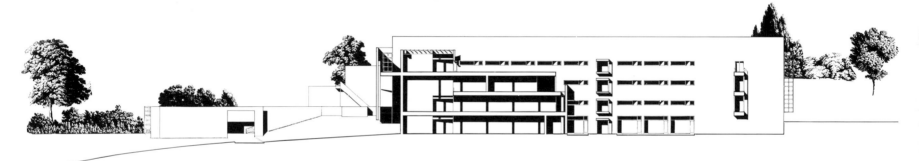

Longitudinal section facing west

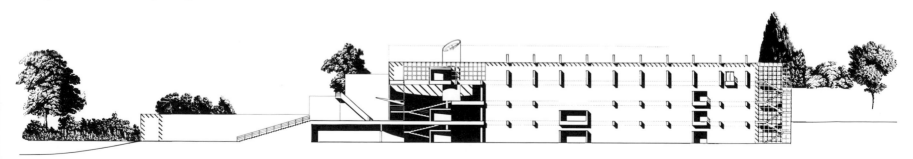

Longitudinal section facing west

The Getty Center

Los Angeles, California
1984–1997

The Getty Center occupies a unique, hilly site that stretches along the San Diego Freeway, jutting southward from the Santa Monica Mountains into the residential neighborhood of Brentwood. As a result of restrictions imposed by the residents in the area, the buildable volume is limited in extent and height by a strict conditional use permit. Within these finely delineated boundaries, the layout of the complex has been largely dictated by the fall of site, covered with chaparral, and affording, on all sides, spectacular views over the city, the mountains and the ocean.

Most of the buildings are thus organized along two natural ridges that form the southern end of the 110-acre parcel. These twin axes meet at an angle of 22.5 degrees, an intersection that corresponds exactly to the inflection of the San Diego Freeway as it bends northward out of the Los Angeles street grid in order to traverse Sepulveda Pass.

In all its particulars, the layout establishes a dialogue between the angle of intersection and a number of curvilinear forms that are largely derived from the contours of the site inflected by the Freeway, the metropolitan grid, and the natural topography. The overall *parti* relates to both the city of Los Angeles and the Santa Monica Mountains.

Three-quarters of a mile to the north of the main complex, an underground parking garage and a tram station establish the public entrance to the 110-acre site. Museum visitors will drive under a freeway overpass, park in the garage, and board a funicular for a five-minute trip to the top of the "acropolis."

At the termination of the funicular and vehicular access, the Getty Center opens out around an arrival plaza with official parking situated under the entry podium. To the northeast, the visitor finds a 450-seat auditorium, the Trust offices, the Art History Information Program, the Getty Grants Program, and the Getty Conservation Institute. All these central administrative and general reception facilities will occupy a single building. The remainder of the complex, the art holdings and academic facilities, extend southward along one of the ridges in seven buildings. The Food Service building and the Center for the History of Art and the Humanities occupy strategic positions on the other ridge to the southwest. However, because of the conditional use permit, much of the overall complex is below the hilltop grade of 896 feet and many of its facilities are connected below ground at the 876-foot level.

After arriving, a visitor will have to choose between entering the museum at once or exploring the gardens and other facilities at leisure. Those who choose to see the collection will immediately ascend a wide esplanade of steps and enter the museum lobby, which gives onto a central cylindrical volume, the full height of which provides views through the courtyard beyond to various galleries arrayed in a continuous sequence. The smaller buildings break down the scale of what would otherwise be an overwhelming institution, while the spaces between the pavilions allow glimpses of the outside world and permit interplay between inside and outside spaces.

The overall exhibition sequence is organized by period and medium. A clockwise internal progression around the court presents the collection chronologically, with different media divided between upper and lower levels. Thus, painting will occupy the upper floors in order to take advantage of the top light, which is augmented by a variety of skylights designed to impart a particular character to each gallery. The decorative arts,

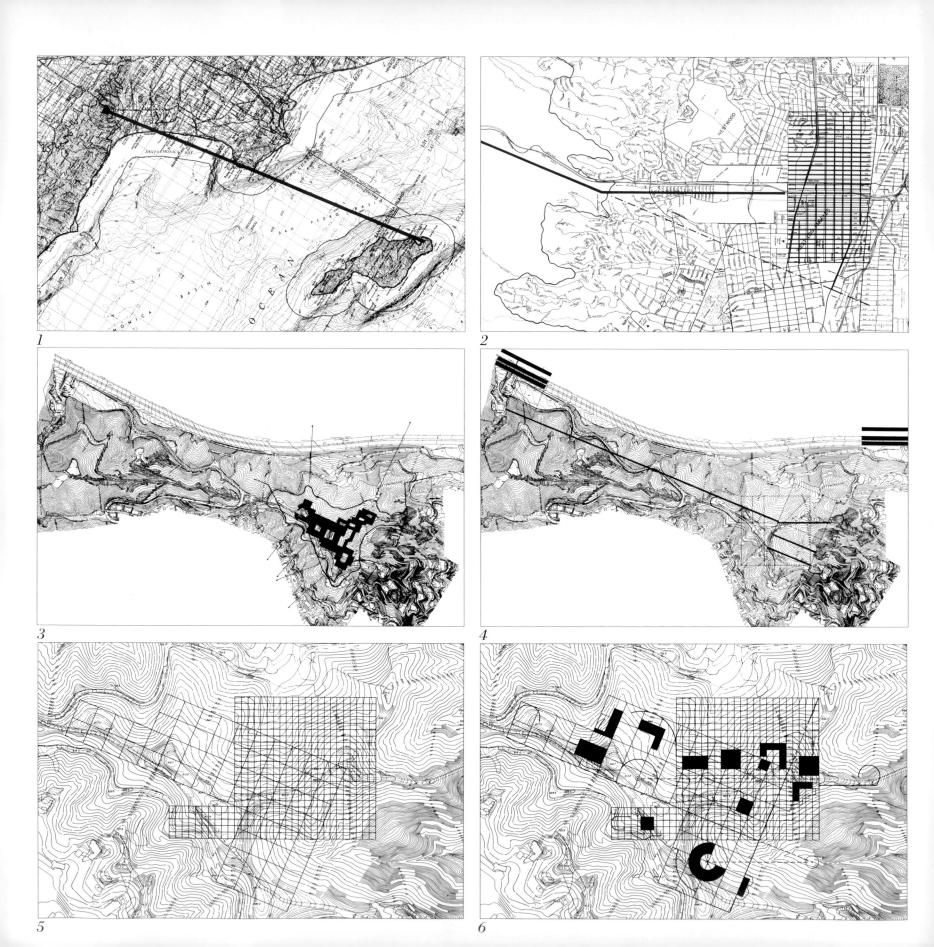

1

2

3

4

5

6

1. *The site organization is generated by the city grid and a north/south axis which aligns with a ravine and bisects the site to provide the central focus for the complex.*

2. *The site for the Getty Center is fourteen miles west of downtown Los Angeles, in the southern region of the Santa Monica Mountains. From this elevated promontory, many of the city's dominant urban and geographical features are visible.*

3. *A dialogue is established between curvilinear forms derived from site contours and the building grids which relate to the city fabric and freeway axis.*

4. *The building envelope is limited in plan and elevation by a conditional-use permit. Due to site line limitations set by this permit, part of the twenty-four-acre envelope is unbuildable.*

5. *The garden extensions reach beyond the building envelope to register the composition with prominent site features.*

6. *The geometric relationships are articulated along ridges to establish the placement of building masses.*

manuscripts, photography, and works on paper will be in the lower level to exclude the ultraviolet light that is so destructive to such works. By moving from one level to the next within each cluster, visitors will be able to experience different media drawn from the same period, or, if they prefer, they will be able to follow the evolution of one medium through time by remaining on one particular level. Several special exhibition spaces, including a larger one for mid-size travelling shows, will offer relief from this purely chronological sequence through the galleries. Visitors who only want to view a part of the collection will be able to take a secondary route, thereby bypassing certain galleries.

Although the museum is the most public part of the J. Paul Getty Trust, its galleries do not by any means occupy the entire complex. The other programs at the Getty Center will eventually employ an even greater number of people, and the structures they occupy will undoubtedly be of interest to casual visitors as well. In addition, the complex will include a number of public buildings that are not program specific.

Since most visitors will come to the Getty Center for a half day or more, it is expected that the Food Service building will be a major attraction. With separate dining rooms for staff and visitors, as well as private rooms for meetings, the Food Service building will account for most of the dining facilities provided on the site. Its siting close to the central plaza gives convenient access to most parts of the complex, while its windows and terraces provide outstanding views to the mountains on the north and to the ocean on the west.

The other major public building, a 450-seat auditorium for lectures, concerts, and other cultural events, is on the other side of the plaza. It stands west of the Trust offices and the Art History Information Program, and terminates the building's long east elevation. Between the Trust building and the museum are the Getty Conservation Institution, the Getty Center for Education in the Arts, and the Getty Grant Program, which can take advantage of the benevolent Southern California climate, with loggias, pergolas, and full-height glazing, since they all have relatively loose security requirements. This spirit will also extend to the circulation for the open-air museum.

Along the more secluded western ridge, the Getty Center for the History of Art and the Humanities completes the complex. The building comprises a million-volume library, reading rooms, study carrels, a small exhibition space, and offices for staff and scholars. It has been given a radial organization, focused about a central, circular building. The information, however, is not centralized, but organized into a series of smaller sub-libraries. The plan is designed to encourage scholars to explore incidental areas in the open stacks while pursuing specific materials. Also, the building's curvature expresses the Center's essentially introspective and analytical nature.

Most of the employees cataloging the collection will retrieve material from the closed stacks, housed below grade. Visitors and scholars gain access to the same material in the reading room and carrel spaces above, and scholars will be able to take materials back to their offices for further study. Some of these offices are arrayed around the top of the main building, with twelve cloistered spaces located in the so-called Scholar's Tower—a smaller, secluded building at the southern end of the ridge.

Throughout the hilltop, landscaping will integrate the buildings into the topography, with gardens extending into the entire site, where water will play an essential role in uniting the structures with the heavily planted terracing. Fountains and raceways cascading down the principal buildings will eventually drain into the central garden water course between the natural ridges.

Various forms of cladding will not only help to integrate the complex with its site, but will also represent the status and use of different parts of the complex. Since the museum sequence is the most public part of the program, it will have traditional stone revetment throughout. All the major buildings will have stone-faced earthworks that will naturally flow into retaining walls throughout the site. In some less prominent instances stucco, the other traditional earthen material for the finish of incidental walls, will be used.

Since the Center for the History of Art and the Humanities, the Conservation Institute, the Trust offices, the Auditorium, and Food Service facilities are all more curvilinear in their external form and more open in their architectural expression, they will be faced in matte-finished metal panels with liberally glazed areas for natural light views. While almost as permanent as stone, matte metal panelling emphasizes lightness and transparency of a building without being shiny and, in combination with stone and vegetation, harmonizes exceptionally well with the Southern California landscape.

The larger, long-term mandate for the Getty Center is the preservation and progressive assimilation of cultural artifacts, with the ultimate intention of making this repository more available for future enjoyment and use. Given this mandate, the architecture of the complex has been designed to combine an axial, if not classical, organization with asymmetrical, organic forms to suggest a balance between the humanism of geometry and the spontaneity of associational form.

Site plan

| 100 | 200 | 400 | 800 |

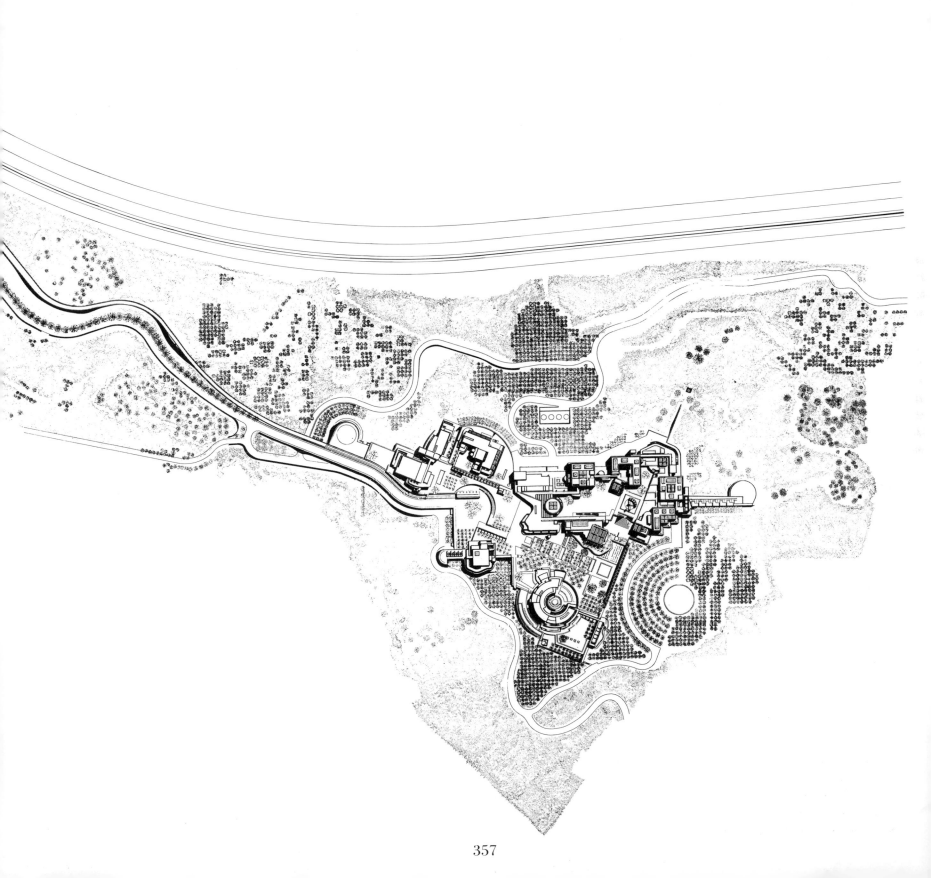

357

The spectacular site of the Getty complex invites the architect to search out a precise and exquisitely reciprocal relationship between built architecture and natural topography. This implies a harmony of parts; a rational procedure; concern for qualities of proportion, rhythm, and repose; precision of detail, constructional integrity, programmatic appropriateness; and, not least, a respect for human scale. All of these issues relate intimately to the choice of materials.

Site plan

1. Museum
2. Center for the History of Art and the Humanities
3. Conservation Institute/ Center for Education/Grant Program
4. Art History Information Program/Trust
5. Auditorium
6. Restaurant/Cafe

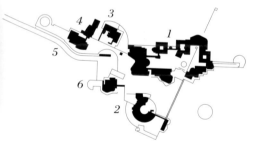

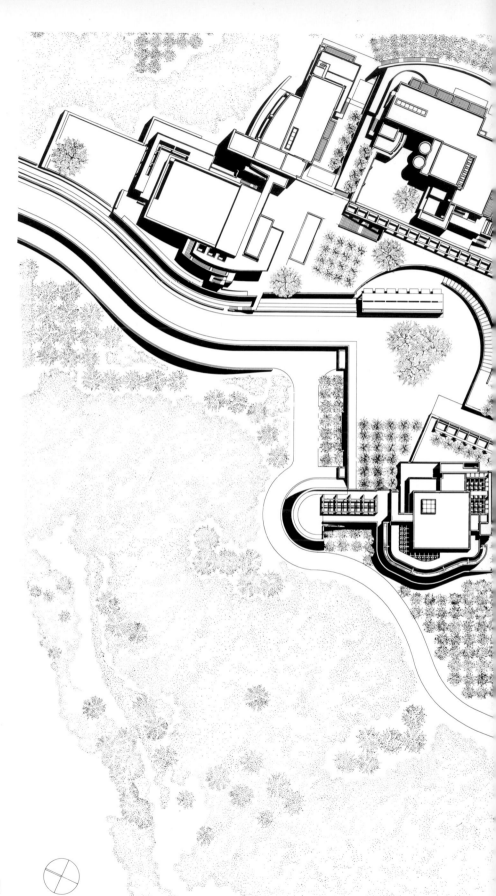

25| 50| 100| 200|

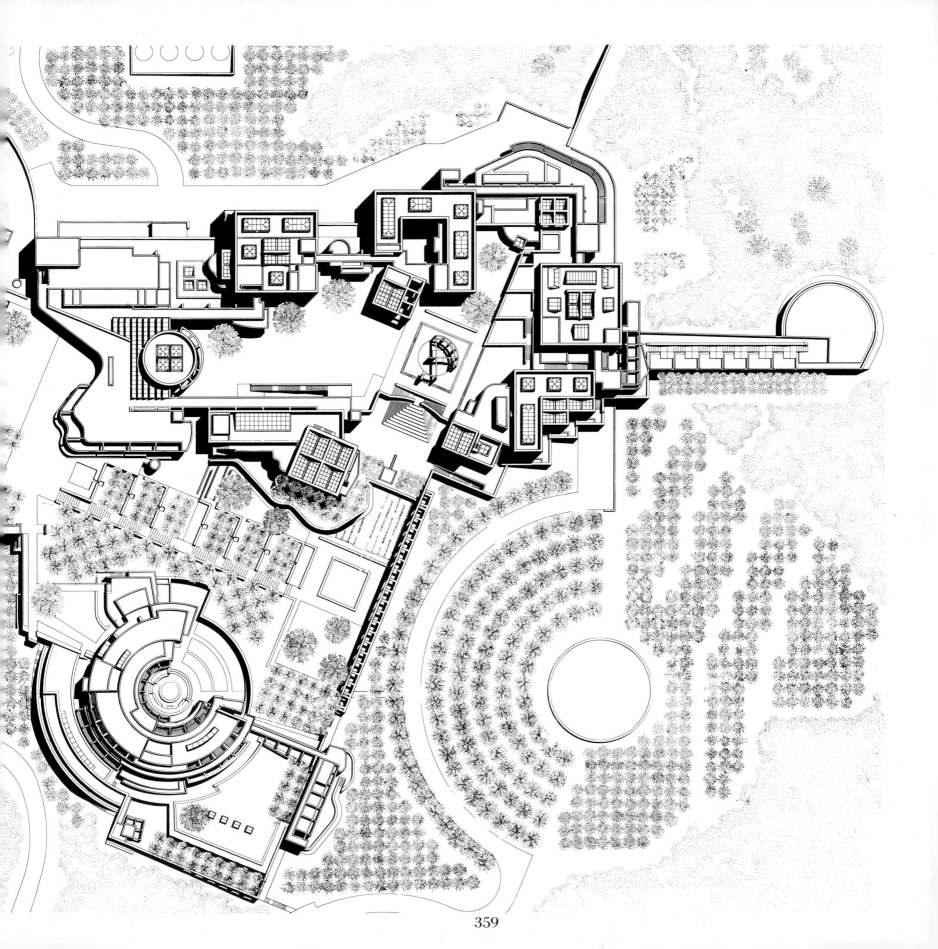

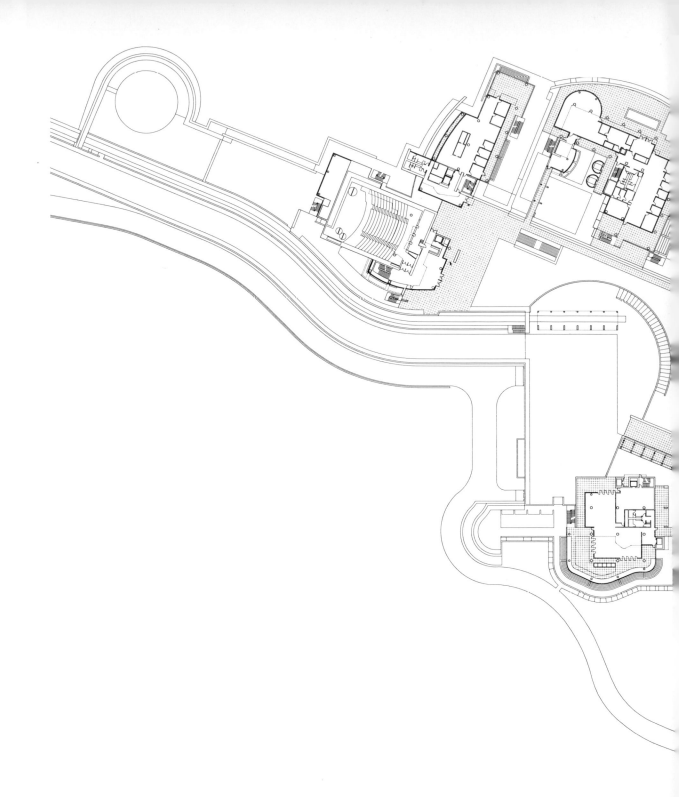

Architecture is an art of substance, of materialized ideas about space. Between the demands of program, site, locale, and building technology the architect has to find a means of making the building communicate in the language of materials and textures. Buildings are for the contemplation of the eyes and the mind, but also, no less importantly, to be experienced and savored by all the human senses. You cannot have form in architecture which is unrelated to human experience; and you cannot approach an understanding of experience, in terms of architecture, without a strongly sensuous and tactile attitude toward form and space.

Besides its topography, the most powerful aspect of the Getty site is the quality of the light that is natural to it, which is astonishingly beautiful. That clear, golden California light is, I must say, intoxicating to an Easterner. I long to see that glorious light flooding through, casting crisp, delicious shadows. I am eager to see built structures set against that brilliant blue sky of southern California. I can envisage this complex based on a horizontal layering of spaces that relate both to the site and to the nature of the collection.

Ground level plan

25| 50| 100| 200|

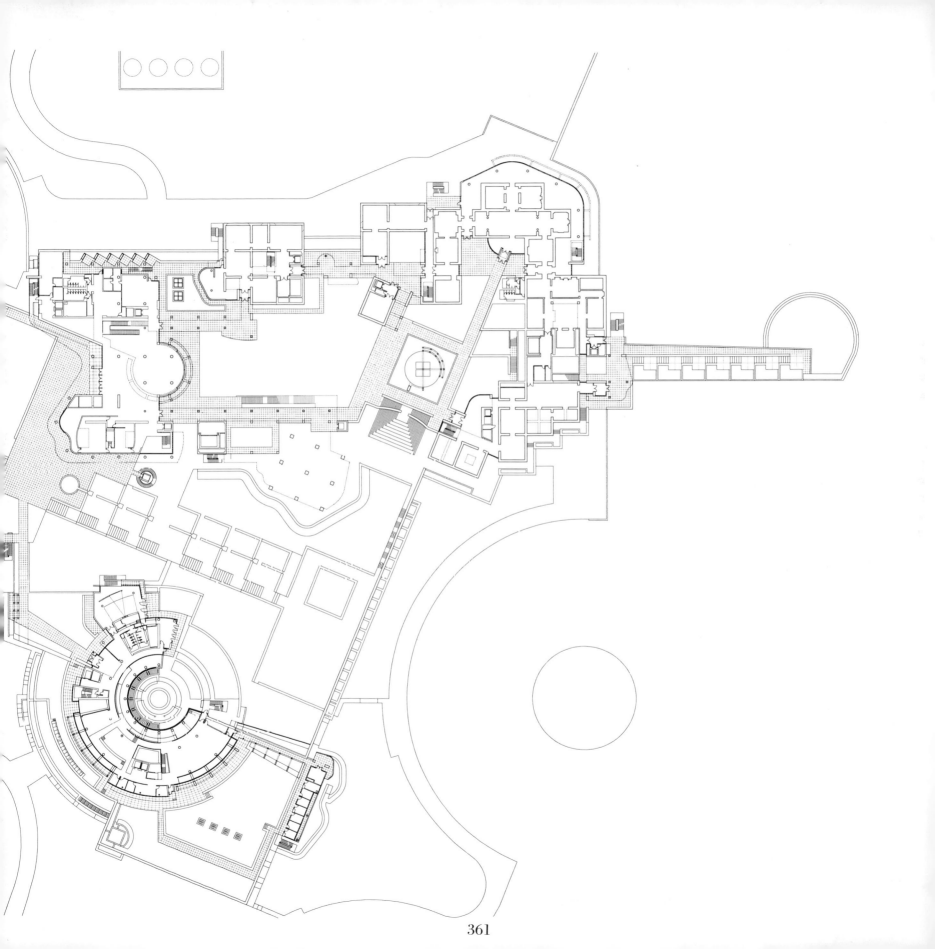

In my mind's eye, I see a classic structure, elegant and timeless, emerging, serene and ideal, from the rough hillside, a kind of Aristotelian structure within the landscape; and sometimes I see the structure as standing out, dominating the landscape. The two are entwined in a dialogue, a perpetual embrace in which building and site are one. In my mind, I keep returning to the Romans—to Hadrian's Villa, to Caprarola—for their sequences of space, their thick-walled presence, their sense of order, the way in which building and landscape belong to each other.

The Getty Center will declare an essential and classical drive—the drive to find enlightenment in the highest achievements of humankind. Getty Center's regular rhythms and axial organization will accentuate the rational, the human. At the same time, the buildings of the Getty Center will take shape on a wild, empty hilltop, or, more accurately, around and within the hilltop. Their alternately fluid and massive forms—and the materials we will use to express these forms—will strike a balance between classical human concerns and the more immediate natural substance of the rugged setting.

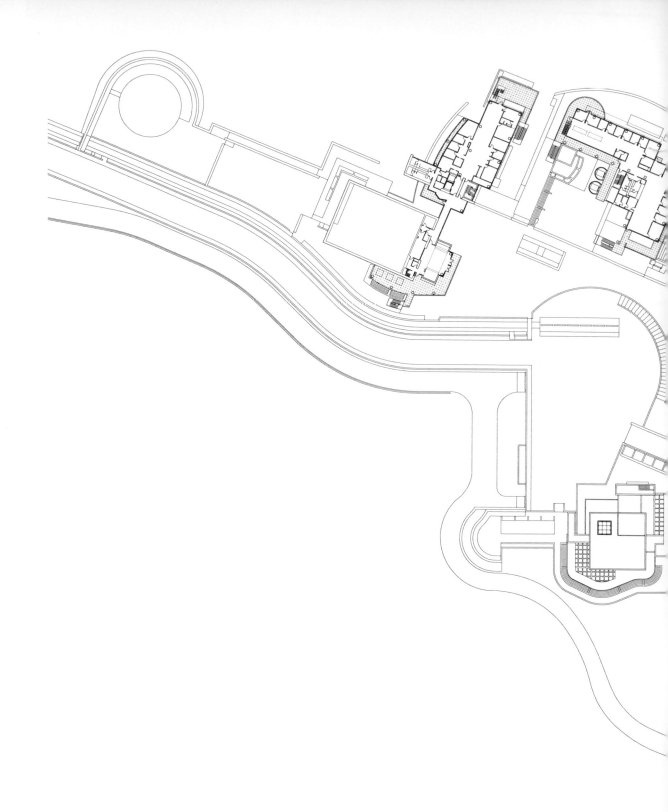

Upper level plan

25 50 100 200

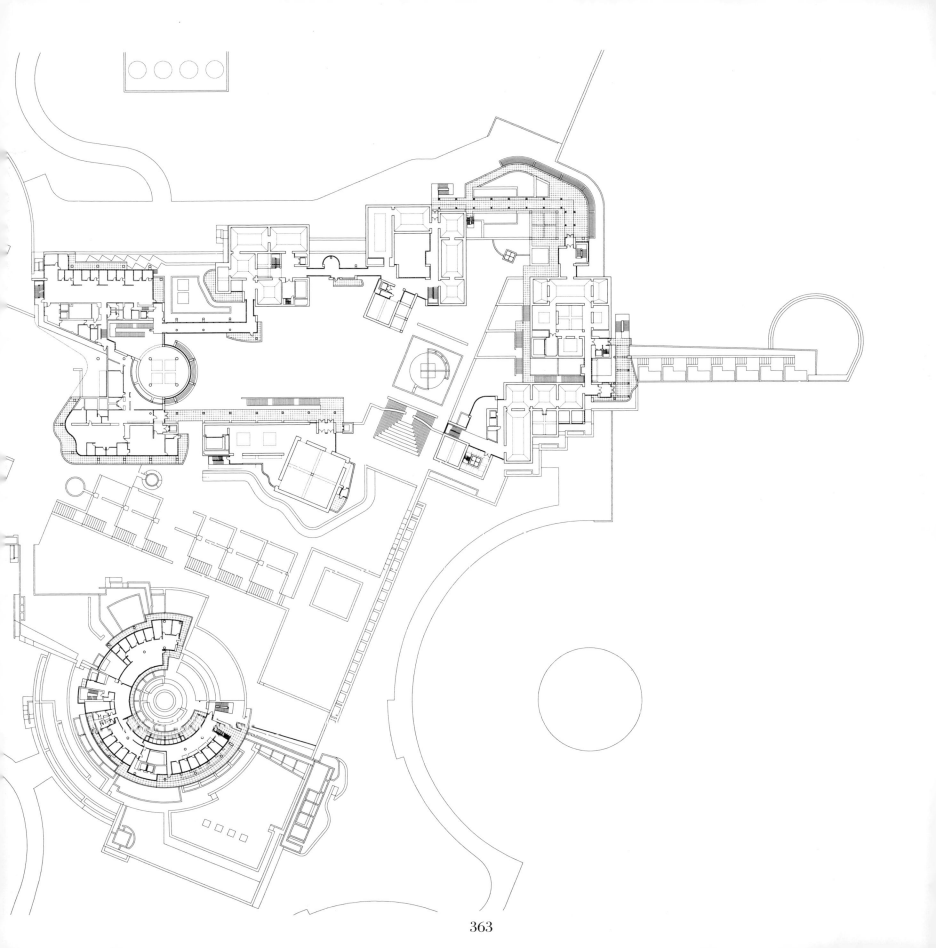

North elevation

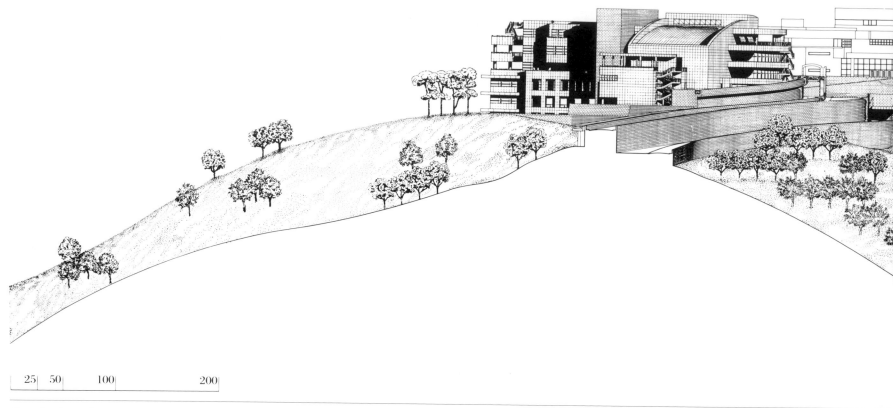

25 50 100 200

South elevation

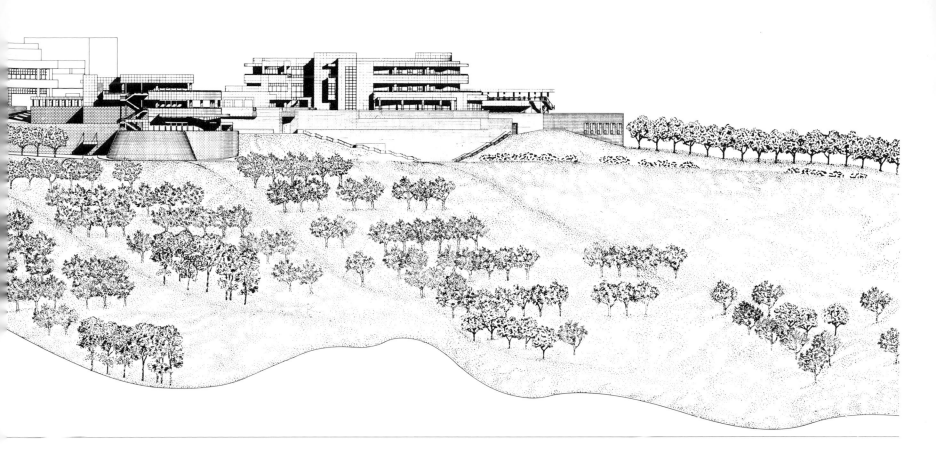

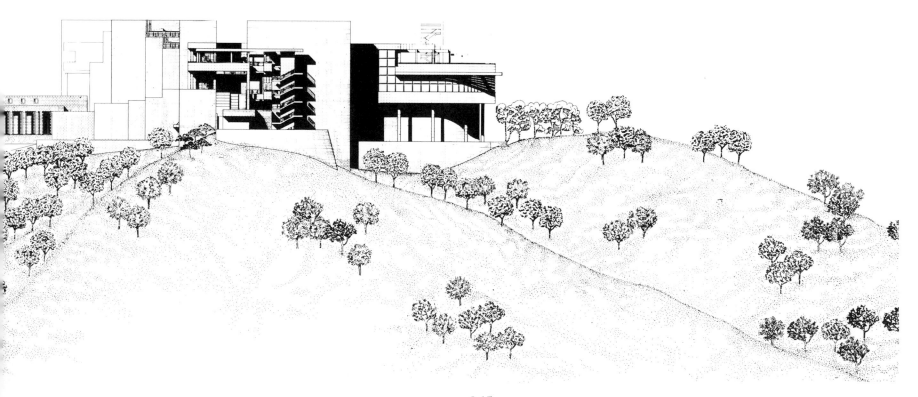

West elevation

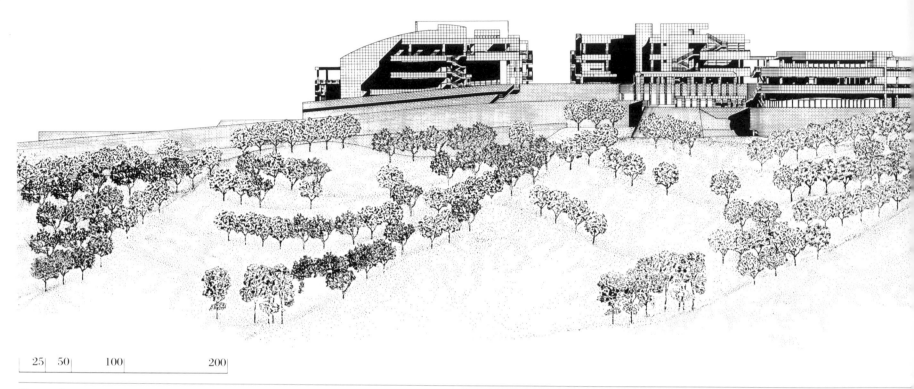

25 50 100 200

East elevation

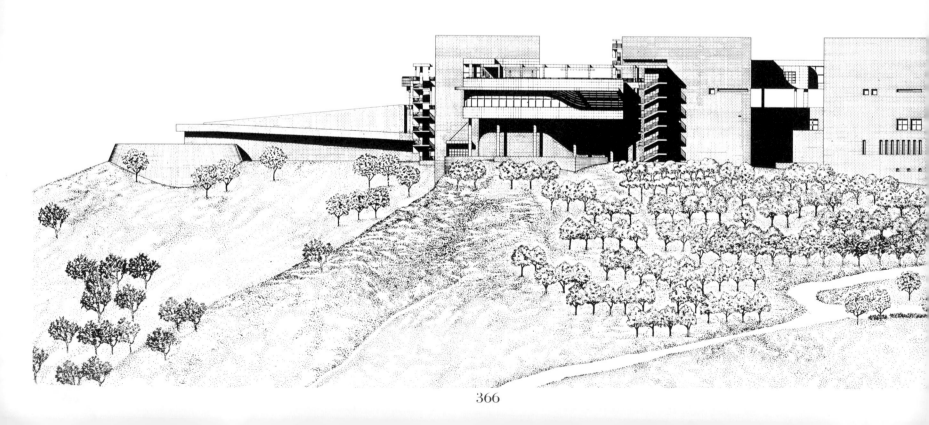

Perspective view of the museum lobby

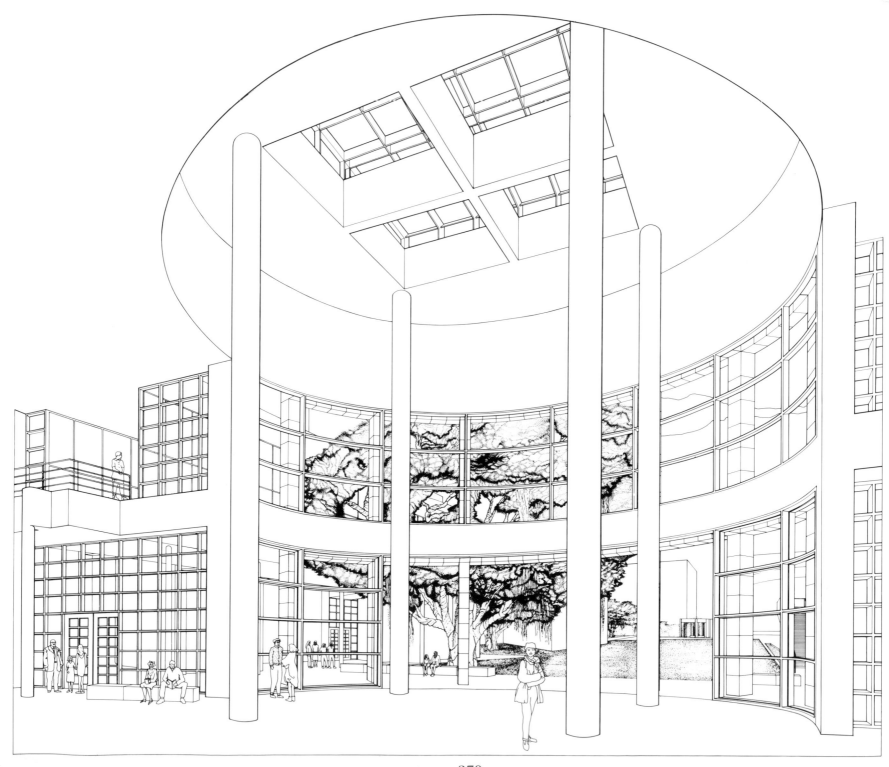

Perspective view of the museum entrance

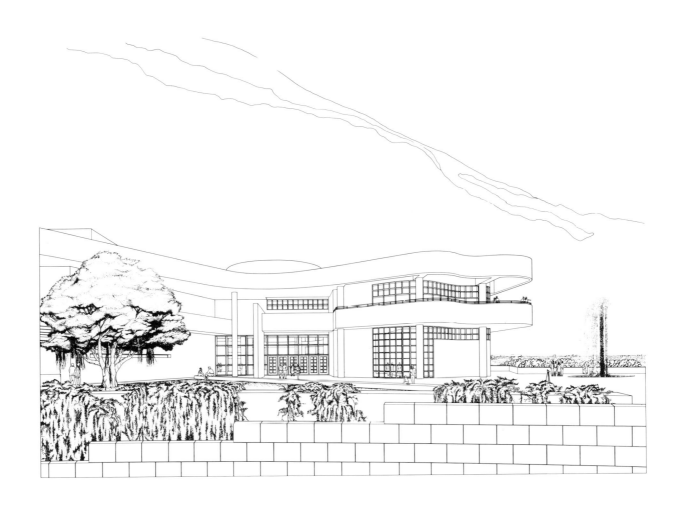

Perspective view of the Auditorium entrance

Perspective view looking south to the central gardens

Perspective view looking north to the central gardens

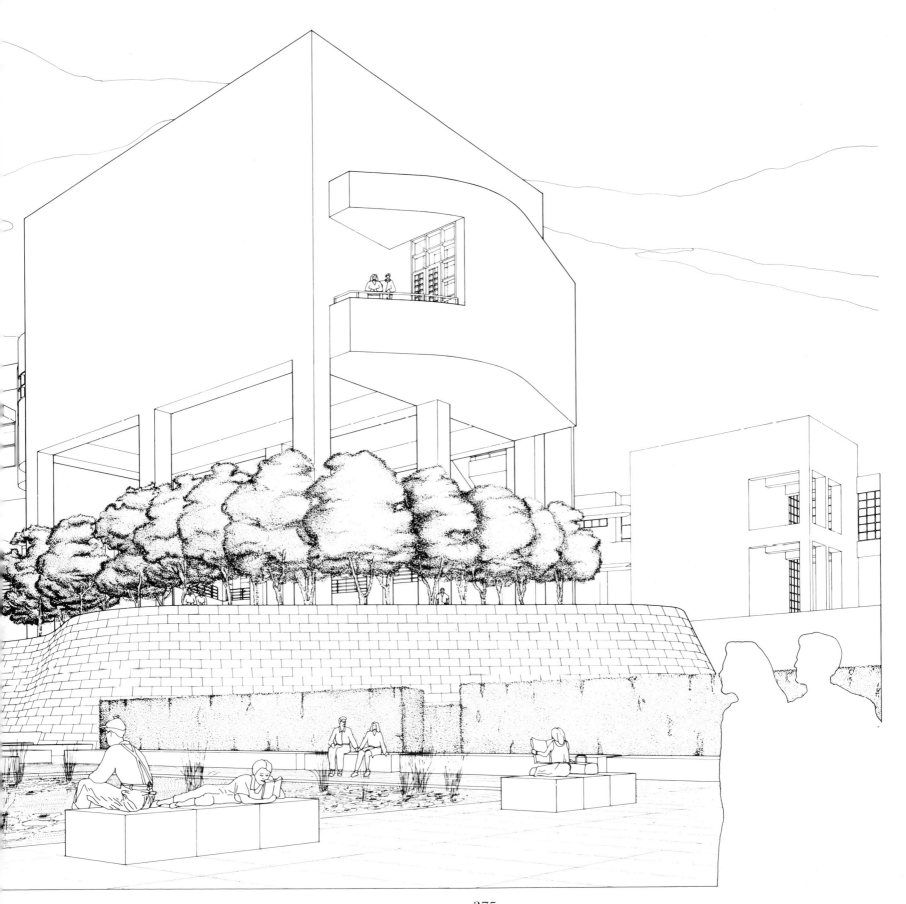

Perspective view of the entrance to the Center for the History of Art and the Humanities

Perspective view of the Restaurant terrace

Perspective view of the courtyard of the Conservation Institute

Perspective view of the entrance to the Conservation Institute

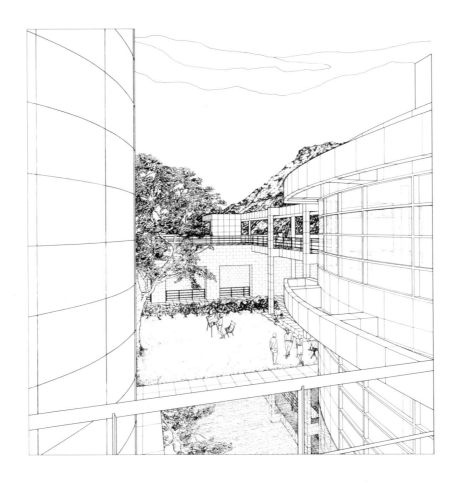

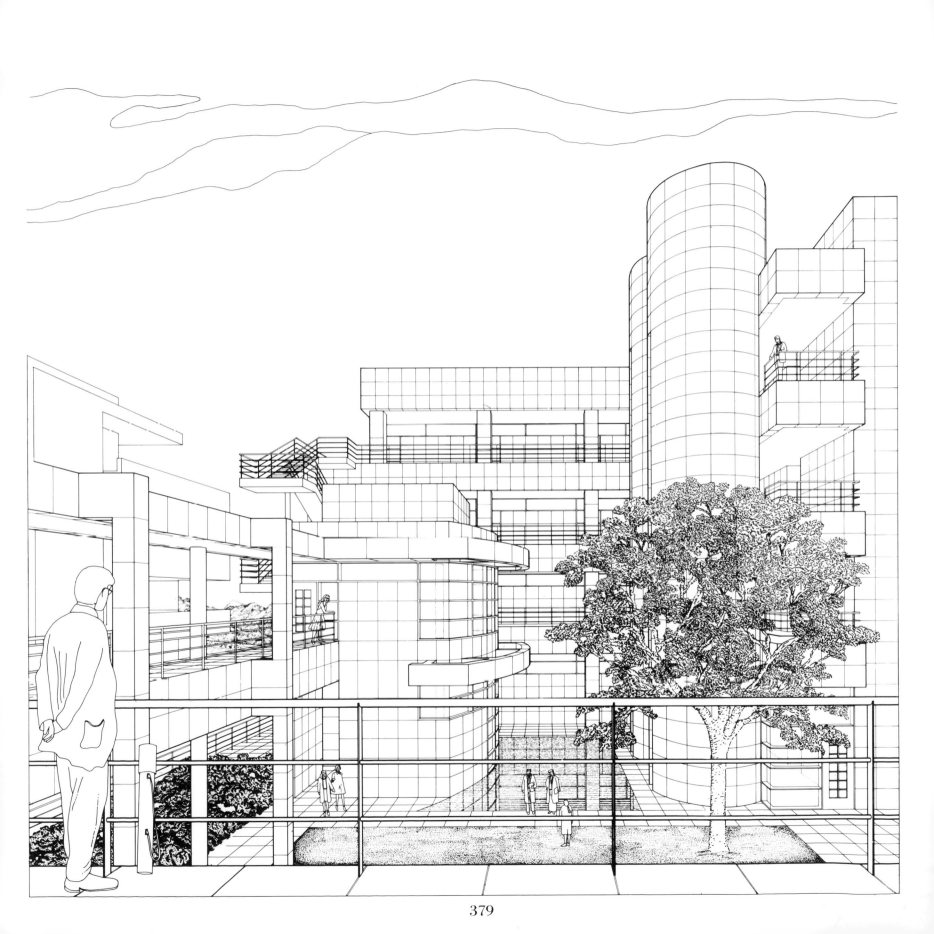

Partial axonometric view of the museum lobby

Partial axonometric view of the first gallery pavilion

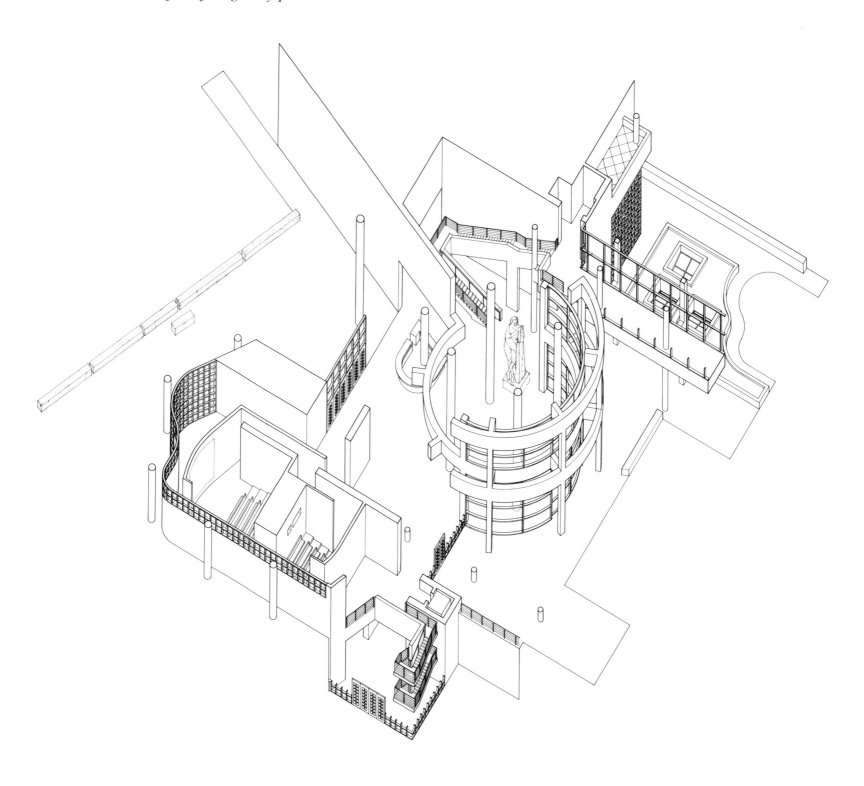

5|10| 25| 50|

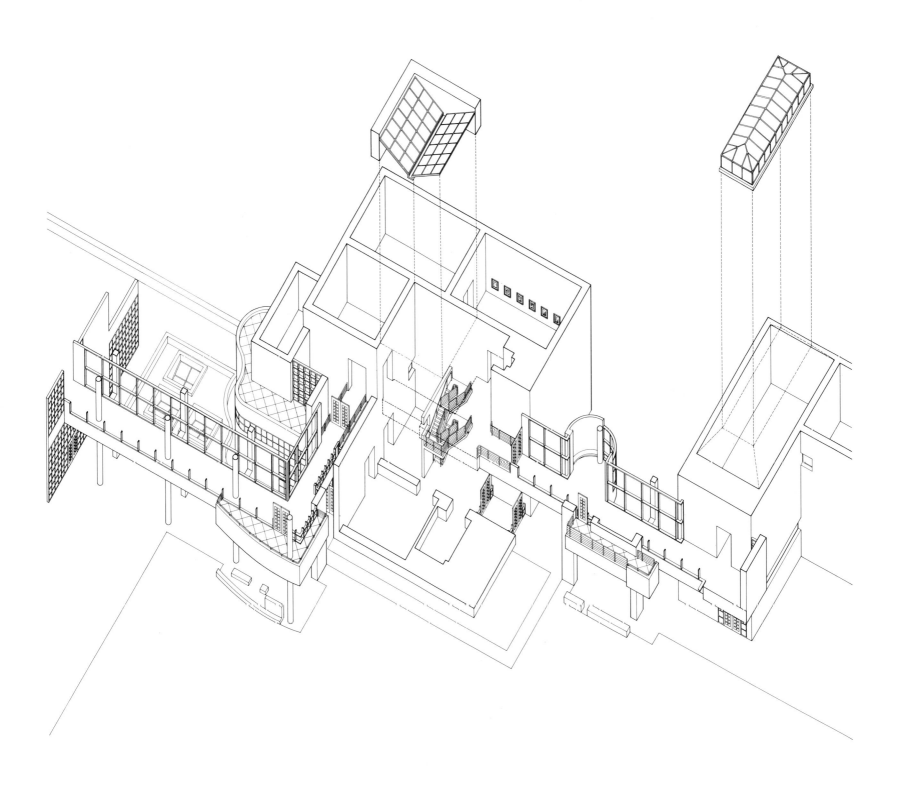

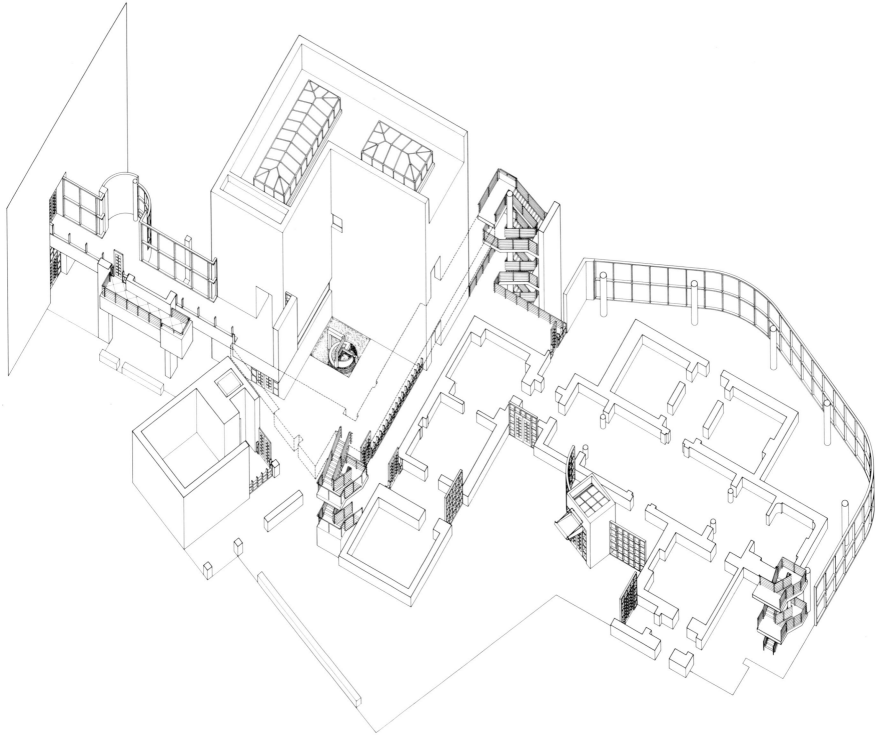

5 10   25   50

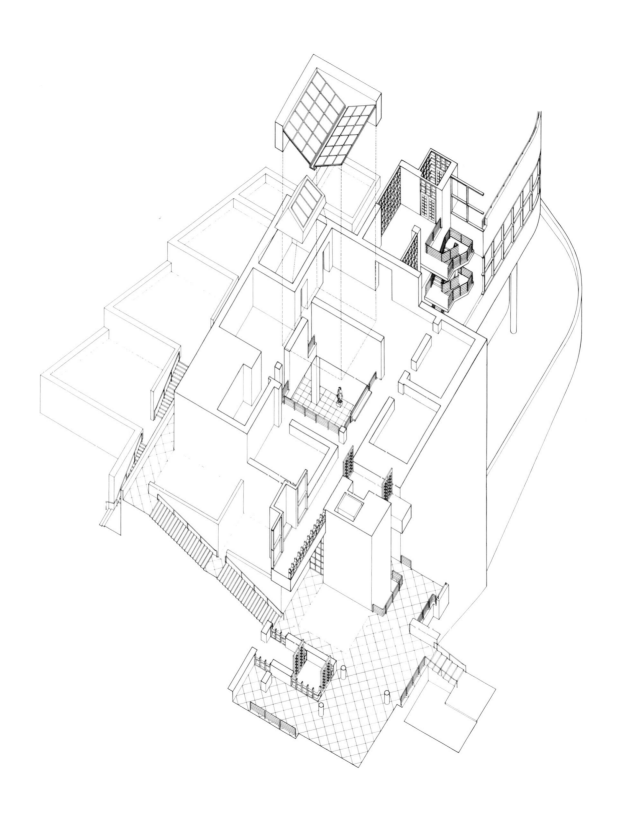

Partial axonometric view of the fourth gallery pavilions

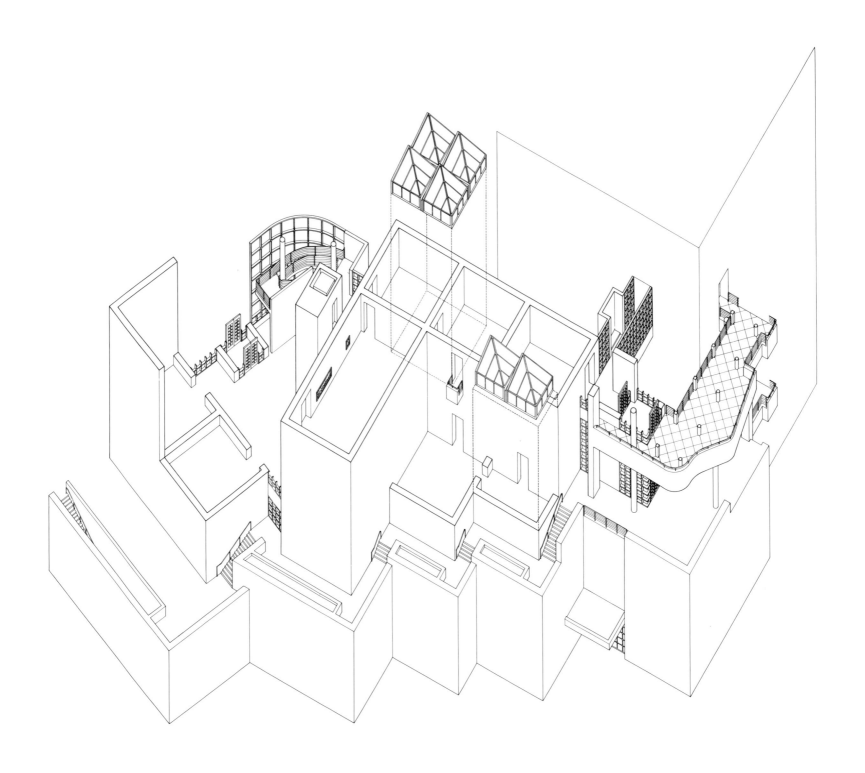

5|10| 25| 50|

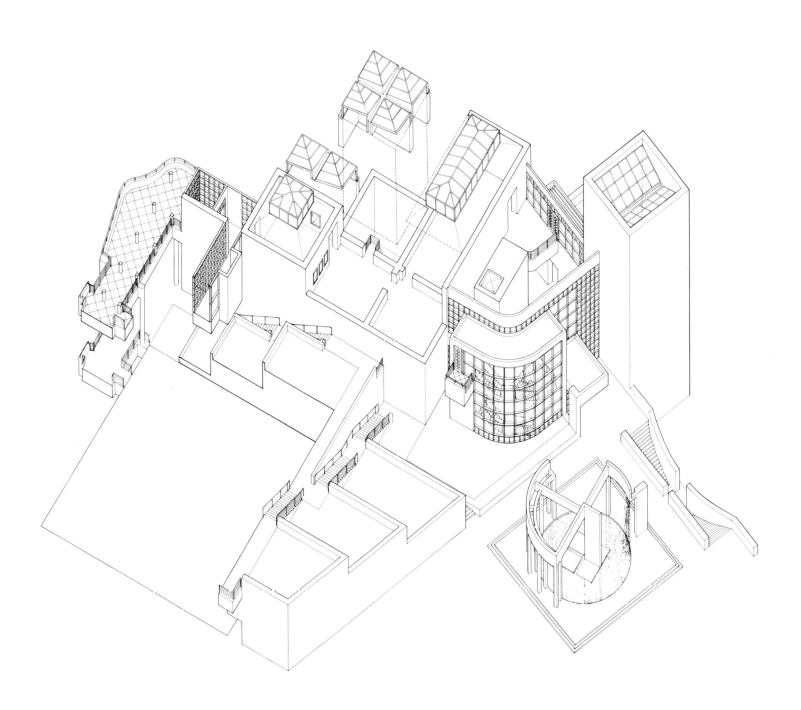

Partial axonometric view of the lobby of the Center for the History of Art and the Humanities

Partial axonometric view of the Auditorium

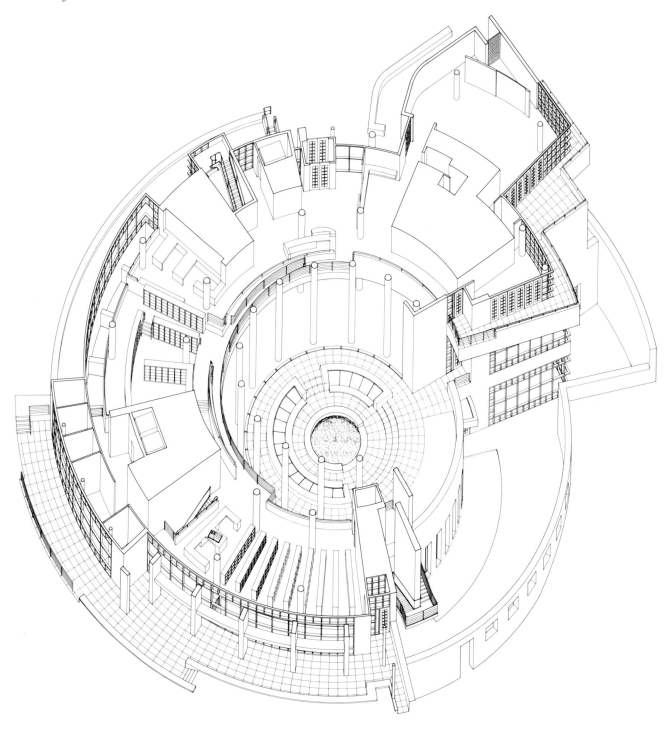

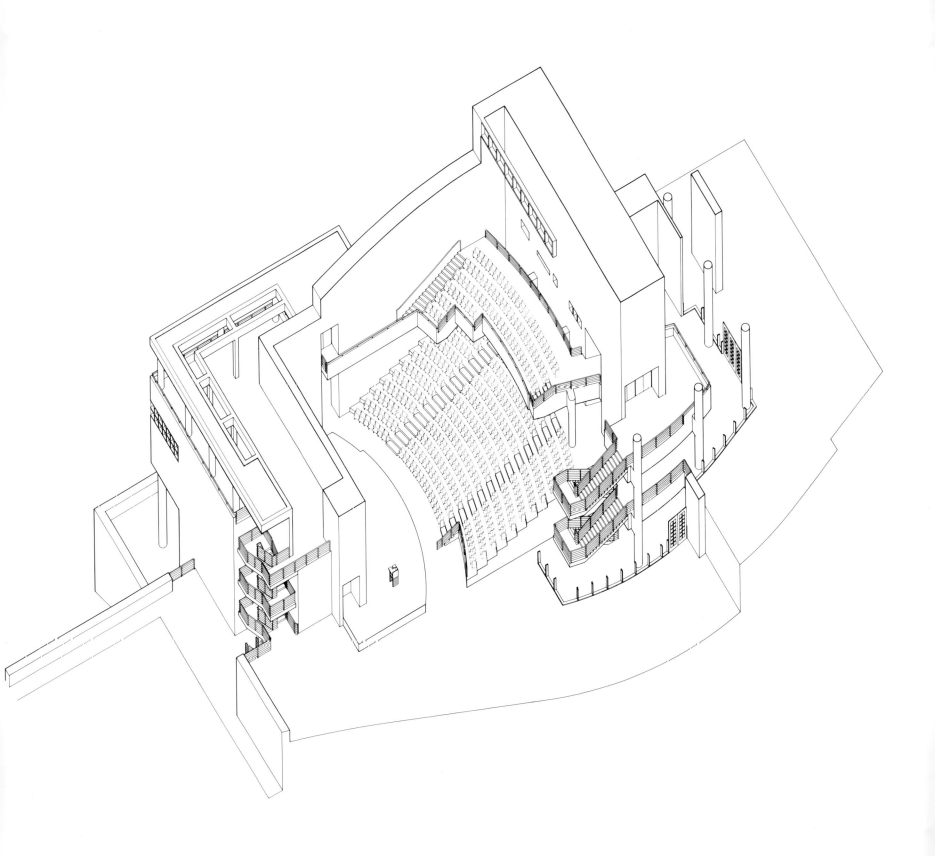

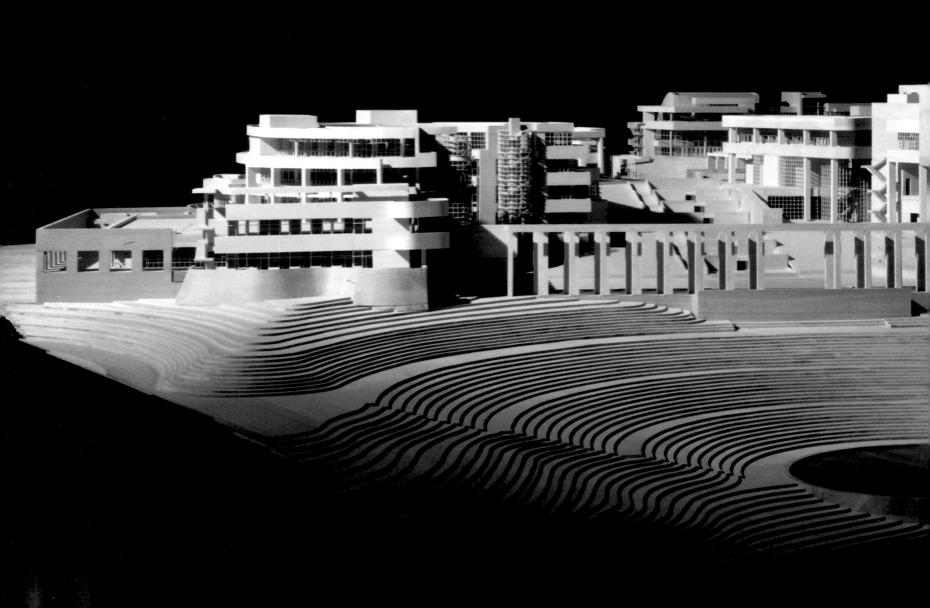

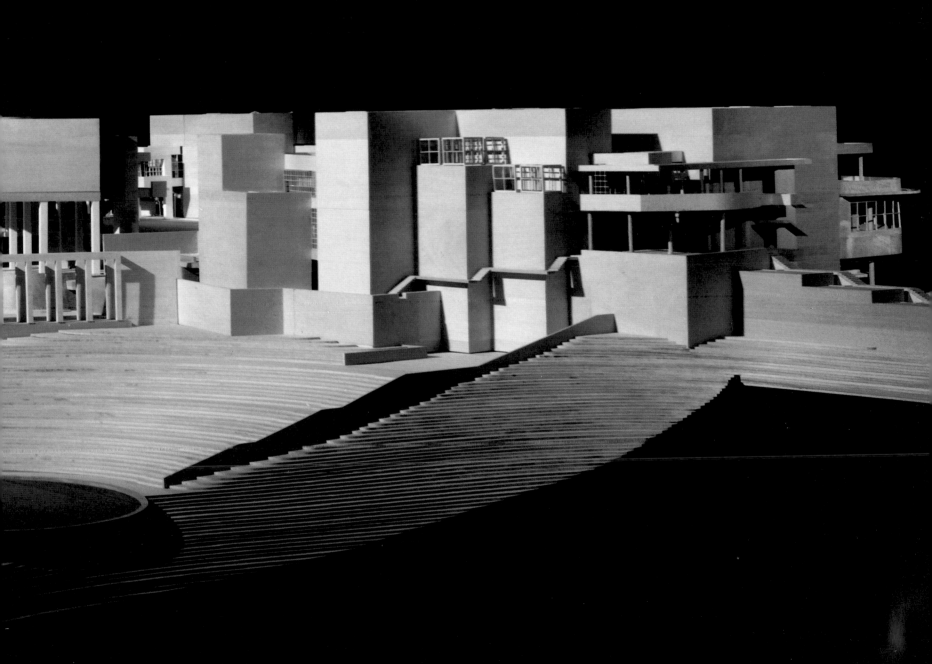

Object Designs

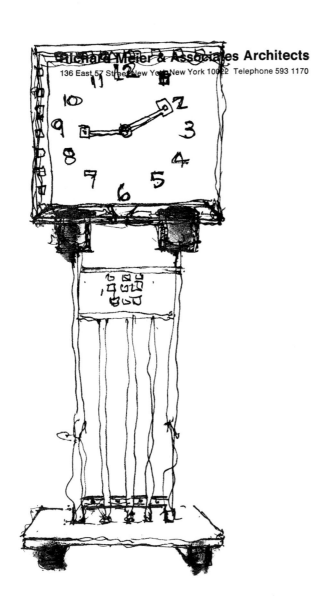

The designing of household objects offers an architect the opportunity to work on a smaller, more intimate scale, and to see projects realized relatively quickly. It is a tradition that has a long and distinguished history, in which architects such as Frank Lloyd Wright, Josef Hoffmann, Alvar Aalto, and Walter Gropius have stressed, in varying degrees, the design of the "total environment," which for them meant not merely the basic structure and interior detailing, but also the furniture and everyday household objects used.

In his product designs, Meier employs, as in his architecture, a classically modernist vocabulary. Such objects as picture frames, candlesticks, stemware, bowls, and dinnerware are all exquisitely proportioned and elegantly scaled and, like his architecture, reflect Meier's fascination with space, form, and light, as well as with geometric clarity. Meier has also experimented with a number of different semiprecious materials, as seen in his mantle clock and silver collection designed for Swid Powell.

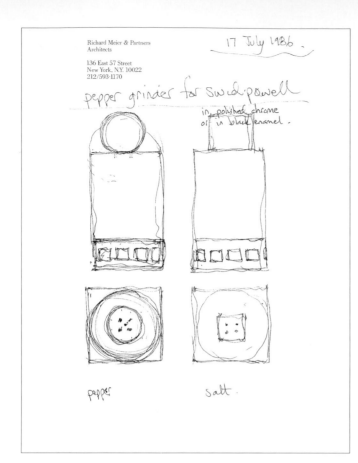

Richard Meier & Partners
Architects

136 East 57 Street
New York, N.Y. 10022
212/593·1170

17 July 1986.

pepper grinder for swid powell

in polished chrome
or in black enamel.

pepper   salt.

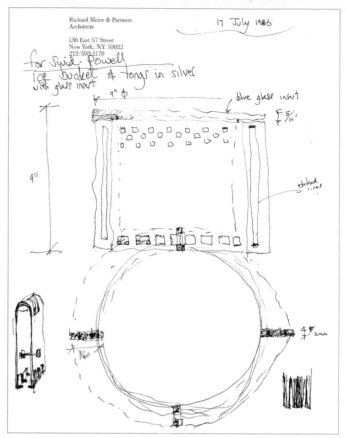

Richard Meier & Partners
Architects

136 East 57 Street
New York, N.Y. 10022
212/593·1170

17 July 1986

for Swid· Powell
Ice bucket & tongs in silver
with glass insert

9" Ø

blue glass insert

5½"

4"

etched lines

3/4"

2mm

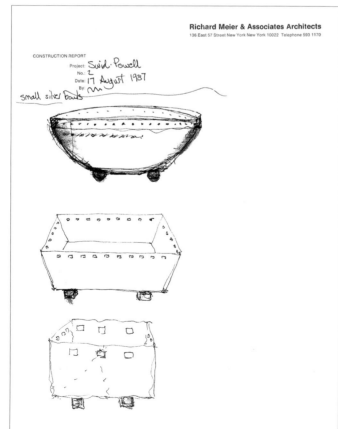

Richard Meier & Associates Architects
136 East 57 Street New York New York 10022 Telephone 593 1170

CONSTRUCTION REPORT
Project: Swid·Powell
No.: 2
Date: 17 August 1987
By:

small silver bowls

Richard Meier & Associates Architects
136 East 57 Street New York New York 10022 Telephone 593 117

CONSTRUCTION REPORT
Project: Swid·Powell
No.: 7
Date: 18 August 1987
By:

silver sugar & creamer on a silver tray

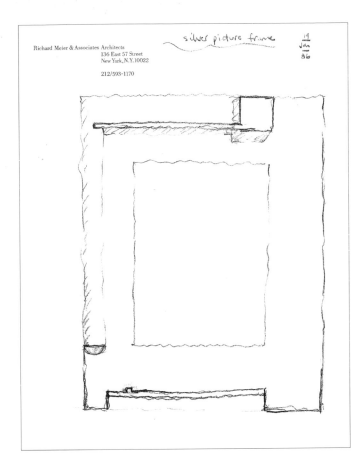

silver picture frame

19
Jan
86

Richard Meier & Associates Architects
136 East 57 Street
New York, N.Y. 10022

212/593-1170

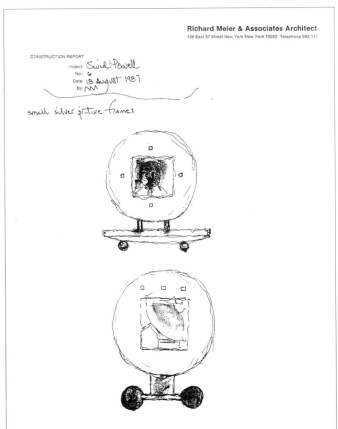

Richard Meier & Associates Architect

136 East 57 Street New York New York 10022 Telephone 593 117

CONSTRUCTION REPORT

Project: Swid Powell
No.: 6
Date: 18 August 1987
By: M

small silver picture frames

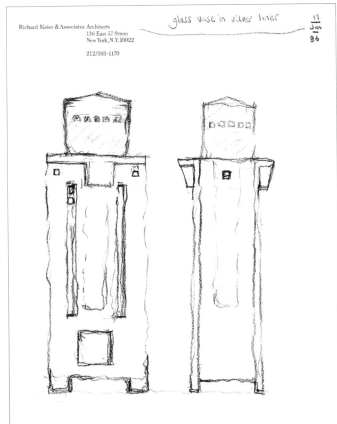

glass vase in silver liner

19
Jan
86

Richard Meier & Associates Architects
136 East 57 Street
New York, N.Y. 10022

212/593-1170

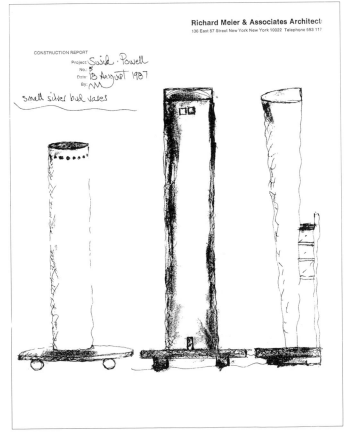

Richard Meier & Associates Architect

136 East 57 Street New York New York 10022 Telephone 593 117

CONSTRUCTION REPORT

Project: Swid · Powell
No.: 5
Date: 18 August 1987
By: M

small silver bud vases

400

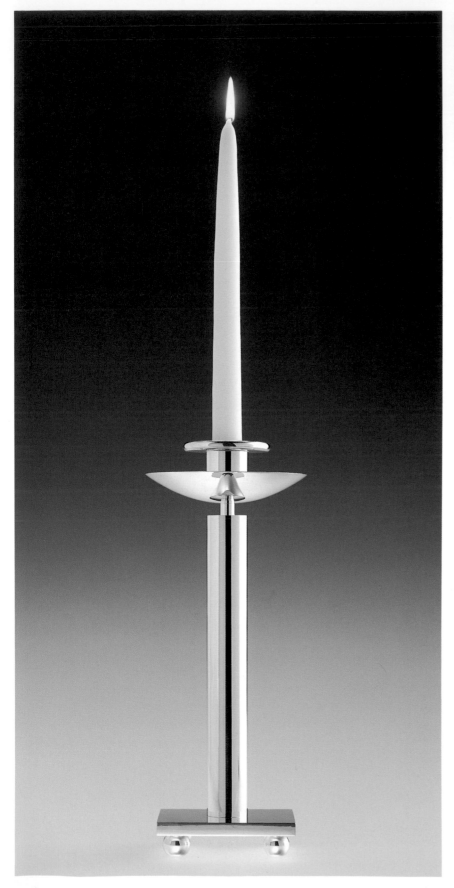

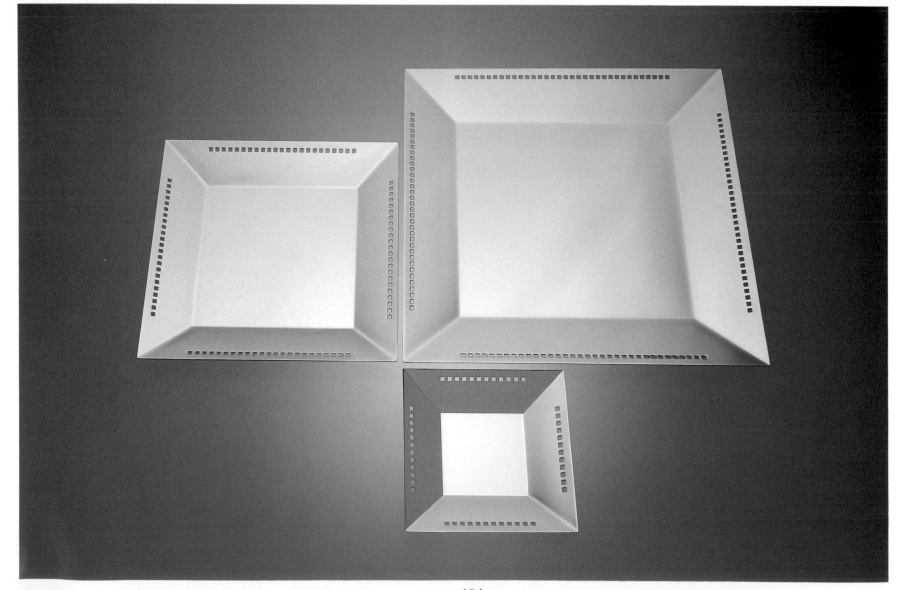

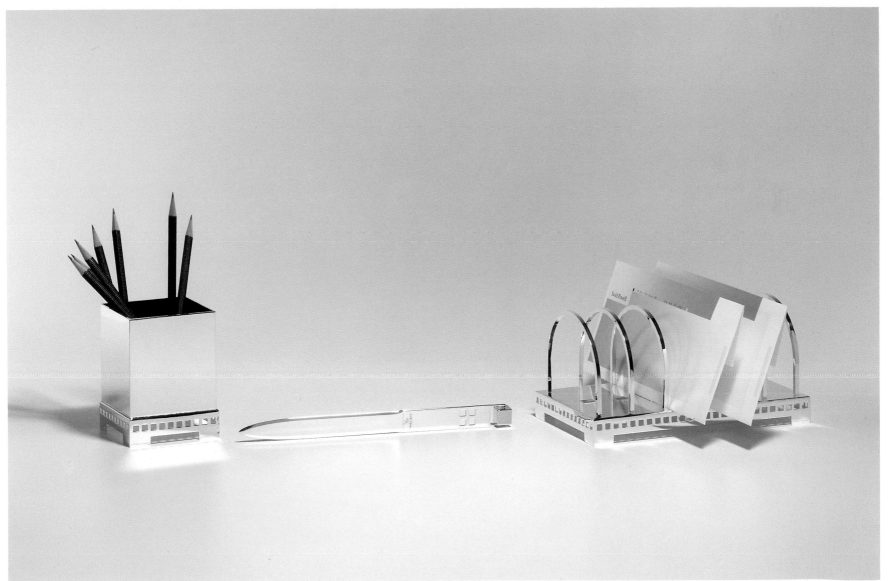

Postscript

No one would deny that architecture is a complicated enterprise. Think of how often its everyday elements—plan, structure, surface and function—seem to defy integration. Yet, when these parts do fall into place, a confident, sometimes glowing, whole results. Suddenly, obvious details reveal sources of coherence and pleasure and strength.

With Richard's work fenestration holds the key to success. It is the obvious detail that arrests our attention. The openings, through which goods, people, light and air pass, create an animated, controlled space. At the same time, the resultant smooth flow of objects and atmosphere gives evidence of a deft touch. We see division and support, architecture's irreducible elements, function as throughway markers rather than, as is unfortunately the more common case, dead-end signs.

The first thing I noticed working with Richard on the Giovannitti House was how little difference there was between the windows and the walls or, for that matter, between the doorways and the support columns. What one could see through or walk through was nearly the same as what was opaque or impenetrable. This sensation seemed to flow from an easy (easy, that is, for Richard) rhythm of placement which fixed walls and windows for the convenience of the viewer/user. It created a kind of flexible habitat that gives design a good name.

Since light is such an active factor in the living space, or spaces, Richard builds, one is forced to interact with it. Drawing on translucent window shades became a nice way to mark the flow of light through the house without getting in its way.

It was exciting to take the cue from Richard that light is life. It was even more exciting, in fact really wonderful, to realize how full his buildings are of both.

Frank Stella
New York
1991

Biographical Chronology

1984

Awarded the National Honor Award by the American Institute of Architects, the Distinguished Architecture Award by the New York Chapter of the American Institute of Architects, and the Atlanta Urban Design Commission's Award of Excellence; named Officier de l'Ordre des Arts et des Lettres by the Ministry of Culture of France.
Recipient of the Pritzker Prize for Architecture.

Westchester House
Westchester County, New York
1986

Helmick House
Des Moines, Iowa

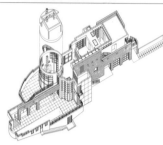

Ackerberg House
Malibu, California
1986

Bridgeport Center
Bridgeport, Connecticut
1989
People's Bank

Barnum Museum
Bridgeport, Connecticut
1989

Grotta House
Harding Township, New Jersey
1989

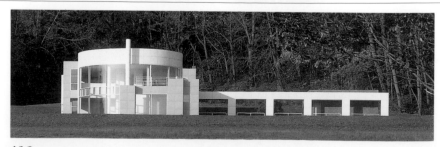

The latest addition to Meier's distinguished roster of residences is among the most exquisitely realized of them all: a weekend house in a rural part of a county suburban to New York City. It is reminiscent of other Meier designs in that it continues his exploration of how much variety he can extract from an extremely limited range of colors, materials and forms. Yet it has distinctively individual qualities that render it instantly recognizable as a definite advancement in the "patient search," as Meier's revered Le Corbusier perceptively characterized the architectural process.

Sitting in the glass-walled dining rooms looking north over hundreds of acres of gently rolling landscape, the observer feels the kind of harmony with nature often disclaimed as possible for such a highly abstracted house as this. It flouts all the Wrightian precepts about a structure being sited into, and not on, a hill; it uses declaratively man-made materials instead of natural substances more in harmony with the surroundings; and takes almost no heed of those age-old symbols of domestic living which are supposed to give the inhabitants of a house an intuitive security. Without any of the trappings we have lately been urged to believe are essential for a home to have what the architect Donlyn Lyndon has called the "indwelling spirit," this bracing and yet calming house shows beyond a doubt that in the right hands reduction can also mean enrichment.—Martin Filler, "Eminent Domain," House and Garden, April 1987

At fifty-three, Meier is beyond doubt one of the leading architects of his generation. His style is utterly distinctive but never a cliché, and it responds better than some of his critics think to the changing requirements of his site and use. It is based on and inspired by the ideal of the "White World" enunciated in Corbusier's early masterpieces of the 1920s, particularly the Villa Savoye, and has acquired—thanks more to reproduction in architectural magazines than to firsthand acquaintance with his actual buildings—a sort of instant recognizability. The curving screen walls, the glass blocks, the punchy square windows, the cylindrical columns, the ramps, the ocean-liner pipe railings, the ceramic tiles: one knows them at once.

Compared to Meier's larger and more complicated public buildings, the Ackerberg house is a fairly straightforward affair. All the same, this house shows very clearly what a romantic Meier actually is. He is infatuated with natural light; its division, reflection and modulation in space, its subtle transitions, from the open air to the cool white privacies within, provide the essential subject of his work; the infolding geometry of his buildings, from which the ghost of Palladio is rarely distant, is not a designer's "look" but the uncompromised result of poetic conviction. The Ackerberg house is one more proof that no living architect is better at balancing the sensuous pleasures of architecture against its practical needs than Richard Meier.—Robert Hughes, "Architecture: Richard Meier," Architectural Digest, October 1987

The tower faces Main Street with a large plaza, and there is something genuinely spectacular about marking one side of a plaza with a 16-story-high concave wall. The splendid visual element of this curving front is not a pure abstraction, set alone in open space; it is tightly woven into a complex building form that relates intelligently to the demands of the street. A low, projecting wing sheathed in red granite closes off the plaza, defines one corner of the site, and helps relate the building to the public square diagonally across the street; the other end of the plaza is enclosed by the rich romanesque mass of the building's neighbor, the Barnum Museum, a splendid 19th-century building that the People's Bank has renovated as part of this project.

The exhilaration of viewing this façade continues inside the main lobby, in the glass-roofed atrium behind it, and in the curving banking hall. These are all spectacular public spaces, rooms in which Mr. Meier's skillful manipulation of geometry produces lyrical results. Like much of Mr. Meier's best work, they manage the nearly impossible trick of being at once energetic and serene. And light is handled with particular grace here; the sun breaks in and sends shadows like frozen streaks across the high, white walls.—Paul Goldberger, "A Short Skyscraper with a Tall Assignment," New York Times, 26 March 1989

This nineteenth-century landmark building, renovated in conjunction with the adjacent Bridgeport Center project, houses a collection of circus paraphernalia that belonged to the great impresario P. T. Barnum, as well as extensive material related to the rich history of Bridgeport. The two buildings have a symbiotic relationship: the museum benefits from increased traffic of the office building, while the museum provides a more diverse and varied pedestrian ambiance to the downtown area. All interior finishes were restored wherever possible and the original wall configurations were put back in place. The ground floor of the museum is connected to Bridgeport Center by a gallery space for changing travelling exhibitions.

This is the sixteenth house Meier has designed, and in it he continues to employ recurrent themes, but some of them reappear with significant new twists. For example, there is the characteristic way in which he sites a house in relation to its view. In several of his early houses of the sixties and seventies, Meier made the actual front into the veritable back. Entered via a narrow bridge from a hillside arrival point, those houses had almost anonymous entry façades, played down in telling contrast to the spectacular facades looking out over the principal vistas, in the American picturesque tradition. At the Grotta house, there is a similar configuration. The bridge bisecting the west facade is not, after all, the front door but merely a rear exit.

This is one of the architect's simplest houses but also one of his most accessible and appealing. If the Grotta house lacks the staggering excitement of Meier's vertiginous Douglas house perched high above Lake Michigan or the sprawling splendor of the house in Old Westbury, New York, it also provides a calmer view of country life than those famous antecedents. Meier is one of the few architects of international reputation who, having moved up to buildings on the civic scale, continues to design houses as a matter of principle. Architects inevitably find that the amount of care required to produce a house of this quality cannot be rewarding in any sense but artistically. And at that Richard Meier, solitary traveler on a narrow but ever-extending pathway, has succeeded once again.—Martin Filler, "Modern Idyll," House & Garden, June 1990

Office and Laboratory Complex
Munich, Germany
1989
Siemens A.G.

1985
Awarded the National Honor Award by the American Institute of Architects, the Distinguished Architecture Award by the New York Chapter of the American Institute of Architects, and the American Institute of Graphic Arts Certificate of Excellence.

The Getty Center
Los Angeles, California
The J. Paul Getty Trust

1986
Awarded the Distinguished Architecture Award by the New York Chapter of the American Institute of Architects.
Elected to the International Institute of Architects.
Relocated to larger offices at 475 Tenth Avenue, New York. Established office in Westwood, Los Angeles.

Office, Richard Meier & Partners
New York and Los Angeles

Supreme Court Building
Competition Entry
Jerusalem, Israel

Progetto Bicocca
Competition Entry
Milan, Italy
Pirelli, Spa

Exhibition and Assembly Building
Ulm, Germany
Stadt Ulm

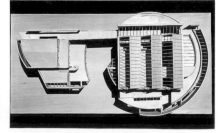

It was European cities like Frankfurt, Munich and the Hague—where urban forms and functions often overlap and interpenetrate—that would most dramatically refine Meier's reductive aesthetic. Without sacrificing their characteristic transparency, his recent projects have assumed a new density and dignity. Most have been conceived for prominent and highly problematical sites—

at the heart of the Hague, in the shadow of Ulm Cathedral, on Munich's cluttered "Ring." Frankfurt posed a particular challenge in requiring that the new museum be wedded to an existing neoclassical villa, but it offered as setting a riverside park that hinted, at least, at the pastoral context.

At Munich's Siemens Stadt—production headquarters for the electronics giant—the

task is infinitely more complex. Dating from the late 19th century, the city-within-a-city has grown with abundant reason but little rhyme. Erecting new structures there is somewhat like tying fishing flies with your fingers thrust through the ends of a matchbox. In a series of four construction phases to extend over eight years, older structures will be demolished and new laboratories and offices slotted into the

gaps. Of greater consequence, however, is the new administration building planned for the Oscar von Miller Ring. If, after a series of Teutonically bureaucratic stumbling blocks, the final permits are issued, this will become the first consequential postwar building at the heart of the Bavarian capital.—David Galloway, "A Heightened Urbanity: The Recent Works of Richard Meier," *A + U*, March 1988

From a strictly architectonic point of view it could be claimed that this is Meier at his most "baroque," where the principle of collage risks between being carried to excess and being brought to a point where one can no longer establish a field of reference for each autonomous form. And while one may argue that this is the inescapable sensibility of our fragmented age, and point to the mode of "deconstruction" running like a

phantom through these exfoliating forms, one can also easily arrive at a moment where legibility disintegrates, where figures lose their reciprocal focus, where interest flags and the object, stripped of its catharsis, dissolves. In this state the overstimulated subject sinks into a state of distraction, so that Eliot's "distracted from distraction by distraction" becomes the final nemesis in which architecture consumes itself.

This is the danger of which Meier is only too aware and he knows, as he moves from the schematics stage, that everything will now depend on how well these multiple works can be profiled, proportioned, fenestrated and clad in different materials in such a way as to sharpen the figure against the ground and to resolve each into an institutional entity. Subtle topographic inflections, ambiguities, the picturesque, the lyrical, et

arcadia ego of contrapuntal form and material richness will hardly be lacking here but the ineffable qualities of presence and emptiness, these touchstones of the real in terms of a direct aesthetic experience, these are the attributes that will have to be fought for as the work unfolds.—Kenneth Frampton, "City in Miniature," *AD*, 1989

Meier creates a world of order wherever he goes. In Manhattan, his office occupies a floor of an old building on Tenth Avenue—the beginning of the rest of the world in Saul Steinberg's celebrated New Yorker cartoon. Though the view out Meier's window might have been painted by Edward Hopper—blank brick facades and a gas station on an unnaturally empty street—the office interior has the serenity of a Robert Irwin light

piece. The high-ceilinged conference room is occupied by a long table, Corb's favorite bentwood chairs (perfectly aligned), a display model, and a phone. Meier's Los Angeles office, housed above a frozen yogurt outlet in a laughably bad building in Westwood Village, is a miniature of his New York digs—right down to the chairs in the conference room.—Michael Webb, "King of the Hill," *Buzz*, February/March 1991

The building is on a plinth slightly above grade to distinguish it from the surrounding area. The parti is based on two organizational grids. One is derived from the proximity of the site to the Knesset and the Kiryah and the axial-view relationship from the site to Mount Scopus; the other is developed in relation to the Ministry Buildings on one side and to views to the old city on the other. These two grids

establish the basic disposition of the courthouses and also include the gardens, thus unifying both inside and outside spaces.

The symbolic character of the Court of Law for the State of Israel and its relation to the City of Jerusalem is reflected in the integration of these two grids with a new center in the city. In this way, the building

projects an image of belonging both to the city and to the larger context, the three Authorities of Government of the State of Israel.

The technological pole, as an urban settlement, is an interesting experience in the process of de-industrialization of the centers and of the peripheries of our old towns. These areas have acted as urban barriers, and this has made it impossible for them, from a hygienic and mechanical point of view, to co-habit with other functions. The industrial settlements derived from high technology present new characteristics:

lesser needs for large spaces, less pollution, more relationships of communication and of participation when compared to non-industrial activities. These characteristics allow the new industrial settlement to adapt to traditional urban rules, integrating with other functions such as teaching trade, residential accommodation, leisure, culture. . . . Another theme is represented by the solution of the contradiction between a . . .

flexibility for varied processes of interaction . . . and the project's own formal and symbolic characteristics, whose image should be strong enough to survive in spite of those alternatives. Richard Meier's project is one of those that best manages to find an equilibrium between the fundamental points on which this analysis rests: the continuity of urban form and the creation of an understandable image. In a sense it is a

reinterpretation of the system of superblocks, whose external shape follows the lines of the road networks and of the continuity of the urban form, and whose interiors allow the co-habitation of different, even contradictory forms.—Oriol Bohigas, "Character and Process," *Casabella*, May 1986

Meier's proposed design for Ulm occupies a special position in his architectural work. With the Ulm project, the demands of city planning on architecture became public and were realized. Thus, it is not so much its outward appearance that especially distinguishes his concept, but rather its urbanistic significance. Meier's design for the Ulm Stadthaus—and particularly by comparison with the submissions of other

architects—represents a concept that demonstrates the effectiveness of a combination of the new and the traditional where public building is concerned, and turns a new stage in urbanistic thinking into reality.

The disproportionately large scale of the Münsterplatz is transformed by Meier's design into an unconstrained abstract

interpretation of urban density of the kind that we know from Italian squares. The function of the Stadthaus as symbol of public life, community, and democratic freedom exceeds the functional heritage of architecture; Meier's plan for the building alludes in a subtle way to the significance of the "square" as the focal point of communal and urban life and in this way gives back to the city center its lost identity.—Stephen

Barthelmess, "Richard Meier's Stadthaus Project at Ulm," *Journal of Architectural Education*, Spring 1990

City Hall and Central Library
The Hague, The Netherlands
Algemeen Burgerlijk Persiuenfonds

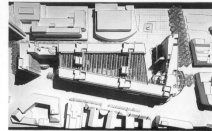

Eye Center
in association with GBD Architects
Portland, Oregon
Oregon Health Sciences University

Progetto per Napoli
Naples, Italy
Università degli Studi di Napoli

Rachofsky House
Dallas, Texas

1987
Awarded the National Honor Award by the American Institute of Architects and the Distinguished Architecture Award and the Architectural Projects Award by the New York Chapter of the American Institute of Architects.
Elected to the Royal Institute of British Architects.

National Investment Bank
The Hague, The Netherlands
Nationale Investerings Bank

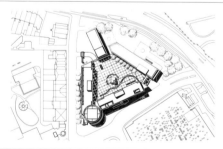

Santa Monica Beach Hotel
Competition Entry
Santa Monica, California

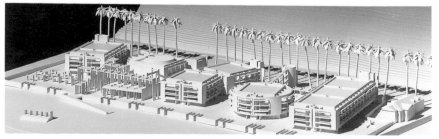

Despite the projects' high degree of definition, we feel that a critical position would be pointlessly premature. In a fairly short while, in fact, the big "fabbrica" will be a real, built object ready to be judged as such. Yet we do not think it is either premature or pointless to present the project's drawings, particularly because they mark a new stopping place in Meier's development: that of a direct confrontation with the

European city. Unlike what happened in Frankfurt, where his design for the Museum of Decorative Arts was still basically a large villa immersed in a green garden facing the river Main, with the Hague not just a building but a part of the city, was required. Meier's architecture thus takes on a new dimension: that of urban planning.

It is not too soon or rash to surmise that the

new dimension is working very successfully. The Hague project, we believe, is confirmation. It was, in any case, a dimension that had already for some time been inherent in the works of Meier, whose villas have, in recent years, transcended the boundaries of their traditional typology. They have been increasingly articulated to the point that they have become almost small settlements in themselves, like

transplants of minuscule Mediterranean towns into the heaths of Long Island or Connecticut. This time, however, the "artificial" city is grafted onto the historic one.—Vittorio Magnago Lampugnani, "Richard Meier: Municipio e Biblioteca, L'Aia," *Domus*, November 1987

The divide between expensive private architecture and poor public architecture is too often all too clear. So when you find an architect, one of the architects of affluent corporate culture, designing a hospital, there is a sense that there is some order, some sense in the world. For Richard Meier is one of those architects who has dined at the tables of some of the most affluent clients in the world.

But, although the new Eye Center of the Oregon Health Sciences University is necessarily a multivalent building, housing a number of complex and related medical functions, Meier is able to translate even this building into a symbol of successful corporate culture. As one of the world's most sophisticated architects, Richard Meier is also one of its most ritualistic and fetishistic.

On one level, his buildings are beautiful, cold, rational architectural games, as complex as a Rubik's cube. Meier's architecture presents an ordered, optimistic view of the world. The buildings are serene. They are classical and nearly always presented without people. Meier's buildings are perfect in the sense that an athletic American movie star or a Greek temple is perfect. If poor, ill or ugly people inhabited

them they would be intruders, upsetting an image of geometric and constructional perfection. You cannot be sloppy in a Meier building. Humans have to live up to Meier's architecture. — Jonathan Glancey,"As Cold, and as Passionate as the Dawn." World Architecture, no. 3, 1989

The Spanish Quarter holds a prominent place in Naples due to its central location in the historic and commercial zone of the city. But it is an isolated area, inaccessible to most Neapolitans, due to poor circulation patterns between its two main borders, Corso Vittorio Emmanuele and Via Roma, and the lack of points of entry and egress along Corso Vittorio Emmanuele. The Quarter needs to have improved quality of

residential life and more pedestrian traffic brought into it if it is to have any hope of reviving its vitality and eliminating its reputation as one of the worst neighborhoods in Naples.

Faced with the critical problem of how to put a new building in a historical context, we have proposed a series of housing units that preserve the fabric of the area.

Contrary to the Corbusian vision in which housing slabs are isolated from their context, we have literally extruded the building volumes from the street plan. In this way, the proportions of the space as well as the context are retained, while improving living conditions through new construction.

Meier's villas exhibit an inward quality; a self-awareness of their objecthood, distancing of their banality as objects of use through an idealization of function in general; all this in conformity with the overreaching aim in evolving a language. By their use of porcelain facings, along with steel frame, masonry enclosures, plywood skins, they are well adapted to their different conditions of production and to their

particularity in place and time. In this respect, while they are ahistorical in their formalism, they also appear to be free from nostalgic sentiment. They are clearly American.—Robert Maxwell, "Modern Master," *Building Design*, 16 September 1988

This proposed office building is an extension of the National Investment Bank of the Hague. It is situated on a triangular parcel of land within the unique district of the Peace Palace, and several salient characteristics of this part of the city have been acknowledged and incorporated into its design. The five-story height was established in deference to its context and to allow for the bank's existing eight-story

tower to remain the point of reference for the building. The addition will be clearly marked by its cylindrical headpiece, which will create a strong corner presence and give the new building its own identity. The V-shaped plan responds to the typology of surrounding courtyard buildings, and the orientation of the southeast wing and courtyard relate to the grid of the old city to the north.

Meier's fractures and collisions signify "imperfect perfection," "unclear clarity," "irrational rationality"—the oxymoronic... meanings which destabilize the certainty of the Modernist white-aesthetic. And here lies the essence of Meier's contribution to the "new tradition," to Late-Modernism or Neo Modernism (I would use the terms interchangeably in his case): it is the note of celebration amidst a questioning doubt, an

affirmation of the "Modern project," of reason and the Enlightenment, at the same time as it's a sensuous denial of the dogmatism of the ideology through the play with sculptural form and light. Those who want to find in Meier's work an intellectual ordering—the abstract distinction between public and private, geometry and nature, necessity and freedom—will continue to be transported by this abstract language,

because it is played with brilliance that would have pleased Le Corbusier. It won't please everyone—no architecture does in an age of pluralism and where the limits of abstraction are known. But unlike so much modernism today, Meier's is kept taut and fresh, reminding us that architectural languages don't die, but rather that certain architects get tired of using them.—Charles Jencks, "Meier and the Modern Tradition,"

Architectural Design, *Volume 58, Number 9/10, 1988*

**Madison Square Garden Site
Redevelopment**
Competition Entry
New York, New York
Olympia & York Companies (USA)

Weishaupt Forum
Schwendi, Germany
Max Weishaupt GmbH

Royal Dutch Paper Mills Headquarters
Hilversum, The Netherlands
Koninklijke Nederlandse Papierfabrieken

1988
Recipient of the Royal Gold Medal by the
Royal Institute of British Architects.

**Cornell University Alumni and
Admissions Center**
Ithaca, New York
Cornell University

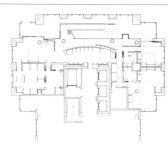

Apartment Interior
Chicago, Illinois

Espace Pitôt
Montpellier, France
URBAT

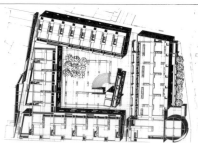

The architecture speaks of the primacy of perception over and above the primacy of mere architecture alone. Inside the very tradition of the Modern Movement of its heroic period one must note that there is no built precedent at the scale of Madison Square Garden to demonstrate how, if at all, its language is capable of bounding and binding a statement stretched vertically to these extremes. In the end, to speak of

Richard Meier's architecture is to point out to the research of how a language can be actually critically reinvented through its application to new aspects of building in the present, for example, a scale not encountered before.

Richard Meier is discharging his responsibilities in an exemplary fashion. He learns from the past, he learns from his own

experiments. His Twenty-first Century is happening for him every day. He is not interested in being a guru, he is a fortune-teller. . . . He is not joining assorted bands of charlatans in predicting the end of the world. He is a master of a great steel compass, a very exacting instrument which seems to be today copyrighted in the USA, in a joint venture with some parts of Switzerland.—Livio Dimitriu, "Richard

Meier," Architetture Per Il Terzo Millennio, Ipotesi e Tendenze, *Perugia: Fondazione Adriano Olivetti, 1991*

Richard Meier's architecture is so evocative of the originating phase of the modernist style, in all its purity, and particularly in the depth of its Corbusian loyalty, that it does not strike one as simply another manipulation of images. By a hallucinatory effect, the sheer consistency of the manner suggests that it has not been adopted arbitrarily, but is the application of a rule of measure. . . .

One great advantage of this approach is that it restores a consistent relation between form and function. The play of large and small openings, of glass walls and windows, of canopied entrances and unmarked exits, of ships' rail and solid-fronted balconies, all work together to ensure that the formal importances are made clear. Because these small differences are strictly controlled, they take on meaning as coded markers of the

building's function. It is as if Meier has renounced self-expression, client adulation, image mongering, whim, and all accidental effects in order to purify the material of architecture and render it transparent to the function. That, to do this, he has had to seize arbitrarily on a predetermined style, seems a small matter. In one sense, we may think that he is taking advantage, as with a takeover bid, of another's achievements. In

another sense, we may be grateful to him for purging architecture of excessive levels of noise and disturbance, allowing us to see, as it were, the underlying realities of building.—Robert Maxwell, "Modern Master," Building Design, *16 September 1988*

This apartment, located on the top two floors of a new, prominently located skyscraper on Michigan Avenue, has dramatic, panoramic views of Chicago from downtown to Lake Michigan. Upon entering, a sculptural staircase/fireplace focuses views and creates an organizing element for the open, two-story living space. A linear gallery on the second floor houses the owner's extensive art collection

and provides a balcony view to the living space below.

This mixed-use development is on the periphery of the old city, near the Palais de Justice and the Arc de Triomphe. In developing the site, the goal has been to provide modern public facilities that have been lacking in the adjacent historic neighborhoods. The program includes housing, commercial office space, retail facilities, a public swimming pool, and a gymnasium.

The project is organized around a large public square with the fitness facilities below ground level and the office, retail, and housing spaces arranged so that their public functions are on the busy Rue Pitôt. The residential areas are oriented to benefit from their close proximity to the eighteenth-century Promenade du Peyrou. A historic city ordinance limits all building height in the area to three stories, so not to interfere

with views from Promenade du Peyrou. Roof gardens and terraces will integrate the buildings with nearby formal gardens.

Canal+ Headquarters
Paris, France
Canal+

Museum of Contemporary Art
Barcelona, Spain
*Consorci del Museu d'Art Contemporani
de Barcelona*

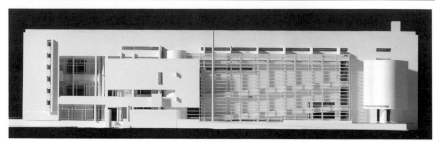

1989
Awarded the Chicago Architecture Award,
the Progressive Architecture Award, and
the Architectural Projects Award by the
New York Chapter of the American
Institute of Architects.

**Administrative and Maritime Center
Master Plan**
Antwerp, Belgium
EPMC

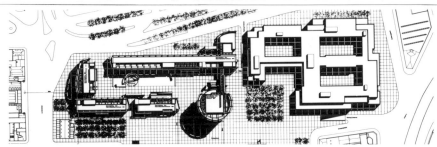

Headquarters, CMB
Antwerp, Belgium
CMB International NV

Bibliothèque de France
Competition Entry
Paris, France
*Association pour la Bibliothèque de
France*

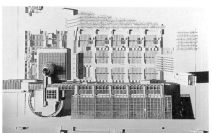

Office Building
Frankfurt, Germany
Harald Quandt Holding

With his building in Paris for the French television company Canal+ about to be completed, Richard Meier has once again demonstrated the virtues of the approach to architecture his name has come to stand for: loyalty to the brief, loyalty to the crystalline, geometric, formal elegance, and loyalty to the concrete nature of whiteness which gives the volume bathed in light that unmistakable spatial note.

The brief, which prescribes a combination of office space and production facilities, demands exactly the kind of ingenious strategy for the manipulation of light which Meier, as a choreographer of light, masters in an impressive manner. What goes on behind the hermetically sealed walls of the television studio during production can be seen as a chamber music version of the orchestral score performed in the building's

exterior. Here the architect as the director of light uses the various instruments of the artistic repertoire at his disposal—light captors, filters and modulators—distributed over the wall and roof surfaces. From the plain pane of glass, to tinted or milk glass, right through to perforated aluminum sheeting, everything technology has to offer is used to make this building into an optical instrument—from the classical brise-soleil,

the skylights and reflectors to multilayered glass and metal filters.—Fritz Neumeyer, *Aedes Gallery Exhibition Catalogue,* Berlin, 1991

Barcelona prepares for the future by assigning its Olympic projects to renowned figures of international architecture, and behind the election of Richard Meier for this museum is that same attitude marking said gamut of commissions and competitions. Meier is undeniably a renowned figure in his own right in the field of museums, responsible for some of the past decade's most outstanding examples and having

consecrated himself with the commission for the Getty Center in Los Angeles. The program had hardly been drafted when the American architect was summoned to design a far-reaching museum building that would give form and content to Barcelona's avant-garde tradition. Regardless of the cost of the building, any significant collection of modern works the museum musters will be worth more than its container, and yet this

endeavors to be a great building, an attraction to the city. Due to the remodelling of Ferlandina and Montealegre streets, the New Yorker has more than 100 square meters to work on between two access-providing squares, linked to the old Casa de Caridad by an exhibition patio. Meier and his team have satisfied expectations regarding style and photogene by designing a signature product of the firm: a rectangle

articulated by three main bodies and exquisitely worked in the unique and white late manner of the old Five.—"The Great White Hope," *A & V,* 1990

This master plan for a new mixed-use development, including the Port Authority, a hotel, restaurants, and office facilities, aims to tie this presently isolated and unutilized area to the adjacent docklands and the center of the old city, thus creating a vibrant new district. By altering traffic patterns and placing substantial parking below grade, the plan would increase circulation in the area and connect it to the

waterfront area. It will become the main point of entry to the waterfront area from the city to the north. It is hoped that the Center would act as a catalyst for future growth in this potentially fertile area.

Designed as a component of our master plan for the Administrative and Maritime Center in Antwerp, this headquarters building is the central element in that plan. On axis with the large Willemdock section to the west, it is a visual beacon that unites the new district with the waterfront and symbolizes the potential for new development. The rounded form was selected to take advantage of the views of the nearby harbor and old city.

For the Bibliothèque de France in Paris Meier works in a space bordering the Seine, in a decaying area that is to be reclaimed for the city. The presence of the river conditioned the project. The linear references are quite precise; they connect the surrounding habitat and confront it, with the library's entrance and public spaces serving as an extension of the surrounding urban fabric. The complex's various volumes

function as mediating elements between the urban fabric on one side and the riverbank on the other. A main concourse emphasizes the library's large forms and acts as a link between the ancient center of Paris and the new fragments of the city, reuniting with unusual naturalness and perfect continuity the project's double reference: its urban context and its site, a continuity between old and new that is reached using simple

elements suggested by the city's classical constructions. Respect for the Bibliothèque's historical environment is the inevitable result of a process of getting to know the site. This does not mean adapting to the existing structures but rather using them as a "meaningful point of departure for the project."

Meier's compositional methods, facing in

Europe a new aspect, that of a confrontation with the historical city, passed the test, using a bilingual idiom: the language of an awareness of place, and the language of the "poetics of continuous invention," which is the hallmark of the modern.—Alberto Izzo, "Facing Europe," *in* Richard Meier Architetture/Projects 1986–1990, Florence: Centro Di, 1991

Edinburgh Park Master Plan
Edinburgh, Scotland
Enterprise Edinburgh

Daimler-Benz Research Center
Ulm, Germany
Daimler Benz AG

Hypolux Bank Building
Luxembourg
Hypo Bank International, SA

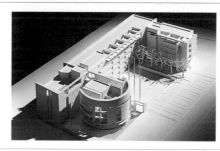

Museum of Ethnology
Frankfurt am Main, Germany
Stadt Frankfurt am Main

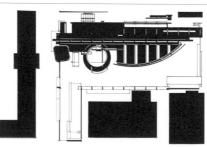

1990
Awarded the National Honor Award by the American Institute of Architects, the Progressive Architecture Award, and the Distinguished Architecture Award and the Architectural Projects Award by the New York Chapter of the American Institute of Architects.
Elected to the Belgian Royal Academy of Art.

Fox Inc. Studio Expansion and Renovation
Los Angeles, CA
Fox, Inc.

Sextius-Mirabeau Master Plan
Competition Entry
Aix-en-Provence, France
Bouygues

Like many architects, Meier has gradually moved up the scale of projects from collage to furniture making to buildings and now to whole townships. Some designers find the transition difficult but Meier apparently applies the same general principles to all. That is, firstly, that local references should be sought, distilled, abstracted and finally reinterpreted; secondly, that a kind of geometric order underpins all design;

thirdly, that structure should be modified by concerns for space and time; and fourthly, that rotational and volumetric disjunctions enliven design.

All four of these considerations are evident in the master plan of the Maybury Business Technology Park for Enterprise Edinburgh Ltd., a company established by Edinburgh District Council. Yet now Meier's concern for

abstract Modernism is more heavily tempered by contextual issues than usual, and these characteristically are rationalized into a formal debate about order and spatial structure. What the master plan shows us in particular is that Meier has looked closely at the New Town of Edinburgh and the relationship between urban blocks and landscaped gardens, at the integrating function of streets as visual and development

corridors, and the separating of big development into discrete but related parts.—Brian Edwards, "Meier's Maybury Master Plan," *RIBA Journal*, September 1989

Contrary to those critics and architects who trade and think only in terms of style and who overemphasize the image of the immediate appearance rather than the experience of the spatial whole, Meier's legacy is not so much stylistic (since all style is inimitable) as it is the substance of a certain tactical approach, in which emphasis is invariably given to such factors as topography, context, volumetric

movement (promenade architecturale), *the interaction of nature and culture, and, above all, the ever-changing pattern of light. Indeed, the unique quality of Meier's architecture is perhaps most singularly characterized by the radiant quality of its internal light. This, more than any other factor, serves to remind us of the influence of Balthasar Neumann on his work.*

The other salient contribution of Meier, of more recent date, is one that he has mainly achieved as a European architect, that is to say, as a Jamesian American working in Europe. I have in mind his incisive proposals made at the level of urban form. Perhaps it would be more correct to refer to these urban fragments, projected for Germany, France and Holland, as essays in the "city in miniature." These essays, despite any

reservation one might entertain as to their detailed development, are patently convincing at the level of their overall morphology and this is surely the most compelling lesson they hold for us.— Kenneth Frampton, *Richard Meier Architect*, Academy Editions, 1989

Richard Meier's Kunsthandwerk Museum is persuasive evidence that a sharp contrast in style from one's neighbors is not necessarily discordant. Promenading through the galleries, it's impossible not to notice the contrast between the whiteness without and the whiteness within: the former tarnished by time and climate, the latter as pristine as the day it opened. In a sense, Meier's is an idealized architecture of the interior, into

which nature encroaches gloriously. The principal features of the building are not bits of architecture that have been put there, but bits of the landscape that haven't been taken away: the two magnificent chestnut trees in the courtyard, whose branches—leaves almost touching the windows—one sees from a new perspective from the upper galleries.

Transparency and tree preservation are also the governing conditions behind Meier's Museum of Ethnology, whose design—in the customary vocabulary of white enamel metal panels, stone and stucco—is unveiled in the current DAM exhibition. Due for completion in 1992, it will sit back from the Schaumainkai, with a long glazed ramp taking advantage of the park which it shares with the Kunsthandwerk Museum. A giant

totem, a boat and a meeting hut will lure visitors through the trees to the top-lit cubic galleries, with a bridge across Metzlerstrasse taking them to a further pavilion housing African and American collections on the first and ground floors, with more ritual objects displayed in open-air courts.—Janet Abrams, "Banking on Culture," *Blueprint*, October 1990

This master plan for Fox Inc. includes two prominent new buildings on the 20th Century Fox lot: a new administrative office building and a new commissary and news station. The office building, prominently located on the corner of Pico Boulevard and Avenue of the Stars, is composed of distinct office blocks that define a series of outdoor spaces organized around a central activity core.

The commissary/news station is centrally located, on access with the new main entry to the lot from Avenue of the Stars. Dining facilities are on the ground and second levels and the news station is in a level below. Interpenetration of the news studio through all three levels creates a visual connection between it and the commissary.

Arp Museum
Rolandswerth, Germany
Fondation Jean Arp

Swiss Volksbank
Basel, Switzerland
Schweizerische Volksbank

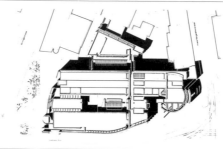

Grange Road Medical Center
Singapore
Pontiac Land Private Limited

1991
Awarded the Architectural Projects Award
by the New York Chapter of the American
Institute of Architects and the Progressive
Architecture Award.
Received honorary doctorate degree from
the University of Naples.

Office Building
Berlin, Germany
Beteiligungen GmbH & Co., KG

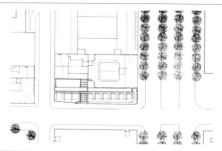

Fabric Designs
DesignTex

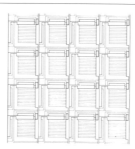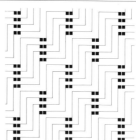

Furniture Studies

The Norwegian architect and architectural critic Christian Norberg-Schulz reminds us of what architecture is called upon to do; namely, to create identifiable places, to interpret spaces and the world we live in not with metaphorical tricks but by exploiting their most basic resources: opening and enclosure, load and load-bearing, concentration and expansion, economy and extravagance. The past must, he says, serve the present and lead us back to former principles which we have to reinterpret with the means and materials of today.

Art moves and has its being in the triangle between studio, gallery and museum, with the museum serving as a repository where what has proved to be of lasting worth can be exhibited. The museum is built for permanence; the object of art may be subject to constant change. This is why there can be no equivalence between building and art, only reciprocal stimulation. Good architecture has always been used for a multitude of purposes. An open plan makes for freedom in combination and variation. It is this ability to adapt the interior to other needs as they arise that makes the excellence of good architecture. The building derives its form from what the interior is actually called upon to express.—Werner Blaser, Building for Art. Zurich: Birkhauser, 1990

This building houses the regional headquarters of a prominent Swiss bank and also includes prime retail and commercial office space. The building is located on the former site of one of the gates to the old city center, and its four main elevations respond to the four sides of the site. Retail facilities along Viaduktstrasse on the south facade give way to a recessed entry plaza for the banking hall and for the offices centered around an interior courtyard. A cylinder marks the location of a light-filled, two-story banking hall.

This new Medical Center, located at the intersection of Orchard Boulevard and Grange Road in Singapore, responds to a number of site demands. Since a low, massive block building would visually have closed off the street, we have designed a slender tower that occupies less than 25 percent of the net site area, thus leaving a greater amount of open space for public use. The portion not occupied by building has gardens and reflecting pools, and this outdoor space extends through and below the building to create an outdoor lobby with shops and a small cafe, which is in turn linked to a covered walkway—a significant urban element required in Singapore. Such space which, in a typical development, might have been enclosed has been displaced to the upper floors here, thus creating a slender and vertically proportioned tower. The building has a carefully articulated facade with sunscreens and balconies that will give human scale and relief and is compatible and sympathetic to the adjacent residential towers.

Located a few blocks east of the Brandenburg Gate on the Unter den Linden, this seven-story office building will cap the end of the block as the only modern piece of architecture in this otherwise intact nineteenth-century block. Cornice heights and setbacks of adjacent neoclassical buildings have been respected, and the regulating lines of their facades determined responses in the new building. The short facade on the Unter den Linden is more solid than the bowed glass-curtain wall on the side street. The building has a five-story sky-lighted atrium cutting through it with bridges connecting the office floors. Shops and cafes are on the ground level.

The three new groups of Design Tex fabrics are, predictably, very different. . . . Richard Meier, whose architecture is purist, minimalist, geometric, and closely akin to some of Le Corbusier's early work, has produced a series of understated, geometric patterns that range from Cartesian geometrics to—oddly enough—Wrightian patterns in stained glass! Although one assumes that Meier would have preferred a color range somewhere between white and off-white (and possibly white-on-white), his fabrics do venture into pale pastels, reluctantly; but the patterns are graphlike, equally adaptable to upholstered surfaces and overlapping draperies. The effort to break with his minimalist palette was obviously a bit wrenching for Richard Meier—but the results are worth every wrench: understated, clean, and very elegant.—Peter Blake, "3 Directions in 3 Dimensions," Interior Design, March 1991

Selected Bibliography

General

Abercrombie, Stanley. "Bravado Variations in a Consistent Theme." *Architecture*, May 1985, p. 325.

Abrams, Janet. "A White Knight." *The Independent*, 25 October 1988, p. 16.

Arthur, John. "Alternative Space, Richard Meier." *Art New England*, April 1986, pp. 8–9.

Blaser, Werner. *Richard Meier: Building for Art*. Basel: Birkhäuser Verlag, 1990.

Cook, Peter. "Richard Meier: Perfect Whiteness." *RIBA Journal*, June 1988, pp. 19–20.

Diamonstein, Barbaralee. "Richard Meier." *American Architecture Now II*, New York: Rizzoli, 1985, pp. 161–168.

Dimitriu, Luvio. "Richard Meier: l'architettura verso il terzo millennio." *Controspazio*, March 1990, pp. 9–25.

Fischer, Volker. "Architektur-Import." *Der Architekt*, May 1990, pp. 236–237.

Flagge, Ingeborg. "Richard Meier." *Haüser*, January 1989, pp. 59–74.

Fort, Jaume. "Richard Meier, la Arquitectura blanca." *El Pais Semanal*, 24 November 1985, pp. 53–62.

Frampton, Kenneth. "Richard Meier & Partners in Europe: Recent Work." *Casabella*. December 1990, pp. 4–10.

Galloway, David. "A Heightened Urbanity: The Recent Works of Richard Meier." *A + U*, March 1988.

Garcias, Jean-Claude. "Consruit par Blanc." *Beaux Arts*, June 1985, p. 70.

Glancey, Jonathan. "As Cold, and as Passionate as the Dawn." *World Architecture*. no. 3. 1989, pp. 40–51.

Glusberg, Jorge, ed. *Vision of the Modern. UIA, Journal of Architecture Theory and Criticism*. London: Academy Editions, 1988, pp. 88–96.

Graaf, Vera. "Alles Weiss in Weiss." *Männer Vogue*, March 1986, pp. 177–181.

———. "Richard Meiers Museums-Welt." *Architektur & Wohnen*, June/July 1990, p. 143.

Gregotti, Vittorio. "The Revival of the Avantgarde." *Architettura*, 28 August 1988, p. 20.

Hansen, Jorgen Peder. "Arkitekten Richard Meier." *Architekten*, March 1986, pp. 85–93.

Henning, Larson, et al. "Interview with Richard Meier." *Skala*, August 1987, pp. 11–15.

James, Warren A. "Meier's Opus: *Richard Meier, Architect 1965–1984*." *Progressive Architecture*, June 1985, pp. 149–155.

———. "Interview: Richard Meier." *Arquitectura*, July/August 1990, pp. 138–153.

Jencks, Charles. "Meier and the Modern Tradition." *Architectural Design*, vol. 58, no. 9/10, 1988, pp. II–V.

———. "Richard Meier and the Modern Tradition." In *The New Moderns*. London: Academy Editions, 1990, pp. 239–255.

Jordy, William H. "Which Terrace for the Sunset?" *The New York Times Book Review*, 17 March 1985, p. 13.

Kaplan, Sam Hall. "Getty Architect and Others." *The Los Angeles Times Book Review*, 7 April 1985, p. 6.

Kelly, Lore. "Ein Gespräch mit Richard Meier." *Neue Zürchner Zeitung*, 26 May 1989, p. 67.

Lemos, Peter. "Richard Meier." *Northwest Orient Magazine*, March 1985, p. 58.

Maxwell, Robert. "Modern Master." *Building Design*, 16 September 1988, p. 28.

Meier, Richard. "Essay." *Perspecta 24*, New York: Rizzoli, 1988, pp. 104–105.

———. "On the Road Again." in *Architecture, Shaping the Future*. San Diego: University of California, 1990, pp. 25–35.

"The Met Grill: Interview with Richard Meier." *Metropolitan Home*, September 1986, p. 24.

Middleton, Faith. "Architecture's White Tornado." *Northeast Magazine/The Hartford Courant*, 30 September 1984, pp. 37–43.

Nesbitt, Lois E. *Richard Meier: Collages*. London: Academy Editions, 1990.

Papadakis, Andreas C., ed. *The New Modern Aesthetic*. Includes the following: "Richard Meier and the City in Miniature" by Kenneth Frampton; "The Tate Gallery Discussion" with Richard Meier, Charles Jencks, Daniel Libeskind and Conrad Jameson; a transcript of the lecture given by Richard Meier at "The Annual Architecture Forum." Great Britain: Art and Design, 1990, pp. 10–19, 30–31, 45–46.

Rapaport, Mariana. "Estaos en un Perisodo de Resonstruccion Modernista." *Clarin*, November 1987, p. 4

"Richard Meier: 'Die Postmoderne ist Passe.' " *Ambiente*, March 1985, p. 160.
Richard Meier. Includes "Richard Meier and the City in Miniature" by Kenneth Frampton; "Richard Meier Interviews 1980–1988" by Charles Jencks; "RIBA Royal Gold Medal Address 1988" by Richard Meier. Great Britain: Academy Editions, 1990. Reprinted in German. Stuttgart, Germany: Deutche Verlags-Anstalt GmbH, 1990.
Richards, Ivor. "The Meier Way." *The Architect's Journal*, 23 May 1990, p. 73.
Sabisch, Christian and David Galloway. "Visionen in Weiss." *Expression*, February 1986, pp. 54–57.
Stoller, Ezra. *Modern Architecture*. New York: Harry N. Abrams, Inc., 1990, pp. 188–202, 210–213.
Tung, Roseanne. "Architecture Alum Lectures about Museums, Modernism." *Cornell Daily News*, 21 February 1986, p. 7.
Vaudou, Valerie, ed. *Richard Meier*. Includes: "Avant-propos" by Richard Meier; "La Modernite comme seuil" by Hubert Damisch; "Radieuse modernite" by Henri Ciriani; "Sur Richard Meier" by Diane Lewis; "La capture du regard" by Jean Mas. Paris: Electa Moniteur, 1986. Reprinted in Italian. Milan: Electa, 1986.
Webb, Michael. "King of the Hill." *Buzz*, February/March 1991, pp. 64–68.
Williams, Hugh Aldersey. "The White Knight." *Blueprint*, October 1988, pp. 51– 52.
Wolf, Deborah. "Dit Is De Meest Opinwindende Opdracht Sinds Het Parthenon." *Avenue*, May 1985.

Ackerberg House

Contal, Marie-Helene. "Meier à Malibu." *Architecture Intérieure Crée*, February/March 1989, pp. 92–97.
Futagawa, Yukio, ed. "Ackerberg House." *Global Architecture Houses 22*, December 1987, pp. 6–21.
Graaf, Vera. "Luxusdampfer am Strand." *Architektur & Wohnen*, June/July 1990, pp. 22–28.
Hubeli, Ernst. "Unsichtbare Konstruktion als Allegorie." *Werk, Bauen + Wohnen*, December 1988, pp. 9–11.
Hughes, Robert. "Architecture: Richard Meier." *Architectural Digest*, October 1987, pp. 152–159.
Papadakis, Andreas C., ed. "Richard Meier, Ackerberg House, Malibu, 1984–86." *Architectural Design*, vol. 58, no. 7/8, 1988, pp. 24–33.
Prichett, Jack. "Richard Meier's Ackerberg House: Beauty at the Beach." *Inside*, vol. 6, February/March 1990, pp. 5–13.
Rykwert, Joseph. "Richard Meier: Two New Houses in USA." *Domus*, March 1987, pp. 29–45.
Stephens, Suzanne. "Malibu Modernism." *Progressive Architecture*, December 1987, pp. 94–101.
Van den Dungen, Mabel. "Richard Meier." *Avant Garde*, October 1990, pp. 120–125.

Bridgeport Center

"Bridgeport Center." *A + U*, April 1990, pp. 8–24.
Berman, Karen. "There's a new kid on the block." *Bridgeport Post Telegram*, 23 April 1989, sec. H, pp. 1, 2.
Branch, Mark Alden. "Bridgeport Center." *Progressive Architecture*, July 1989, pp. 19, 24.
Canella, Guido, ed. "Bridgeport Center." *Zodiac 1*, Milan: Rizzoli, 1989, pp. 92–107.
Dietsch, Deborah. "New Directions." *Architectural Record*, August 1989, pp. 70–77.
Dimitriu, Livio, ed. "Bridgeport Center." *New York Architects 3*. New York: U.S.A. Books, 1990, pp. 173–177.
Futagawa, Yukio, ed. "Bridgeport Center." *GA Document 24*, August 1989, pp. 76–91.
Goldberger, Paul. "A Short Skyscraper with a Tall Assignment." *The New York Times*, 26 March 1989, p. 32.
Hartoonian, Gevork. "Bridgeport Center: Re-Minding Richard Meier." *Journal of Architectural Education*, November 1990, pp. 33–36.

Canal+ Headquarters

"Canal Plus." *Bauwelt*, October 1989, p. 1910.
"Canal+ Headquarters." *Progressive Architecture*, January 1990, pp. 92–93.
Canella, Guido, ed. "The Canal+ Headquarters, Paris." *Zodiac 4*. Milan: Rizzoli, September 1990.

Mas, Jean. "Siège de Canal Plus: Richard Meier." *L'Architecture d'Aujourd'hui*, September 1989, pp. 64–65.

Des Moines Art Center Addition

Blunk, Mark E. "An Experiment in Contextual Evolution." *Inland Architect*, May/June 1989, pp. 70–73.
Dean, Andrea Oppenheimer. "Eliel Saarinen, Then Pei, Now Meier." *Architecture*, October 1985, pp. 32–41.
Demetrion, James T. "Des Moines Art Center." *Iowa Architect*, March/April 1984, pp. 16–20.
"Des Moines Art Center: One Museum with Three Architects." *Baumeister*, January 1987, pp. 52–56.
"The Des Moines Art Center." *A + U*, September 1985, pp. 44–70.
Futagawa, Yukio, ed. "Des Moines Art Center Addition." *GA Document 13*, September 1985, pp. 4–41.
Goldberger, Paul. "Museums Designed for Tight Quarters." *The New York Times*, 20 October 1985, p. 28.
Jodidio, Philip. "Quand Les Cathedrales Etaient Blanches." *Connaissance des Arts*, July/August 1985, p. 20
Lampugnani, Vittorio M. "Des Moines Art Center Addition." *Domus*, April 1986, pp. 37–43.
Lucas, Mary. "The Richard Meier Addition." *Des Moines Magazine*, April 1985, p. 43.
Meier, Richard. "Des Moines Art Center." *Iowa Architect*, March/April 1984, pp. 21–25.
Papadakis, Andreas, ed. "Richard Meier: A Personal Manifesto"; "Des Moines Art Center Addition, Des Moines, Iowa." *Architectural Design*, vol. 55, no. 1/2, 1985, pp. 56, 58–69.

Getty Center

Banham, Reyner. "Who's the King of the Mountain?" *California*, August 1984, pp. 94–103, 120–121.
Boaga, Giorgio. "J. Paul Getty Center a Los Angeles di Richard Meier." *Casabella*, April 1990, pp. 32–33.
Chazanor, Mathis. "Architect Vows Getty Museum will Blend into Brentwood Hills." *The Los Angeles Times*, 23 February 1986, sec. W, part IX, p. 5.
Diamonstein, Barbaralee, "Designer of the Decade." *Vanity Fair*, January 1985, pp. 86–88.
Ghirardo, Diane. "Invisible Acropolis." *Architectural Review*, June 1990, pp. 92–95.
Goldberger, Paul. "Architect Chosen for Getty Complex." *The New York Times*, 27 October 1984, sec. 1, p. 13.
———. "A Romantic Modernist Wins a Plum from the Getty." *The New York Times*, 11 November 1984, sec. 2, pp. 32, 34.
Kaplan, Sam Hall. "Getty Designer Stresses Flexibility." *The Los Angeles Times*, 16 December 1984, pp. I, VI.
Ketcham, Diana. "Chaste Geometry in Los Angeles." *Metropolis*, October 1987, p. 26.
Kieran, Kevin, et al. "The Getty Trust and the Process of Patronage." *The Harvard Architecture Review*, no. 6. New York: Rizzoli, 1987, pp. 122–131.
"Meier's Museums: A Tale of Two Cities." *The Journal of Art*, April 1989, pp. 50–53.
Muchnic, Suzanne. "Catching up with the Getty Center." *The Los Angeles Times*, 22 October 1990, pp. F1, 12.
Muschamp, Herbert. "Herbert Muschamp on California Architecture." *Art Forum*, October 1990, pp. 31–33.
Pastier, John. "J. Paul Getty Museum Unveils Preliminary Scheme by Meier." *Architecture*, July 1987, p. 18.
Pristin, Terry. "Getty Center Challenges a Premier U.S. Architect." *The Los Angeles Times*, 19 May 1989, pp. 1, 28, 29, 30.
Rikola, Taina. "California Perpective." *Building Design*, 16 September 1988, pp. 30–33.
Stephens, Suzanne. "Richard and Famous." *House and Garden*, February 1985, p. 54.
Stevens, Mark and Douglas Davis. "The Golden Eye of Los Angeles." *Newsweek*, 26 November 1984, pp. 80–82, 87–89.
Von Eckardt, Wolf. "Taking on an Imperial Task." *Time*, 12 November 1984, p. 111.

Whiteson, Leon. "The Man who got the Getty Job." *The Los Angeles Herald Examiner*, 6 December 1984, p. B1.

———. "Put-Up-Or-Shut-Up Time at the Getty." *The Los Angeles Herald Examiner*, 23 March 1986, sec. E, pp. 1, 6.

Grotta House

Balint, Juliana. "Det Perfekta Samspelet." *Sköna Hem*, March 1990, pp. 94–101.

Filler, Martin. "Modern Idyll." *House & Garden*, June 1990, pp. 150–157.

Futagawa, Yukio, ed. "Grotta House." *Global Architecture Houses 28*, March 1990, pp. 46–47.

———, ed. "Grotta Residence." *Global Architecture Houses 30*, December 1990, pp. 8–31.

"Grotta House." *A + U*, December 1990, pp. 16–23.

Murphy, Jim. "A Collaboration." *Progressive Architecture*, November 1990, pp. 90–95.

Rasch, Horst. "Herr Meier Und Die Liebe Zur Geometrie." *Häuser*, May 1990, pp. 16–23.

The Hague City Hall and Central Library

Buddingh, Hans. "Directuer De Ridden Vevlaat Planbureau." *NRC Handelsblad*, 1 December 1988, p. 1.

Diaz, Tony. "El sentido de la práctico: Richard Meier en La Haga." *Arquitectura Viva*, March 1989, no. 388, pp. 17–19.

"The Hague City Hall & Central Library." *New York Architects II*. Cefalu, Italy: Medina, 1988, pp. 50–51, 157–165.

Heuvel, Wim J. van. "Drie varianten stadhuis-ontwerp Meier." *Architectuur/Bouwen*, January 1989, pp. 41–44.

Lambert, Donald. "La Haye Grands Projets." *L'Architecture d'Aujourd'hui*, June 1988, pp. 22–24.

Lampugnani, Vittorio M. "City Hall/Central Library, The Hague." *Domus*, November 1987, pp. 25–31.

"Rathaus mit Zentralbibliothek in Den Haag, Niederlande." *Architektur + Wettbewerbe*, September 1988, pp. 28–38.

Westerman, Maks. "De giest van Berlage: Richard Meier over zijn Haagse Stadhuis." *Elseviers*, 23 May 1987, pp. 23–25.

Library of France

Pelissier, Alain. "Concours Pour La Bibliotheque de France." *Techniques & Architecture*, October 1989, pp. 34–45.

Welsh, John. "Salon de Refusees: Speaking Volumes." *Building Design*, 6 October 1989, pp. 18–29.

Madison Square Garden Site Redevelopment

Dimitriu, Livio, ed. "Madison Square Garden Site Redevelopment." *New York Architects 3*. New York: U.S.A. Books, 1990, pp. 178–181.

Futagawa, Yukio, ed. "Madison Square Garden." *GA Document 23*, April 1989, pp. 7–11.

"Madison Square Garden Site Redevelopment." *OZ*, vol. 11, 1989, pp. 40–41.

Museum of Contemporary Art

"Museum of Contemporary Art." *Progressive Architecture*, January 1991, pp. 94–95.

"Museo de Arte Contemporáneo." In *Barcelona: Arquitectura y Ciudad 1980–1992*. Includes essays by Oriol Bohigas, Peter Buchanan, Vittorio Magnago Lampugnani. Barcelona: Editorial Gustavo Gili, S.A., 1990, pp. 124–129.

Museum for the Decorative Arts

"Architektur: Ein 'Juwel' für Frankfurt." *Der Spiegel*, 20 July 1981, pp. 132–134.

"Arts and Crafts Museum Frankfurt." *Architectural Review*, October 1980, pp. 196–97.

Brenner, Douglas. "The Frankfurt Museum for the Decorative Arts: Theme and Variations." *Architectural Record*, April 1981, pp. 87–95.

Cannon-Brooks, Peter. "Frankfurt and Atlanta: Richard Meier as a Designer of Museums." *The International Journal of Museum Management and Curatorship*, vol. 5, no. 1, March 1986, pp. 39–64.

Cobb, Henry N., and Richard Meier. "Richard Meier's Museum für Kunsthandwerk." *Express*, April 1981, p. 7.

Cook, Peter. "White Magic." *Interiors*, July 1985, pp. 202–205, 217–218, 231.

———. "Meier Handwerk." *The Architectural Review*, November 1985, pp. 48–57.

"Crafts Museum, Frankfurt." *Space Design*, February 1986, pp. 29–44.

Dean, Andrea Oppenheimer. "Serene, Ordered Presence in a Park." *Architecture*, January 1986, pp. 56–63.

"Die Erste Skizze." *Daidalos*, 15 September 1982, pp. 46–47.

"Einfach Reinlatschen." *Der Spiegel*, 22 April 1985, pp. 202–207.

Flagge, Ingeborg. "Museum für Kunsthandwerk, Frankfurt." *Lichtbericht*, June 1985, pp. 64–71.

Frampton, Kenneth. "Il Museo come Mescolanza." *Casabella*, July/August 1985, pp. 11–17.

Futagawa, Yukio, ed. "Museum für Kunsthandwerk." *GA Document 13*, September 1985, pp. 4–41.

———. "Winning Scheme, Museum for the Decorative Arts Competition, Frankfurt am Main, West Germany." *GA Document 2*, Autumn 1980, pp. 66–71.

Galloway, David. "The New German Museums." *Art in America*, July 1985, pp. 74–89.

———. "New Museum Graces Frankfurt's Cultural Skyline." *International Herald Tribune*, 11–12 May 1985, p. 7.

Goldberger, Paul. "New Museums Harmonize with Art." *The New York Times*, 14 April 1985, sec. 2, p. 1.

———. "Harmonizing Old and New Buildings." *The New York Times*, 2 May 1985, p. C23.

Hoyet, Jean-Michel. "Made in U.S.A.: Trois conceptions recentes de Richard Meier & Associés." *Techniques & Architecture*, November 1982, pp. 140–47.

Huse, Norbert. *Richard Meier Museum für Kunsthandwerk, Frankfurt am Main*. Berlin: Wilhelm Ernst & Sohn Verlag für Architektur und Technische Wissenschaften, 1985.

Irace, Fluvio. "Radiant Museum." *Domus*, June 1985, pp. 2–11.

Jaeger, Falk. "Schimmernde Perle." *Deutsche Bauzeitung*, August 1985, pp. 28–33.

Jodidio, Philip. "Quand Les Cathedrales Etaient Blanches." *Connaissance des Arts*, July/August 1985, p. 20.

Klemm, Gisela. "Museum für Kunsthandwerk." *Detail*, September/October 1985, pp. 457–466.

Klotz, Heinrich, ed. *Jahrbuch für Architektur: Neues Bauen 1980–1981*. Includes "Der Wettbewerb für das Museum für Kunsthandwerk in Frankfurt am Main" by Frank Werner. Braunschweig/Wiesbaden: Friedr. Vieweg & Sohn, 1980, pp. 22–29, 30–39.

Knobel, Lance. "Meier's Modules." *Architectural Review*, July 1981, pp. 34–38.

Lampugnani, Vittorio Magnago. "The Jewel with All Qualities." *Lotus International 28*, 1980, pp. 34–38.

———. *Museums Architektur in Frankfurt 1980–1990*. Includes "Magnificent Chaos" by Kenneth Frampton. Munich, Germany: Prestel-Verlag, 1990, pp. 106–115.

Lemos, Peter. "Museum as Masterpiece." *Pan Am Clipper*, September 1985, pp. 57–62.

Maas, Tom. "Een Bron Van Architectonisch Genoegen." *De Architect*, June 1985, p. 33.

Montaner, Josep M. and Jordi Oliveras. "Museum of Arts and Crafts, Frankfurt." *The Museums of the Last Generation*. Barcelona: Gustavo Gili, S.A., 1986, pp. 102–105.

Murray, Peter. "Frankfurt's Carbuncle." *RIBA Journal*, June 1985, pp. 23–25.

"Musée des Arts Décoratifs, Francfort." *L'Architecture d'Aujourd'hui*, September 1980, pp. XI–XII.

"Musée de l'Artisanat et des Metiers d'Art Francfort." *Techniques et Architecture*, April/May 1985, pp. 103–108.

"Museum für Kunsthandwerk." *Werk, Bauen & Wohnen*, no. 12, December 1984, pp. 36–41.

"The Museum für Kunsthandwerk." *A + U*, September 1985, pp. 15–48.

"Museum für Kunsthandwerk in Frankfurt." *Baumeister*, August 1980, pp. 767–73.

"Museum für Kunsthandwerk in Frankfurt." *Baumeister*, August 1985, pp. 22–33.

"Neue Tempel fur die Kunst." *Stern*, 25 April 1985, pp. 46–66.

Papadakis, Andreas, ed. "Richard Meier: A Personal Manifesto"; "Museum for the Decorative Arts, Frankfurt, West Germany." *Architectural Design*, vol. 55, no. 1/2, 1985, pp. 56, 58–69.

"Richard Meier: Museum für Kunsthandwerk." In *AMC*, December 1985, pp. 20–33. Includes: "Décalages et Dynamisme: an Interview with Richard Meier," by Henri

Ciriani and Jacques Lucan; "Le Musée de Francfort: 'Apprendere à voir l'architecture'," by Jacques Lucan.

Rumpf, Peter. "Museum für Kusthandwerk, Frankfurt am Main." *Bauwelt*, May 1985, pp. 766–777.

Ruthenfranz, Eva. "Nobler Kulter-Park für die Bürger." *Art, das Kunstmagazin*, September 1983, pp. 68–74.

Sabisch, Christian. "Kein Manhattan in 'Manhattan.'" *Der Apotheker*, July 1985, p. 5.

Schilgen, Jost. *Neue Hauser für die Kunst*. Dortmund: Harenberg Kommunikation, 1990, pp. 82–105.

Schreiber, Mathias. "Weisses Bauhaus Schloss." *Frankfurter Allgemeine Zeitung*, 27 April 1985.

Stephens, Suzanne. "Frame by Frame." *Progressive Architecture*, June 1985, pp. 81– 91.

Stock, Wolfgang Jean. "Richard Meier: Museum für Kunsthandwerk in Frankfurt am Main." *Bauen in Beton*, November 1988, pp. 32–41.

"Ten Star Museums: White on White." *Monografias de Arquitectura y Vivienda*, no. 18, 1989, pp. 57–63.

Van Dijk, Hans. "Richard Meier in Duitsland: Museum für Kunsthandwerk, Frankfort." *Wonen Tabk*, 15 July 1985, pp. 20–28.

Wilson, William. "Germany's Grand Designs." *The Los Angeles Times*, 3 November 1985, pp. 74–77.

Zardini, Mirko. "Il Bianco e Il Grigio." *Casabella*, July/August 1985, pp. 4–10.

Museum of Ethnology

Lampugnani, Vittorio Magnago. *Museums Architektur in Frankfurt 1980–1990*, Munich, Germany: Prestel-Verlag, 1990, pp. 116–123. Includes: "Unity in Diversity" by Dieter Bartetzko.

Peters, Paulhans. "Museum für Völkerkunde in Frankfurt." *Baumeister*, June 1990, pp. 40–45.

Portland Eye Center

Montrasi, Fabio. "Centro Oculistico a Portland, Oregon, di Richard Meier." *Casabella*, April 1989, pp. 30–32.

"Portland Eye Center." *Progressive Architecture*, January 1989, pp. 100–102.

Ulm Exhibition and Assembly Building

Barthelmess, Stephen N. "Richard Meier: Stadthaus Project at Ulm." *Journal of Architectural Education*, vol. 43, no. 3, Spring 1990, pp. 2–19.

"Exhibition-Assembly Hall, Munsterplatz, Ulm, West Germany." *Progressive Architecture*, February 1988, p. 39.

Futagawa, Yukio, ed. "Exhibition-Assembly Building, Ulm, West Germany." *GA Document 18*, April 1987, pp. 7–12.

Lampugnani, Vittorio M. "Richard Meier: Davanti alla Cattedrale di Ulm." *Domus*, October 1987, pp. 8–9.

Montauer, Josep M. *Nuevos Museos*. Barcelona: Gustavo Gili., S.A., 1990, pp. 44–49.

"Neuggestaltung des Munsterplatzes in Ulm." *Architecture + Wettewerbe*, December 1987, pp. 52–58.

Schuster, Jan-Richard. "Ulm[. . .] Die Schöne Waeße Welt du Richard Meier in der Region." *Schwabischer Zeitung*, 11 March 1989, p. 59.

Westchester House

Adam, Peter. "Ein Meister der Moderne." *Ambiente*, July 1987, pp. 44–52.

Filler, Martin. "Eminent Domain." *House & Garden*, April 1987, pp. 162–169. Reprinted as "Precision au Sommett." *Vogue Decoration*, September 1987, pp. 114–117, 212.

Futagawa, Yukio, ed. "Westchester House." *GA Houses 22*, December 1987, pp. 22– 33.

James, Warren. "Casa en Westchester, Nueva York 1984–87." *Arquitectura*, November/December 1987, pp. 80–89.

Rykwert, Joseph. "Richard Meier: Two New Houses in USA." *Domus*, March 1987, pp. 29–45.

Van den Dungen, Mabel. "Richard Meier." *Avant Garde*, October 1990, pp. 120–125.

Vogel, Carol. "Classic Modern." *The New York Times Magazine*, 1 February 1987, pp. 60–64.

Other Projects

Arnott, Ian. "Meier at Maybury." *Prospect*, Spring 1990, pp. 40–41.

Borras, Maria Lluisa. "Los Collages de Richard Meier." *La Vanguardia*, 26 July 1988, p. 38.

Brausch, Marianne. "Montpellier. L'Enprente de Richard Meier." *Le Moniteur*, 26 May 1989, pp. 110–113.

Chapman, Irv. "Alumni Profiles: Richard Meier: Celebrated architect, Cornell ready for each other again." *Cornell '87*. Summer 1987, p. 3.

Cohen, Edie Lee. "Richard Meier & Partners: Two Offices by and for the Architectural Firm." *Interior Design*, May 1988, pp. 278–284.

Collins, Glenn. "A Showplace for a Showman." *The New York Times*, 6 June 1989, pp. 15–16.

Edwards, Brian. "Meier's Maybury Master Plan." *RIBA Journal*, September 1989, pp. 28–29.

Firlotte, Gregory. "Intent or Smut: Conversing with Richard Meier, Ed Ruscha and DeWain Valenlul." *Designer's West*, January 1988, pp. 114–115.

Fortier, Bruno. "Il Concorso Per Il Quartiere Sextius-Mirabeau a Aix en Provence." *Casabella*, October 1990, pp. 62–9.

Giordano, Paolo. "Progetti per Napoli." *Domus*, March 1987, pp. 79–84.

Izzo, Alberto, et al. *Progetti per Napoli*. Napoli: Guida Edition, 1987.

Papadakis, Andreas C., ed. "Richard Meier: The Art of Abstraction." *Art and the Tectonic*, Great Britain: Art and Design, 1990, pp. 86–91.

Rinaldi, Rosamaria. "Due Studi d'Architettura: Da New York a Los Angeles." *Interni*, March 1989, pp. 8–13.

Timmerman, Jacques. "Antwerpen: Den Entrepot." *A + Architektuur*, February 1990, pp. 40–44.

Photographers